Grundtvig in International Perspective

Grundtvig in International Perspective

Studies in the Creativity of Interaction

Edited by A.M. Allchin, S.A.J. Bradley, N.A. Hjelm,
and J.H. Schjørring

AARHUS UNIVERSITY PRESS

Skrifter udgivet af Grundtvig-Selskabet, bind XXXIII

Published with the financial support of the Aarhus University
Research Foundation

AARHUS UNIVERSITY PRESS
Langelandsgade 177
DK-8200 Aarhus N
Fax (+ 45) 8942 5380

73 Lime Walk
Headington, Oxford OX3 7AD
Fax (+ 44) 1865 75 00 79

P.O. Box 511
Oakville, CT 06779
Fax (+ 1) 860 945 9468

www.unipress.dk

ANSI/NISO
Z39.48-1992

Cover: Drawing of N.F.S. Grundtvig by Peter Christian Thomsen Skovgaard
located at Det Nationalhistoriske Museum på Frederiksborg Slot, Denmark

Acknowledgements

The contents of this book give an indication of the way in which the international discussion of Grundtvig's work has developed since the publication of the previous volume Heritage and Prophecy. Grundtvig and the English-Speaking World in 1993. This volume comprises material from the Grundtvig conference held in Chicago in July 1995, from the conference at Køge, Denmark, in August 1997, which marked the 50th anniversary of the Grundtvig Society, and also from the conference held in January 1999 at Jadavpur University in Calcutta, India.

The editors are deeply grateful to Aarhus University Research Foundation, Kirkeligt Samfund, Copenhagen, and N.F.S. Grundtvig's Fund for their generous support.

The editors owe a debt of gratitude to Dr. Kim Arne Pedersen, Research-coordinator at the Centre for Grundtvig Studies in Aarhus, for his untiring work on behalf of the Centre, and also in connection with this book. We are also deeply indebted to the Revd. Susanne Gregersen and – last but not least – to Birgit Winther-Hansen for their skilful assistance in the editorial work on this volume.

The editors

Contents

Abbreviations and Frequently Quoted Books ix

Preface 1

A.M. Allchin
Introduction 5

Philip Hefner
Theology and Creation:
Joseph Sittler and N.F.S. Grundtvig 27

Michael Root
Generous Orthodoxy:
Regin Prenter's Appropriation of Grundtvig 45

Axel C. Kildegaard
Danish Grundtvigians in the United States:
Challenges Past and Present 59

R. William Franklin
Grundtvig Within the Ecclesiological Revival
of 19th-Century Europe 75

Vítor Westhelle
"The Noble Tribe of Truth"
Etchings on Myth, Language, and Truth Speaking 87

Jakob Balling
Old Europe and its Aftermath:
Poetry, Doctrine, and Western Culture 103

Christian Thodberg
Grundtvig's View of the Bible 115

A.M. Allchin
The Holy Spirit in the Teaching of N.F.S. Grundtvig 135

S.A.J. Bradley
"A Truly Proud Ruin":
Grundtvig and the Anglo-Saxon Legacy   147

Gustav Björkstrand
Grundtvig's "Education for Life" and the Cultural
Challenge Facing the Baltic and Nordic Countries Today 163

Asoke Bhattacharya
Adult Education in India:
Relevance of Grundtvig   173

K.E. Bugge
Some International Varieties of Grundtvig Inspiration   185

Holger Bernt Hansen
Education for Life or for Livelihood?
Grundtvig and the Third World Revisited   193

List of Authors   207

Abbreviations and Frequently Quoted Books

Danne-Virke. Et Tidsskrift af N.F.S. Grundtvig, I-IV (Copenhagen, 1816-19, reprint 1983).

Den Danske Salmebog (Danish Hymnal Book). [DDS]

A Grundtvig Anthology. Selected from the Writings of N.F.S. Grundtvig, ed. and tr. N.L. Jensen and E. Broadbridge (Cambridge, 1984).

Grundtvigs Erindringer og Erindringer om Grundtvig, eds. H. Høirup and S. Johansen (Copenhagen, 1948).

Grundtvigs prædikener 1822-26 og 1832-39, bd. I-XII (Copenhagen, 1983-1986) (Grundtvig's sermons). [GP]

Grundtvigs Sang-Værk til den danske kirke, I-V (reprinted Copenhagen, 1982) (Grundtvig's Song Work). [GSV]

Heritage and Prophecy. Grundtvig and the English-Speaking World, eds. A.M. Allchin, D. Jasper, J.H. Schjørring, and K. Stevenson (Aarhus, 1993).

Martin Luther, *Kritische Gesamtausgabe* (Weimar). [WA]

Martin Luther, *Works*. [LW]

N.F.S. Grundtvig, *Mands Minde (1788-1838). Foredrag over det sidste halve Aarhundredes Historie*, ed. Svend Grundtvig (Copenhagen, 1877) (Within Living Memory).

N.F.S. Grundtvig, *Selected Writings*, ed. and with an introduction by Johannes Knudsen (Philadelphia, 1976).

N.F.S. Grundtvig, *Tradition and Renewal. Grundtvig's Vision of Man and People, Education and the Church, in relation to World Issues Today*, eds. Christian Thodberg and Anders Pontoppidan Thyssen (Copenhagen, 1983).

N.F.S. Grundtvig, *Udvalgte Skrifter*, I-X, ed. H. Begtrup (Copenhagen, 1904-1909). [US]

N.F.S. Grundtvig, *Værker i udvalg*, I-X, eds. G. Christensen and H. Koch (Copenhagen, 1940-1949).

N.F.S. Grundtvig, *What constitutes authentic Christianity?*, tr. Ernest D. Nielsen (Philadelphia, 1985).

N.F.S. Grundtvigs, *Breve til hans Hustru under Englandsrejserne 1829-1831*, ed. Stener Grundtvig (Copenhagen, 1920).

Preface

In 1993 a first volume of essays entitled *Heritage and Prophecy. Grundtvig and the English-Speaking World* was published through the initiative of the Centre for Grundtvig Studies at the University of Aarhus. The collection was intended to promote a wider international discussion of the significance of Grundtvig's work and teaching, considered historically and in relation to today. The dialogue partners represented in that volume were almost all either from Denmark or from England. Only one contributor came from across the Atlantic; and he was a scholar of British origins, Professor Geoffrey Wainwright.

Now, some seven years later, in this second volume, the circle of exchange has widened significantly. There are five transatlantic contributors here, four from the United States and one from Brazil. All of them, in very varied ways, are concerned with seeing Grundtvig in an international and ecumenical context. Four of them, Michael Root, Philip Hefner, Vítor Westhelle and William Franklin, suggest strongly the relevance of Grundtvig's thought to urgent current questions, social and theological, questions which are concerned with Christian unity, with the ecological crisis of our century and with the nature of theological discourse itself. The fifth contribution to this section is of particular value to all concerned with the theme of Grundtvig and the English-speaking world, since it looks carefully and sensitively at the influence of Grundtvig in the United States of America through the actual communities formed by the movement of Danish immigration into the United States in the second half of the 19th century. This influence was never numerically powerful, but it had a remarkable quality, as emerges from Axel Kildegaard's essay.

If these essays are primarily concerned with seeing Grundtvig in relation to other theologians and other movements of thought, the following four essays are more concentrated on looking closely at Grundtvig himself. At first sight this might not seem to be true of Professor Jakob Balling's contribution on the relation of poetry to doctrine in the heritage of "Old Europe". But the implications of this paper for the understanding of Grundtvig are, as will be argued in the introduction to this volume, very far-reaching. This is followed by Professor Christian Thodberg's masterly discussion of Grundtvig's attitude to the Bible. It is an essay which shows both the elements of change and development which took place in Grundtvig's mind and the elements of continuity of view which are also to be found. It reflects an outstanding knowledge of Grundtvig's work as a preacher, an area in which the writer, as the editor of the ongoing edition of Grundtvig's sermons, is the outstanding authority. The same combination of development and continuity in Grundtvig's views can be seen in my own contribution, which looks at his insistent affirmation that spirit and body need to be seen together and not apart. The fourth contribution to our understanding of Grundtvig himself is concerned with Grundtvig's attitude toward the literature of Anglo-Saxon England. It forms part of Dr. S.A.J. Bradley's ongoing study of Grundtvig's reception of the legacy of Anglo-Saxon England. This is a study which establishes Bradley as one of the first non-Danish scholars, if not the first, to make a genuinely original contribution to the study of Grundtvig as a poet, a thinker, a scholar and an historian, and it throws much light on Grundtvig's understanding of tradition.

The following four essays are all directly concerned with the impact, direct or indirect, of Grundtvig's ideas in the world today, in particular in the world of education, in Europe, Asia and Africa. It begins with Professor Björkstrand's careful and balanced consideration of the part which Grundtvigian ideas have played in the development of various kinds of cultural and political interchange between the Nordic and Baltic countries in the last decade, since the fall of communism opened up the paths which link the two sides of the Baltic Sea to one another. It continues with Dr. Bhattacharya's survey of the way in which Grundtvig has been seen, not just in India, but in particular in Bengal, in the light of the educational history of that state, through the last two centuries. Dr. Bhattacharya gives particular consideration to some of the parallels between Grundtvig and Rabindrinath Tagore, which have struck Grundtvig's admirers in India, and he gives us an insight into the ideas which lay behind the remarkable conference on Grundtvig and Continuing Education which was held in Calcutta in January 1999. This conference was in many ways a new beginning for the study and understanding of Grundtvig outside a North American and European context, and it is highly significant that it has given rise to a proposal for the establishment of a *Grundtvig International Centre for Study and Research in Adult Education*, to be based at Javadpur University in Calcutta. This promising initiative can be seen in a more general context through the two following contributions, that of Professor K.E. Bugge and that of Professor Holger Bernt Hansen, which give us a wide-ranging survey of the ways in which Grundtvig's example has, in the second half of the 20th century, been an inspiration in different parts of the developing world for movements to promote democratic forms of human and social development, in particular through new forms of adult education. Both writers approach their subject with a great wealth of experience, academic and practical, which gives their judgement special value.

It is perhaps not by chance that the essays which make up this book should range from detailed studies of particular points of historical, philological and theological research, on the one hand, to considerations of some of the most basic problems about education and the nature of what makes us human, on the other. The introduction, which follows this preface, seeks to draw together some of the ideas presented in these essays and in doing so suggests "strangeness" as one of the categories for understanding Grundtvig. This is a strangeness which makes him at once more scholarly, more learned, than most of the scholars and experts, and at the same time more popular and more willing to engage in the most basic aspects of human existence than the most popular of politicians and publicists. For Grundtvig, spirit, human and divine, can never be separated from the body, our flesh, our dust, the very dirt of the streets. These are indissolubly linked with one another in the love which moves the sun and the other stars. Macrocosm, microcosm and history mutually mirror one another in a coherence of creation and redemption which constantly breaks through our attempt to define or confine them in sentences of prose. There is an interaction here of history and nature, of individual and community, of human and divine which continues to prove itself creative of new forms of life and understanding at the beginning of a new period in human history.

Introduction

By A.M. Allchin

The attempt to create an international forum for the study and evaluation of Grundtvig's life and work is a fascinating, if at times baffling, task. Seven years ago the first collection of essays which was published with the intention of furthering that purpose was entitled *Heritage and Prophecy. Grundtvig and the English-Speaking World*. The title was meant to suggest that while Grundtvig had his roots deeply planted in the past, there was something in his stance which spoke to the future. Indeed there was a suggestion in some of the contributions that Grundtvig was a man who did not fit very well into the century in which he lived, or indeed into our own century, and that while this might be at least one of the reasons why his work has been little studied beyond the boundaries of his own country, it might also be a reason to think that his writings still have a strong future reference.

This suggestion that in some way Grundtvig fits uneasily into the 200 years which stretch from the revolution in Paris in 1789 to the fall of the Berlin wall in 1989 is reinforced by some of the articles in this new collection. As some of his contemporaries felt, H.L. Martensen for instance, Grundtvig seemed to be a man who belonged more to the middle ages than to the 19th century. He was in some ways a very old-fashioned thinker, and he constantly referred to himself as an old-fashioned believer, *gammeldags troende*. But no one could deny that as time went by his political options became more and more aligned with those on the left. He combined radical and conservative elements in his make-up in surprising ways. He has a capacity for holding together within himself viewpoints or characteristics which are often thought of as distinct if not opposed to one another.

On the one hand for instance he was a man of startling and often unexpected erudition. As Sid Bradley remarks of him, in his article in this book, "When, in the period of 1815-20, Grundtvig began seriously to work with the Anglo-Saxon epic poem *Beowulf*, there was hardly anyone in Scandinavia and hardly anyone in England – hardly anyone in the world therefore! – who could adequately read Anglo-Saxon, or who knew very much at first hand of the scope and content of the surviving Anglo-Saxon literature." Yet at the same time this antiquarian scholar with his specialist knowledge of the history and mythology of the early North was also the writer of popular ballad-style songs which tell the stories of the people of Israel in the Old Testament and of the people of Denmark in the middle ages. They are songs written with such directness and simplicity that children still delight in singing them today. One cannot help feeling that there is something strange about this man. He is more scholarly than the scholars and more popular than the publicists. He does not like to fit into our usual ways of categorising people, even of categorising people of exceptional ability and vision.

There are signs of this difficulty in understanding him both inside and outside Denmark. Within his own country his name is very widely known, his memory, even though it is now a very stereotyped and legendary memory, is still very familiar. Yet remarkably little of his own writing is in print, and while detailed scholarly studies of particular points in his life and teaching abound, many of them of the highest quality, there is a surprising dearth of general studies of the man, whether biographical or literary or theological. Once you get beyond the boundaries of Denmark the fog of ignorance soon begins to become impenetrable. Even in the neighbouring countries of Norway and Sweden, Grundtvig is very little known and where he is known, he is regarded as impossibly Danish and therefore foreign and therefore incomprehensible. Once we go outside the world of Scandinavia and the North, whether to Germany or France or Spain or Britain, let alone to the United States or Japan or Russia, it is difficult to know where to begin in starting to speak or write about Grundtvig, so unfamiliar is his name.

The few exceptions to this widespread international ignorance are to be found in certain areas of the English-speaking parts of the developing world, where Grundtvig's ideas on adult education and community development have received an unexpected response. This whole phenomenon is considered in two of the most substantial contributions to this volume, those of Professor K.E. Bugge and Professor Holger Bernt Hansen, contributions which in themselves suggest that there is at least some element of prophecy in the legacy which Grundtvig has left us. But in general the gulf between the detailed, loving appropriation of Grundtvig which characterises Danish Grundtvig scholars, and the vague and often imprecise impressions of him received by those beyond the Danish border, remains and we are only gradually beginning to build bridges across the gulf.

Nevertheless we do make new beginnings, and in this collection there are some highly significant ones, as for instance those which have American origins. First among these is Michael Root's study of "Regin Prenter's Appropriation of Grundtvig". Here we have in a very special way, a bridge between the inner and the outer Danish worlds. The writer is an American scholar who has worked for many years in the Lutheran Institute for Ecumenical Research, in Strasbourg, and therefore has a strongly international outlook and experience, and is at the same time a man whose own original doctoral studies were in the theology of Regin Prenter, one of the outstanding Danish theologians of our time. The fact that Prenter himself should have given so much space to the study of Grundtvig and should have been so manifestly influenced by him in many of his own basic theological options already alerts us to the fact that there is material in the inter-relationship of these three writers, two Danish and one American, two of the 20th and one of the 19th century, which promises to be fruitful.

Root's discussion of Prenter's presentation of Grundtvig centres on two points, first the "kirkelige Anskuelse", the vision of the Church which emerged in its full form in 1825, in what Grundtvig himself called his "unpar-alleled discovery", the "mageløse opdagelse", and the second, in the under-standing of the interrelationship between creation and redemption which underlies all Grundtvig's thinking and is also foundational for Prenter him-self. Prenter's own dogmatic theology, published in 1967, was called simply *Creation and Redemption (Skabelse og Genløsning)*.

On the first subject it is instructive to compare Root's discussion of the theology of the view of the Church with Christian Thodberg's careful ac-count of how it actually emerged in Grundtvig's preaching and hymn-writ-ing in and around the year 1825. For both it is clear that something of major and lasting significance in Grundtvig's development happened then, and, I should dare to add, something of major significance, at least potentially, in the life and history of Western Christendom. This moment in 1825 is one in which a major representative of the tradition of the Protestant Reformation finds it necessary, without in any way repudiating that tradition, to go be-yond it, in a movement of creative reappropriation, the reaffirmation of some-thing which is so basically and universally Christian that it belongs not only to the past which it recalls but also to the future to which it leads.

Root and Thodberg both, from their different perspectives, insist that in placing the worshipping Church at the heart of the Christian tradition of faith and life, Grundtvig sees the baptismal and eucharistic life of the congregation as the place above all where the risen Christ makes himself known to his peo-ple and enables his people to make their response of faith to him. In doing this Grundtvig is not simply saying that the Church is to replace the Bible at the heart of our faith, nor is he running himself into a kind of "confessional fundamentalism", in which it is held that the clauses of the Apostles' Creed were taught by Jesus to the disciples in the 40 days between Easter and As-cension. This theory, a 19th-century reproduction of a pious medieval specu-lation, was in later life at times entertained by Grundtvig himself and was certainly taught by some of his followers, notably for instance Bishop P.C. Kierkegaard. What Grundtvig sees in the discovery of 1825 is something much more many-sided and life-giving than that. He sees the need to reaf-firm the presence of the risen Christ in the power of the Spirit at the heart of the Church. At the heart of all this is "the thought of the living Christ who lives his life now in the community in the word, in which he himself is life and gives life".

This thought of the indwelling of Christ in his people is of the greatest importance. As Root points out Prenter's thought is not "controlled by a rigid separation of divine act and human act". Nor, we must add, is that of Grundtvig. Just as there is a constant interaction between God's work in creation and God's work in redemption, so there is also for Grundtvig a constant interaction of divine and human, in creation and redemption alike, in Christ himself and in his Church and in all who belong to him. Root goes on to say that "the insistence that the indwelling of Christ in the Christian is mediated communally and, more specifically, ecclesially leads to a different valuation of the church and its traditions. Popes, bishops, and councils may err, but if the church in its sacraments is regularly locus of the Spirit's presence, then an essential trustworthiness should characterize the Church. Herein lies, I believe, the central root of the 'catholic' character of Prenter's theology. Prenter is by no means uncritical of the wider, catholic ecclesial and theological tradition, but his writings exude (at least to me) a fundamental trust in that tradition, an at-home-ness there". It is hardly necessary to underline the specifically ecumenical significance of this "Catholic" character of Prenter's theology.

Grundtvig may have had a more dialectical, questioning, anguished mind than Prenter, and his relationship to the tradition as a whole is therefore more open and questioning, but still, it seems clear that the "at-home-ness" is there in him also. We see something of its nature when we come to look at Jakob Balling's contribution to this volume, as we also see it constantly reflected in Bradley's account of Grundtvig's appropriation of the literature of the Anglo-Saxons. In Grundtvig's case, too, it has evident implications for the renewal of understanding and contact between the separated parts of the one Christian tradition.

This "at-home-ness" with tradition, this reinterpretation and reappropriation of the word "catholic", on the other side of the Reformation, is of course one of the features which Grundtvig has in common with the Tractarians, as Franklin points out in his wide-ranging contribution to this volume. As we know, Grundtvig's direct approach to the leaders of the Oxford Movement in 1843 proved in the end to be fruitless, but his determination to go to Oxford in that year, his feeling that he could perhaps make a decisive intervention in the development of the movement even at that stage, are things which in themselves bear witness to his sense of kinship with the Oxford men, Newman and Pusey in particular, despite all their manifest differences.

As Franklin suggests this whole exchange could still be of significance today in the relations between Anglicans and Lutherans, not only in North America but in other places as well. For the Tractarians, as well as Grundtvig, were seeking to hold together attitudes and beliefs which were too often set at odds with one another then and still are today. In this the Oxford Movement leaders can be paralleled by another outstanding Anglican theologian of that time, a man whose thought has sometimes been compared with that of Grundtvig, F.D. Maurice. Maurice, like Grundtvig, was a man who sought to interpret the movements of history, for instance the events of 1848, in the light of God's action in the world. He was also a man who insisted that all Christian thought should begin from our faith in God's goodness revealed in creation, rather than in our perception of human sinfulness and evil. He made a sustained and biting criticism of the tendency in Victorian England to make "religion" into a world of its own, a world of detailed doctrinal disputes and devotional feelings, a world cut off from the public life of every day in which men and women live and suffer and act. He was, above all, concerned to perceive God's work in the whole creation, in flesh as well as in Spirit, in nature as well as in grace. In all this, the parallels with Grundtvig are evident, both in Maurice's view of the historic nature of the Church and still more in his view of the relation of creation to redemption.

It is interesting to note that Franklin's four points held in common by Grundtvig and Pusey might well be extended on the Anglican side to include F.D. Maurice (something which at the time might easily have disturbed both him and Pusey, since both believed their disagreements to be profound).

1) "Both were concerned to make a firsthand 'traditional' religion possible for the common man and woman amid the revolutionary circumstances of the 19th century."

2) "Both wished to stress the universal elements of Christianity as opposed to the denominational elements of it."

3) "Both wished, through liturgical worship to reinforce a sense of universal solidarity not only among the living but also with the dead."

4) "Both Grundtvig and Pusey ultimately believed that this apostolic solidarity is sacramental: it is in the celebration of the sacraments and within the congregation at worship that we hear God's Word to us, creative word, which brings into being the church, the new people of God."

It would be important to explore these parallels further. As we have seen already, for Prenter this whole vision of the Church is based on the thought of the indwelling of Christ in each Christian and in the whole community; "the thought of the living Christ who lives his life now in the community in the word, in which he himself is life and gives life." How deeply this thought is rooted in post-Reformation Anglicanism can be seen not only in the theology of Richard Hooker but also in the prayers of Thomas Cranmer himself. There are common themes here which need further exploration, and which could

renew not only the relationships of Anglicans and Lutherans with one another but also, and more importantly, their common relationship with other
Christian traditions and with the world in which they live.

In the second part of his essay where he deals with the whole question of
the relationship and interaction of creation to redemption, Root again makes
points about Prenter which sometimes apply even more powerfully to
Grundtvig. That there is an intimate correlation of creation with redemption
is fundamental to both of them. This question, which, as we shall see in a moment, is so urgently central to Philip Hefner's contribution to this volume, is
not passed over here, though it is not worked out at length. "The redemptive
word of the gospel does not replace or render superfluous the creative word
… The Church also exists within and is permeated by the structures of creation. The creative word … continues to shape the identity in which persons
are the concrete individuals they are." And all this leads Root to a conclusion
in which he speaks of Prenter's thought in terms of a "generous orthodoxy".
If there is a system here it is open and flexible and leads to an orthodoxy
which is itself open and hospitable, which involves "an openness towards
and an interest in the wider world that too often is missing from the usual
connotations of the word orthodox". This word which has come too often to
suggest a stance which is rigid, defensive, closed in on itself is seen in its original meaning to have quite other connotations.

In Britain, at least, this term "generous orthodoxy" is becoming associated with a new development in the world of theological reflection and research, which can be discerned in writers of varying schools of thought. In
face of the fragmentation of post-modernity, the term "generous orthodoxy"
affirms its roots in the given tradition of Christian faith and life, a tradition
deeply Trinitarian and Incarnational. But in face of the increasing rapidity of
change in our culture and society, the term firmly rejects the conservative
temptation to adopt a reactive or defensive strategy and instead seeks to discern God's action in the world, developing a confident though not uncritical
openness and concern in face of the world in which we live.

It is the imperative need for this openness towards the world, this interest
in all that goes on in it, this confidence that God speaks both in it and through
it, which stands at the beginning of Hefner's essay and indeed runs all
through it. If Root has shown us something of the underlying structure of
Grundtvig's thought in relation to the life and worship of the Church, and the
person of Christ made known within it, Hefner takes us a further step and begins to outline what is perhaps the most vital of all the elements of
Grundtvig's vision of Christian faith, his understanding of the relationship
and interaction of creation and redemption. Although his method is somewhat different, his essay has one notable similarity to that of Michael Root.
He too takes a distinguished Lutheran theologian of the second part of the

20th century, a scholar of international repute, this time Joseph Sittler, and uses him as a partner in a dialogue with Grundtvig. In a text which is animated by a passionate concern, and a certain well-justified impatience, Hefner confronts us with the challenges which the ecological crisis puts before us. How, he asks, is it possible that so little has been done within the Churches to respond to that crisis? How is it that the world of theological reflection and investigation seems so often to run on along its accustomed ways without seeing the revolutionary changes which are made necessary by the development of the world that we live in?

In a striking passage, which he quotes from Sittler, we are confronted with God's judgement present in the state of the environment, as it could be seen already more than 25 years ago. "If, for instance, Lake Michigan is assessed according to its given ecological structure as a place for multiple forms of life, by nature self-sustaining and clean, available for right use and delight, then in a blunt and verifiable way, we are 'justified' by grace even in our relation to the things of nature. The opposite of justification is condemnation … if a lake becomes a disposal-resource, or a dump, or a source for water to cool ingots with, or a bath to flush out oil-bunkers then a repudiated grace that 'justifies' becomes the silent agent of condemnation." Such a vision of things, Hefner insists, involves our understanding that "our life in the natural world [is] to be fully incorporated within the central Christian vision of the Trinity".

Even a first reading of Hefner's essay will show how deep and all-embracing the theological considerations are which underlie its more immediate and pressing interests. Here is a plea to take with unconditional seriousness both the world, the material world in which we live, and the fullness of divine action which we encounter within it. Basing himself on the work of Joseph Sittler, Hefner asks "by what is the actual worldly order in which we live every day normatively defined – by its grounding in God's will and action of creation or by its empirically manifested evil, sin, and finitude?" For him there is no more doubt about the answer to that question than there would have been for F.D. Maurice. " … the world is defined normatively by its status as God's creation and by nothing else. Redemption flows from the living spring of creation and from no other source."

In this way Hefner is able to state with great force the conviction that the fullness of God's grace is present to us in the details of our daily existence. Nothing is too small to be a vehicle of the divine grace, and the divine grace is nothing less than the active presence of the Triune God. "This means, on the one hand, that any occasion of God's presence is an occasion of the presence of the fullness of God. We dare not describe any encounter with God in terms so small that our description in fact betrays – that is, actually commits treason against – the richness of what we actually believe about God. On the other hand, our understanding of the natural occasion in which God's presence is known is also transformed into terms that are commensurate with what we believe about God. In the framework of the Triune concept of God, this means that the situation in which we meet God is the creation of God, that it has been created for redemption, and that the ongoing presence of God as Spirit aims at making actual for us the redemption of the creation in which our lives participate. In other words our concept of the God who is present in our situations requires that we do not settle for too low a concept of the situation which has been the medium of God's presence as grace. ... The situation in which we meet God's grace is not only an occasion of redemption, it is also the creation of God, and redemption constitutes the meaning of the created situation."

One vital aspect of this vision of the present continuing and coherent action of God in the world, as at once creator, redeemer and sanctifier relates to the understanding of the coinherence of the human and non-human parts of the creation. Humankind cannot be separated from the living and the material world of which it is a part. Christian theology can no longer continue in a fully credible and meaningful way, without some serious attempt at a renewed cosmology. "The character we ascribe to God, particularly in God's relationship to Creation, and specifically to humans, no longer makes sense unless we can relate that character of God meaningfully to the totality of the created order. It must be related to our culture because, as Grundtvig said, we must avoid speaking of human beings as if they inhabit 'a life in heaven or in the sky, never on earth. On earth you never find humanity without folk-life'. The character of God must be related to non-human nature, because we now know that God created us humans, even in the inner sanctum of our personhood, from the stuff of non-human nature. We live on earth, not in the sky, and on earth you never find a humanity without physics, geology, biology, and neurobiology."

Hefner's language is of course that of our own time. Grundtvig's is that of the first half of the 19th century. But it is easy to see how, under the differences of idiom, the concerns expressed are the same. We see Grundtvig's insistence that we are shaped not only by the culture we share but also by the world of which we are part. We see his constant affirmation that the earth itself is made in God's image. It is not humankind alone but all creation which is in some sense open to God, apt for God. The world is God's world, he keeps telling us, the world that God made and made very good. "We should not, like our fathers, consider nature in us and ourselves, as the property of the Enemy, but as the work of God which never fell from his hand or slipped from his care ... Yes, we shall consider nature as God's work, in us and around us, which shall in no way be hated, mistreated or destroyed, but loved, cleansed, healed and sanctified, yes which should share in that same glory, which in the Spirit we already rejoice in ... . for which, as the apostle says, the whole of creation longs with a wonderful hope. In no way then should we set *nature* and *revelation* (italics original) in opposition to one another, as things incompatible with one another; rather we should call revelation nature's light and salvation, as our Lord Jesus calls himself the light and salvation of the world."[1]

Again, as I have set out in my own contribution to this book, for Grundtvig, throughout his life, the Spirit (and here we include the created human spirit as well as the uncreated Spirit of God) is never to be separated from bodiliness. For him, body and spirit belong together. There is for him no greater sign of the error of the age in which he lives, than "its abstract conception of Spirit and spiritual reality and its material conception of freedom and personality". In the union and fusion of flesh and Spirit, dust and Spirit, Grundtvig will not hesitate to say our human life consists and can grow. The human person is to grow in the awareness of a double relationship, "the relationship to the world which his body expresses, the relationship to the divine, to which his spirit bears witness". In this way the ancient Christian understanding of humankind as microcosm and mediator gains new force in the 19th century through his stress on the solidarity of the human with the non-human elements in creation.

Of course in Grundtvig the distinctly ecological lines of thought, to which Hefner points us, are latent rather than fully developed. The world has changed greatly in the century and a half which have passed since his time. But it is one of the most basic and all-important facts about Grundtvig's theology that it had much more direct consequences in the world of work, in the social and economic structures of 19th-century Denmark, than was the case with the teaching of most churchmen in that century. In the years after the disastrous war of 1864, the last years of Grundtvig's life, when Germany took almost a third of the territory of Jutland, the economist Dalgas produced the remarkable saying: "Outward loss, inward gain".[2] These are words which could be taken in their purely literal sense to mean "we must gain by land reclamation, in the territory which remains to us, what we have lost in the land which has been taken from us", but they could also be taken in a more spiritual sense "the outer loss shall be the inner gain", and the two meanings ought not to be disjoined. The inspiration of the folk high schools began to be felt across the countryside in these years. Heathland was reclaimed, ditches were dug, trees were planted, methods of pig-breeding were improved, farming cooperatives were established. "Nothing is too small to be a vehicle

1. Quoted in A.M. Allchin, *N.F.S. Grundtvig. An Introduction to his Life and Work* (Aarhus, 1997), p. 148.
2. Quoted in Steven M. Borish, *The Land of the Living. The Danish folk high schools and Denmark's non-violent path to modernization* (Nevada City, 1991), p. 14, see note 16.

of divine grace and the divine grace is nothing less than the active presence of the Tri-une God" at work in human history, to take up again Sittler's way of stating the question.

One of the most moving passages in Steven Borish's remarkable study of Danish society, *The Land of the Living*, particularly significant as the work of an American anthropologist of agnostic Jewish background, is to be found in his chapter on "The Rise of the Danish Folk High Schools" where he quotes from letters written at that time by former students to Ernest Trier, the principle of Vallekilde High School, one of those early folk high school men who had known Grundtvig personally. In these letters we see something of the mixture of practical concerns, careful planning and deeply felt faith which motivated many of these young people. "Yes, dear Trier, I have become engaged to a girl who is young and poor. I hope it is God's will that we have come so close to each other, and I am hoping that when the time comes we will live in our own home, no matter how small it may be. Not just to be a place where we eat our food, sleep our sleep and have a shelter against the weather and the wind, [but] a home where warm hearts beat and noble thoughts are born, where life's best forces are strengthened and developed, because such a home would I wish and ask God to cast anchor in."[3]

If former students of schools such as Askov and Vallekilde were changing the face of Danish farming in the 1870s and 1880s, others from these schools were going out to work with the Danish immigrant communities in the United States of America. Among them were the grandfathers both of Axel Kildegaard and his wife, as he tells us in his contribution to this volume. This essay gives a unique insight into Grundtvig's influence in North America through the life of the Danish communities there. It also shows us, in a vivid picture, another way in which the teaching of Grundtvig did not easily fit into 19th-century Christendom. Amongst the Scandinavian immigrants to the United States, the Danes were the least numerous, and amongst the Danes those who had been influenced by Grundtvig or who felt in general sympathy with his viewpoint were themselves a minority. Thus, among the Scandinavian immigrants and particularly amongst the Norwegians, Grundtvig was regarded with the greatest suspicion. Their strong Lutheran if distinctly Norwegian form of pietism could find itself at home in the religious world of the American mid-West. Grundtvig could not.

These Danes who came to the United States found themselves in a Protestant world very different to the one they had known at home. It had its own history, its own strengths and its own limitations. Its intellectual background in the Calvinism of New England was, if anything, stranger to them than its popular expressions in the revival movements. Axel Kildegaard re-

3.   Quoted in Borish, *The land of the Living*, p. 198.

cords their uneasy reaction to it. "In the church, biblical literalism and doctrinal conservatism ruled. ... Denominations and sects grew in numbers as they grew in competition and intolerance. The separation between the holy and the profane was sharply drawn and exploited. Post-Civil War churches often subscribed to a transcendental belief structure that justified the neglect and avoidance of many human concerns. At the same time, a folk religion reigned that expressed itself in subjective sentimentalities. It was hardly a receptive climate for the Danes, especially those attracted to Grundtvig ... " The Danish preacher and the hymn writer, who in the theology faculties of Europe had looked conservative and old-fashioned, looked positively radical, liberal, soft, humanist and syncretistic in this context.

Nonetheless, as Axel Kildegaard makes clear, within the smaller of the two Churches into which the Danish community split in 1894, a genuinely Grundtvigian pattern of life and thinking continued and indeed flourished for at least two generations. Its milieu was never large but it was true and living, and it produced scholars of the calibre of Johannes Knudsen, Ernest Nielsen, and Axel Kildegaard himself. The name of Grundtvig was not forgotten in at least some Lutheran circles in America. This world also produced men and women of real quality, some of whose voices are reproduced for us in this text.

In preparing his contribution Kildegaard sent round a questionnaire to a representative group of men and women who had been touched by the Grundtvigian ethos. Their testimony is impressive. "One remarked that life is received and celebrated with joy for the wealth that it has – not as the ultimate. But neither is it diminished in any way by being penultimate." This view is echoed by others "who equate being Grundtvigian with unlimited breadth of interest in all life. History itself as an unfolding of life ever new as a witness to a living and creative God. Another wrote: 'When I encounter a perspective that views history, culture and language as a heritage of the Spirit, I am also in touch with my Grundtvigian formation.' ... Some despaired at the captivity of much Christian thought by a sterile literalism of scripture or dogma. They found in Grundtvig a confidence that the Spirit accepts, blesses, and visits our humanness and that its message is one of hope".

As Grundtvig begins to be more widely known in the United States, as he assuredly will be, it will be interesting to see the ways in which he is received in a new millennium. There will surely be circles in which his voice will be welcomed, in which his message will be found penetrating, convincing and relevant. But we may also be sure that suspicion and rejection await him in other circles. Nowhere is Grundtvig's viewpoint more out of sympathy with a large part of conservative American Protestantism than in his conviction about the historic-poetic nature of Christianity and in his determination to detect the goodness and creativity of God still at work throughout the creation, for here the contrast with a way of thinking, determinedly literalist in its attitude towards truth and deeply suspicious in its attitude both towards human history and towards the natural world, is at its greatest.

This poetic-historic aspect of Grundtvig's position, taken together with his capacity for holding together things which ordinarily we leave apart, points us towards one of the deepest elements of his life and thinking, his capacity to hold together in a fruitful, if sometimes difficult interaction, factors, elements, aspects of a situation which are often allowed to remain in separation. This is the subject of the searching investigation in Professor Jakob Balling's study of the nature of Grundtvig's theological vision and its relation to the world of poetry. Balling approaches his subject as a church historian, and as a scholar with a very wide and deep appreciation of the literature of "Old-Europe". Looking at two of the greatest exponents of the theological poetry of that era, Dante and Milton, Balling leads us to see how at least some of the characteristics which he finds in common in them are also to be found in Grundtvig. But this essay not only tells us much about a particular kind of theological poetry, it also tells us much about the character of the poetic theology of "Old-Europe" as a whole. Indeed it tells us much about the nature of theology in general, both in the Christian East and West, as it was in the period before the rise of Western scholasticism. For, as Balling points out, this theology in poetic vein is in many ways very close to "the ancient and medieval biblical and monastic theology", a theology which itself could include, in a coherent, if not strictly systematic way, the whole scope of God's dealings with humanity and all creation.

We are reminded here again of the deeply patristic character of Grundtvig's thought, its biblical and liturgical quality, something we can see in the prose of his sermons – often very poetic prose – as well as in the verse of his hymns. Balling comments on this in relation to two specific Grundtvig hymns. He starts with one of the most famous of all the Easter hymns, a hymn which incidentally is particularly difficult to translate, and he speaks of it as embodying "a genuinely patristic and Old European approach to the Christian message, put to use in fresh and totally un-antiquarian Danish 19th-century speech and thus, by the way, implying an acute challenge to conventional modes of distinguishing between ancient and modern". Having made again, in passing, this point about Grundtvig's capacity to disarrange our sense of past and present and having pointed to the centrality of Easter in his understanding of the gospel, Balling goes on to comment on another even more remarkable hymn; Grundtvig's version of the *Te Deum*, a text which shows how intimate Grundtvig's ties were to that tradition. "Even a cursory comparison between his version and the Latin original (as well as the intermediate versions) makes clear not only that Grundtvig, as we already know, felt comfortably at home in these surroundings but, more significantly, that he felt sufficiently at home to make the *Te Deum* more copiously and densely patristic than it had been in patristic times." Here is a man who has lived himself into the tradition in such a way that the tradition has come to life in him.

At an earlier point in this essay Balling has given us a summary of what he sees as "the sum of the most fundamental tenets of Old European Christian thinking". They deserve pondering, for they help us to see more specifically how it is that Grundtvig as a theologian is so often able to keep together things which get separated. Balling enumerates three points:

1. "the assertion of coherence and mutual illumination between a cosmic, an anthropological and an historical order;

2. the double assertion that God is involved in the world as its Creator and Saviour, knowable as such by way of the world, which he has created and redeemed, and at the same time as the Totally Other, dwelling in an existence unknowable by 'natural' means; and

3. the assertion that everything that has happened in sacred history is relevant for the self-understanding of the now-living individual by being, so to speak, summed up and actualized in him or her."

The great poets of the tradition, a Dante or a Milton, had their own way of articulating and improvising on that basic set of convictions, opening it out and bringing it to life.

"The freedom enjoyed by the poets to build an imaginative universe of meaning by means of interrelated images, open-ended narrative and dramatic confrontation – the freedom, in other words, to establish a mutual 'mirroring' of macrocosm, microcosm and history – enables them to make a statement about the coinherence of creation and of redemption, about God's nearness and otherness, and about the summing up in every human being of God's entire purpose and action that cannot be made by traditional methods of doctrinal exposition."

Only at the very end of that weighty and substantial sentence, with its stress on the possibility of a coherent and all-inclusive vision of things, do I feel the need to register a small note of dissent, by introducing five words of qualification. The statement should read that what the poets can do is make a statement which "cannot be made *in quite that same way* by traditional methods of doctrinal exposition". When we think of the varied forms of doctrinal exposition employed in the Church in the pre-scholastic era, the sermons of the great preachers with their varied rhetorical styles, the liturgical and spiritual texts, which bring doctrine to life in the corporate life of the congregation and in the hidden life of the man or woman of prayer, the different forms of biblical exposition, some more argumentative, some more reflective, the recounting of the deaths of the martyrs and the lives of the saints, and the story of God's doings in the history of his people – think for a moment of the theological value of Bede's *History of the English Church and People*, a text with which Grundtvig was particularly familiar – when we think of all these other ways of opening up the central core of doctrine, many of them at least in some degree poetic, then we have to suggest that the characteristics, which Balling discerns in the outstanding poems of the Christian tradition and in one of the outstanding poems of Grundtvig's own work *New Year's Morning*, are more widely spread, and more frequently embodied through Christian history than he seems to allow, even if at times this happens in ways less radiant and memorable than he describes.

In the whole body of his hymnody, and in the body of his preaching, and it extended over many years until the last Sunday in August 1872, Grundtvig expounds a faith which affirms "that God is involved in the world as its Creator and Saviour, knowable as such by way of the world, which He has created and redeemed". It is a vision of the faith which holds together its different aspects and different dimensions in a remarkably coherent unity and in a living interaction. It seems that it is in and through this world that human beings are called to cooperate with God, to become co-creators with him in the responsible use of their gifts of freedom and creativity.

We are brought back here by Balling's insistence on the patristic nature of Grundtvig's thought, to one particular concern of Philip Hefner's essay, his concern to hear the voice of Eastern Christianity, his determination "to ask whether it is possible for us to reflect with adequacy upon Creation unless we bring both Eastern and Western traditions to bear in equal measure upon this task". As perhaps the most notable Protestant exponent in recent times, of the idea of a fully cosmic Christology, Joseph Sittler found himself indebted not only to the work of the Eastern Fathers, but also to the insights of living Orthodox theologians whom he got to know personally through his work on the Faith and Order Commission, notably John Meyendorff and Nikos Nissiotis. Hefner points to Sittler with Teilhard de Chardin as one of the two great proponents of cosmic Christology in the 20th century. Perhaps we might add to that illustrious pair a third name, a major representative of the Orthodox tradition which has never altogether lost that awareness of the cosmic dimension of theology as a whole. This is the Romanian theologian, Dumitru Staniloae (1903-1993) whose work is accessible to us in a new way since we now have Charles Miller's brief but weighty introduction to his theology, a book which gives us a wonderful overview of its outline and scope.[4]

---

4.   Charles Miller, *The Gift of the World: An Introduction to the Theology of Dumitru Staniloae* (Edinburgh, T&T Clark, 2000).

Staniloae was without question one of the outstanding Orthodox theologians of the last century. But he was little known beyond his own country because he spent the second half of his life until his very last years in the constricting circumstances of communist Romania and indeed in his case spent five years (1958-63) in a prison cell. At the foundation of his thought there is the conviction that the world itself is God's gift and God's word to us, a word and a gift, which humankind is to return in thankfulness and praise. From the opening words of his *Dogmatic Theology* he is concerned to hold together creation and redemption, natural and supernatural, human and divine in a single complex but unified focus. "The Orthodox Church does not separate natural revelation and supernatural. Natural revelation is known and fully understood in the light of supernatural revelation; and natural revelation is given and maintained by God's continual action upon nature." How fully he develops this unified and unifying vision can be seen in Miller's book, particularly in the chapter "Rediscovering Cosmic Christianity", in which he understands the calling of every human person as a participation in the natural priesthood of freely offering back to God God's created gift on behalf of creation itself. In such a perspective "every labour of human mind, imagination or body is therefore a decisive moment. It is either a movement on behalf of natural harmony and human solidarity or else one that fosters the abuse of the natural order and the disintegration of human solidarity with God and one another". Even a first acquaintance with the thought of such a man reveals the theology which, if it has its roots deeply planted in the tradition of Scripture and the first Christian Millennium, is nonetheless urgently contemporary in its living concerns and insights.

Jakob Balling has spoken of "the freedom enjoyed by the poets to build an imaginative universe of meaning by means of inter-related images, open-ended narrative and dramatic confrontation – the freedom, in other words, to establish a mutual 'mirroring' of macrocosm, microcosm and history". Staniloae himself, in his sometimes laborious style, with its elements of poetic and personal eloquence, blended in with passages of academic and philosophical precision, seems to have aimed at realising such a unity and at times to have succeeded in a remarkable degree. Certainly his theology has a wonderful all-inclusive quality to it. But perhaps the most remarkable of all his gifts was that of a friendship which united monks and nuns on one hand with writers and scientists and poets on the other in a single collaborative movement "on behalf of natural harmony and human solidarity". When he was arrested in 1958 there were two things above all that worried the communist authorities, first the inspiration which his writings were giving to the swiftly growing movement of monastic renewal at that time but above all the role which he played in a group of leading Romanian intellectuals who met regularly in his company in Bucharest. Here was a genuinely functioning theology, interactive in its relationship with the world of the arts and the imagination, with the world of economic and technological development and, even if painfully, with the world of social and political action. In a late 20th-century setting we see something of the all-inclusive quality of Grundtvig's own activity as a teacher and writer in the Denmark of the 1850s.

We have been looking at some of the factors involved in a poetic-historic view of Christian truth and life and have been looking at them in what is for the most part a Western European-North American perspective and in categories which are rooted in the thought of the 19th and the 20th century. But in Vítor Westhelle's presentation we are aware of an opening to the South which is also an opening to the further East, an opening to the future which brings us back to the foundation myths, not of one tradition alone, but of many. How many of the topics raised in this exuberantly elusive presentation are topics which relate directly to aspects of Grundtvig's life and experience! We may consider, for instance, languages as means of control, instruments of government; we may consider languages as means of resistance, instruments of subversion; we may consider languages as ways of displaying the truth and enforcing it, or we may think of languages as ways of disguising the truth and saving it from those who would destroy it. Yes, and sometimes it is the same language which fulfils all these functions. Danish, in the first half of the 19th century, on the frontier with Germany, was the language of the peasants, the country people, with no place in law or public administration. At the same time Danish in the Faroe Islands was the language of government and control, the language which threatened the very existence of Faroese, at that stage not reduced to writing, a language which found a defender and advocate in Grundtvig's son Svend, an advocacy which his father strongly supported.

There is in this many-layered text an interpretation of languages and insights which is full of future promise. For someone whose native tongue is English, it is a strange gift to receive John Milton through a mind which is Danish, as it is to see William Shakespeare through a mind which is South American. The amazing many-sidedness, the potential, indefinitely expansive possibilities of meaning, which great texts contain, are opened up in such presentations and through such examples of interchange and interaction. I believe that something of this process is beginning to appear in our work on Grundtvig himself and perhaps especially in the translations of the hymns being made by the English poet and hymn-writer Alan Gaunt. The amazing gift of speech is somehow redoubled when the effort to transpose a poetic word from one language to another is crowned with success.

One small but most interesting and unexpected fact which this book contains concerns this question of language and the juxtaposition of different languages and is to be found in the article by Professor Gustav Björkstrand, rector of the University of Åbo in Finland. It is the fact that the highest concentration of folk high schools anywhere in the world is to be found in the Swedish-speaking region of Finland. It seems as if such schools can flourish best in a region where two languages live close together, side by side, not in mutual antagonism but rather in mutual acceptance and respect. As Björkstrand remarks, it is encouraging to discover that the Swedish-speaking and Finnish-speaking folk high schools make a common affirmation of the culture and heritage which their respective languages convey to them "[without the folk high schools becoming] involved in language squabbles even at the most inflamed periods of linguistic difference".

Is the fact that the Swedish-speaking population of Finland is particularly rich in writers and poets a sign that where different linguistic communities can live together in this way, creative possibilities in both language groups can be released? Might it be possible to see the flourishing state of the literary world in Ireland at the present time where the practice of translation between the Irish and English languages has been very carefully and skilfully pursued for many decades as a similar sign that diversity of language need not always be experienced as part of the curse of Babel? It may also be known as one of the blessings of Pentecost.

If we are rightly, deeply concerned with the loss of plant and animal species in the present growth of the human population of our planet, we need surely to be even more concerned with the number of languages which are dying in these very same years. Within a century it seems probable that the great majority of languages at present spoken by the human race will have died. The loss involved in the destruction of any one language, one of the greatest of human creations, one of the greatest of God's gifts, is altogether beyond calculation. One of the impressive features in Gustav Björkstrand's presentation of the public policies of the Nordic and Baltic countries in the last decade is the stress laid on the importance of cultural and thus of linguistic factors in these relations. The monochrome insistence on the sole importance of economic factors in the life of nations, now taken for granted in large parts of the English-speaking world, is silently rebuked by such wisdom.

Anyone who knows a "minority language" from inside will have some sense of the irreplaceable qualities it embodies and thus a sense of the disastrous loss entailed in the death of any language. It seems as if, in India and Africa as well as in Europe, Grundtvig's sense of the importance of the mother tongue has a particularly urgent resonance in the present time when so many languages are threatened. It certainly seemed to some of those at the Calcutta conference of January 1999 that this was the case. "The multi-ethnic, multicultural, multilingual background of India", of which Dr. Bhattacharya speaks in his paper, calls out for the presence of a way of thought and action which is more sensitive to the irreplaceable value of linguistic diversity than most of our contemporary ideologies are.

Here we come back again to one of the basic and irreducible facts about Grundtvig which we need to explore further. He was both a great poet and a great theologian, the two things together. This gives his utterance a quality which Les Murray, one of the greatest of English language poets of our time, names *Wholespeak*, "properly integrated poetic discourse … ", in an essay called "Embodiment and Incarnation". This *wholespeak* is contrasted in Les Murray's thought with *narrowspeak*, *narrowspeak* being "discourse based on the supposed primacy or indeed exclusive sovereignty of daylight reason … The former *wholespeak*, embraces all the good poetry including that of religion, the latter embraces most of the administrative discourse by which the world is ruled day by day, as well as most criticism … We have come, over the last few centuries, to think that we live in a prose universe, with prose as the norm of all discourse. This is a cause or consequence of the decline in the belief in creation (*poiesis*). In fact descriptive prose doesn't answer to our own inner nature, and so cannot describe the cosmos adequately".[5] Here yet again we discover ways in which Grundtvig does not fit easily into his own century or ours. His highly poetic view of life has its own particular possibilities of meaning and affirmation. The poetic nature of his prose can hold together the many aspects of the one Christian tradition.

It is in this context of the insights of the poet that we can perhaps see the unexpected relevance of Grundtvig's view of things to a widespread but also widely contested religious phenomenon of the English-speaking world during the last 15 or 20 years, the fascination with early Celtic Christianity which is to be found in the United States of America and Australia as much as in Britain and Ireland. That some aspects of this movement have been ambiguous, careless of accuracy or merely sentimental, it would be difficult to deny. But it is possible to argue that behind such things there lie more serious concerns, in particular a desire to recover a sense of the sacredness of the material of which our planet is made and a desire to recover a more forcefully imaginative way of affirming and understanding Christian faith.

One of the less foreseen results of this generalised interest and enthusiasm for all things Celtic has been a renewed study of Celtic Christianity in places where departments of religious studies and departments of Celtic studies are working side by side. Among the more impressive publications, which have come out of this movement, two particularly deserve our attention and are relevant to our purposes. The first is Oliver Davies' major anthology of early Celtic sources (Irish and Welsh), contributed to the series *The Classics of Western Spirituality* and simply entitled *Celtic Spirituality*.[6]

5. Les Murray, *The Paperbark Tree. Selected Prose* (Manchester, 1992), p. 263.
6. Oliver Davies (ed.), *Celtic Spirituality*, preface by James Mackey (Mahwah, Paulist Press, 1999).

In his introduction to this anthology Oliver Davies, having discussed the controversy about the nature of Celtic Christianity, writes, "I maintain that the Christianity that developed in the Celtic countries during the early middle-ages is characterised by a strongly incarnational theology, with an emphasis, in diverse ways, on physicality and materiality … . Nature appears as a theme to an unusual degree, and enjoys its own autonomy … . Human creativity is drawn to the centre of the Christian life in Irish art and Welsh poetry … Features such as the Brigid tradition offer positive and empowering images of women … At a theological level these different aspects find a unity in the centrality of the doctrine of the Trinity, which profoundly shaped the religious imagination of the early Celtic peoples". Needless to say, this world of early Celtic Christianity had a particularly close and complex relationship with the Christianity of Anglo-Saxon England, which Grundtvig studied with such care.

The second work is Ian Bradley's searching, and by no means uncritical study, *Celtic Christianity, Making Myths and Chasing Dreams*.[7] In it the author places the contemporary movement in a long historical context and sees it as the latest manifestation of the desire to rediscover the local origins of the Church which has characterised Christianity in Britain and Ireland since the early middle-ages until today. Such a presentation of the matter makes one look afresh, for instance, at the Celtic enthusiasm of the late 18th century, linked above all with the poems attributed to Ossian. These poems were translated into a number of European languages and aroused great interest. They provide an interesting parallel to the enthusiasm with which the young Grundtvig began to discover the poetry and mythology of his Norse and Anglo-Saxon ancestors. How far these different worlds, Celtic, Norse and Anglo-Saxon, were inter-related in Grundtvig's mind is a matter which deserves more attention. We might well wish that Nugent Wade had been a little fuller in his diary entry in February 1836: "Long evening, intellectual feast with Gruntvig [sic] – on a great variety of subjects – Irish manuscripts – Northern languages – history of the very Northern nations, particularly of Iceland."[8] Here again, in this more serious study of early Celtic Christianity itself and of contemporary interest in it, we find a new context in which the insights of Grundtvig find a remarkable echo.

In working over these texts in the preparation of this volume, I have frequently been reminded of a verse of an Old-European poet of some distinc-

---

7. Ian Bradley, *Celtic Christianity, Making Myths and Chasing Dreams* (Edinburgh University Press, 1999).
8. Quoted in Helge Toldberg, "N. Wade i Helsingør" in *Grundtvig Studier* (1948), pp. 42ff.

tion, Charles Wesley. It is a verse which speaks of this bringing together of things widely separated which we find in so many ways in Grundtvig. It occurs in a Christmas hymn.

> He deigns in flesh to appear
> Widest extremes to join,
> To bring our vileness near
> And make us all divine.

Grundtvig too sees the incarnation as bringing together the world of Spirit, the human spirit and the divine Spirit and the world of dust. It is the same point that Wesley is making here in his use of the word "vileness", a word which in the 18th-century context has a wider and more general meaning than it would have in the English of today; it is not just our sinfulness but our lowness, our everydayness, our triviality, our dustiness, our dirtiness. These things are brought near and made *all* divine. The word *all* in this line – it is one of Charles Wesley's favourite words – may rightly convey two meanings. It is saying that the Word's coming in the flesh makes all of us divine, an inclusive and not an exclusive affirmation. But at the same time it is saying that the coming makes us wholly divine; it brings about an entire transformation in our nature, changing the water of our humanity into the wine of his divinity.

These are the kind of extreme affirmations which Grundtvig makes time and again both in his sermons and his preaching. This is the kind of wholespeak that he uses. It is only our habit of thinking of him as an ordinary 19th-century churchman which blinds us to these facts. As Christian Thodberg points out at the end of his article on Grundtvig's interpretation of the scriptures, the work of God is one work from beginning to end. Thus, for Grundtvig, the resurrection, ascension and second coming are to be understood with the same realism, with the same seriousness as the birth, crucifixion and death of Jesus. All alike speak to us of a transformation of heaven and earth, a transfiguration of flesh and spirit, a bringing together of all things in the divine love which renews all things in God. In a Septuagesima sermon for 1834, Grundtvig comments on the word of scripture, "what God has joined together let no man put asunder" (GP).

"No, just as surely as the creator has brought soul and body together within our human nature, so will the saviour free both soul and body from the bonds of corruption ... and just as humankind is created of the dust of the earth, to be its king, and to eat of its fruit and to live eternally, so the Saviour will in no way abolish or derange this nature's order, but only loose the bonds in which nature has been placed on account of the sins of its king, that is to say of humankind. So, when by the world we understand the world which God created in six days by his Word, which he saw and found to be very good, then we shall also see that what the Lord says is joyfully and trust-worthily fulfilled, that God sent out his son into the world, not to condemn the world but that the world through him might be saved" (GP). The solidar-ity of humankind with creation is total. All creation waits in eager expecta-tion of a new birth into eternal life.

In such ways Grundtvig succeeds in holding together macrocosm, micro-cosm and history; he is enabled to affirm the coinherence of creation and re-demption, God's nearness and God's otherness, and to speak of the summing up in every human being of God's entire purpose and action, in remarkably open-ended and potentially fruitful and creative ways. We see something of his strangeness in his conjunction of intellect, imagination and practical ca-pacity. We see it again in his constant juxtaposition of spirit and dust, created and divine. We see it again in his refusal to be defined, in terms of his own time, as either of the right or of the left.

Speaking in May 1998 in Oxford, on the centenary of Gladstone's death, another great public figure of 19th-century Europe, who resists our attempts to categorise him, Colin Matthew could say of him that no one in public life had been both so radical and so conservative, radical when he was a conser-vative, and conservative when he was a radical, and both running together through the long course of his public life. Just as Grundtvig, in the many-sid-edness of his gifts, overflowed the particular calling of preacher, poet, scholar and educationalist, so too Gladstone was all his life much more than a plain politician, showing himself also as a scholar, a thinker and a theologian. And despite the failures and setbacks of his later years, particularly in his Irish policy, his public personality was one of hope and progress.

It is true that it is difficult to make Gladstone's genius a strongly poetic one, but both men, in their totally different circumstances, were filled with a hope which was rooted not in this world but in a vision of the magnificence and bounty of God, conveyed through the living tradition of the Church in 1,900 years. Both held together sacred and profane, this world and the next in ways which were profoundly untypical of the 19th century. If in one sense both worked with rather than against the 19th century's tendency towards secular-ization, both did it in such a way as to mitigate profoundly the effects of that secularization, indeed in some sense to call into question its very meaning. In Grundtvig's case, as we can see in the pages of this book, there are possibilities in his work, possibilities for reopening old and neglected paths of Christian thought and action and discovering new ways forward for the human family into a time of massive change, without losing touch with the gifts and achieve-ments of the past, without that collective loss of memory which seems at times to threaten our Western societies. If there is prophetic vision here it is one which is rooted in the heritage of the ages and which constantly reveals afresh the necessity and creativity of interaction and reciprocity.

Theology and Creation: Joseph Sittler and N.F.S. Grundtvig

By Philip Hefner

My reflection on Joseph Sittler and N.F.S. Grundtvig takes the following shape: (1) I will set forth the main theme of my discussion by focusing upon one concept from the work of Joseph Sittler that articulates what I take to be also an important concept for Grundtvig; (2) I shall elaborate the significance of that concept; (3) I shall suggest some differences between Sittler and Grundtvig that occur within the common framework of this concept, also illuminating what is at stake in these differences; and (4) I will conclude by posing some questions and challenges that emerge from my discussion. My presentation is largely a reading of one essay by Sittler: "The Presence and Acts of the Triune God in Creation and History" (1971) and four of Grundtvig's short essays: "Folk-Life and Christianity" (1847), "About Folk-Life and Dr. Rudelbach" (1848), "The Christian, the Spiritual, and the Eternal Life"(1855-61), and "The Innate and the Reborn Humanity" (1855-61). I must warn you that since the concepts at issue in this discussion also occupy my own thinking, I cannot avoid interposing myself into this interaction between Grundtvig and Sittler.

I. Grace and the "immemorial placenta of personal being"

Joseph Sittler concludes his essay on the Triune God in nature and history with these words:

Just as humans are unable to envision eternal blessedness with God apart from communion with their fellow human beings, so they are unable even to know an eternal blessedness with God without a conservation and renewal, in that consummation, of that theatre of nature which is the immemorial placenta of our personal being. Any thinkable consummation must be in some sense in continuity with the things that are ... A Christian theology cannot go from grace to nature; the incarnation demands that it so relate grace to nature that the presence of God as grace in nature is not in principle excluded.[1]

1.   Joseph Sittler, "The Presence and Acts of the Triune God in Creation and History" in Vilmos Vajta (ed.), *The Gospel and Human Destiny* (Minneapolis, Augsburg Publ.

"Any thinkable consummation must be in some sense in continuity with the things that are," with the "immemorial placenta of personal being": This, I take it, is a concept that Grundtvig never tired of affirming, and very likely he would have resonated to Sittler's rhetoric of formulation. Grundtvig did state it in epigrammatic form: "Human beings must be confronted where they really exist if they are to be persuaded to believe in Jesus Christ."[2] It is this concept that I choose to make the centerpiece of these reflections on the two thinkers. Even these two sets of quoted passages suggest some differences between the two thinkers, but I shall postpone discussion of such elements to a later section of my paper.

II. The significance of taking seriously "the things that are"

Both Sittler and Grundtvig argued strenuously that the actualities of the human situation constitute the vessel or medium in which God's grace comes to us. God's grace confronts us where we really exist, in Grundtvig's words. This assertion has the appearance of obviousness akin to the child's exclamation that "the emperor has no clothes on." Where else would we encounter God's grace except in the actual situation in which we live every day of our lives? The striking and puzzling thing is that both of these theologians, who were separated by a full century, had to carry on a vigorous polemic against the theological mindset of their times and also provide a reassessment of Christian history, in order to clear the way for their insistence that "where we really exist" is where grace meets us.

Why would such an obvious assertion be strange and even unacceptable to the religious and theological consensus in the second half of both the 19th century and of the 20th? The emphasis on the fitness of the present to carry grace rests on two assumptions that challenged the conventional views that confronted these theologians and continue today to carry an unsettling freight.

Revaluing the place where we live
Firstly, such an emphasis revalues the natural and social order in which we carry on our lives. The conventional view that confronted both Grundtvig

House, 1971), pp. 131-32. Hereafter referred to as "Presence." In all of the quotations that appear in this paper, wherever possible, I have revised unnecessary masculine forms by replacing them with more inclusive forms.
2.   N.F.S. Grundtvig, "About Folk-Life and Dr. Rudelbach" in Johannes Knudsen (tr., ed.), *Grundtvig, Selected Writings* (Minneapolis, Fortress Press, 1976), p. 48. Hereafter referred to as "Rudelbach."

and Sittler, and which also faces us today, holds that the condition in which we live is so flawed, so evil and sinful, that it not only cannot be a medium of God's redeeming grace but on the contrary constitutes precisely the hopeless mess from which God redeems us.

This conventional view may be grounded in an understanding of the Fall that has virtually destroyed the goodness of God's original creation and thereby obliterated the image of God in which humans were made. Or, it may be rooted in a classical Hellenistic worldview that considered the realm of time and space and matter to be inherently inferior. In either case, this present condition is the situation from which we expect relief, from which we expect to be extricated, the very antithesis of the blessedness God has willed for us. We can feel the frustration of the Original Happy Dane as he describes those who hold to the unfitness of the human situation:

It is evidently inconsistent, argumentative, and extremely boring when so-called Catholic or Protestant theologians, evangelical or biblical, admit and insist on the creation of humans in the image of God and the renewal in the same image by faith in the Son of God and the Son of man, our Lord Jesus Christ, when with equal vigor they insist that "the Fall," which occurred between creation and renewal and which makes the reconciliation or renewal indispensable for salvation, has distorted, or rather erased, the life of God's image and destroyed humankind, so that there is nothing left of the created glory or the relation to God ... Then the story of revelation and the whole work of reconciliation become a series of impossibilities which must be surmounted by the dead and powerless written word that whatever is impossible for humans is possible for God.[3]

The concept that stands as the theme of this discussion challenges such viewpoints with a fundamental reordering of sensibilities, a Copernican revolution in perspective.To say that the condition in which we actually live is that *from* which God wishes to extricate us, *from* which we are to be redeemed, is exactly wrong. Such a perspective has missed the point. The natural condition in which we live is that which is to be redeemed, to be brought to term, to be fulfilled in the ways that God imagines and wills.

What is at stake in this dispute is nothing else than the doctrine of Creation. The Dane is rejecting an understanding of Creation that holds it to be for all practical purposes so fully compromised by the Fall and sin that it is no longer a fit vehicle for God's gracious action of fulfillment. He is insisting that what God has created originally is that to which God continues to be faithful, that the natural order in which we actually find ourselves is defined norma-

3.   N.F.S. Grundtvig, "The Innate and the Reborn Humanity" in *Selected Writings*, pp. 75-76. Hereafter referred to as "Innate."

tively by its character as the created work of God and not by its very obvious flaws and sin. This point is fundamental, and it is one in which Joseph Sittler thoroughly concurs: *By what is the actual worldly order in which we live every day normatively defined – by its grounding in God's will and action of creation or by its empirically manifested evil, sin, and finitude?* What is at stake here is the classic Christian theology of Creation and, in particular, the doctrine of creation-out-of-nothing (*creatio ex nihilo*). Whatever may be the popular misconceptions (or learned misconceptions, for that matter!), the phrase "out of nothing" has to do most centrally not with some speculations about conditions at the beginning of time nor with the rooting out of ancient heresies but with the conviction that God and God alone is the ground of the world and its existence. As a consequence, to affirm the "out of nothing" is to insist that the world is defined normatively by its status as God's creation and by nothing else. Redemption flows from the living spring of creation and from no other source. As Sittler puts it, "Grace came by Jesus Christ, but grace was not created by Jesus Christ."[4]

Once this Copernican revolution of perspective takes hold, then it is clear that the natural condition in which we live is the theater of God's grace and the medium of God's presence to us; furthermore, it is literally unthinkable that some alternative medium would be necessary or even possible.

Grace shares in the contours of change

The second assumption which is contained in the Grundtvig-Sittler proposal and which conventional opinion finds unsettling is that since the "place where human beings really exist" locates itself in a continually changing terrain, the shape of God's presence for us as grace shares in the contours of that change.

Grundtvig and Sittler, each in his own situation, found stern resistance to this recognition of change as intrinsic to the coming of divine grace. In Grundtvig's case, the issue of change took the form of an insistence that the presence and grace of God could be carried by the realities of Danish folk-life, including language and national geopolitical placement. Against Dr. Rudelbach, for example, he had to defend himself from the charge that he was identifying Christianity with Danish nationalism. Apparently his antagonist had accused Grundtvig of falling into the same temptation that led the Germans and the French to sanctify their "un-Christian and anti-Christian nationalism." Since the critics apparently identified Christianity with social-cultural forms that were abstracted from any actually existing forms, except perhaps Old Testament and New Testament examples, Grundtvig was obliged to argue for the potential equality of all social-cultural forms, with respect both to their fitness as vessels of grace and also to their flawed character. He held up

4.   Sittler, "Presence," p. 125.

the figure of John the Baptist as one who "revitalized the memories, the hope, and the imagery of the people, and without this awakening to folk-conscious-ness Christianity would not have been known, understood, or believed in Is-rael."[5] Not only do Martin Luther and the other Reformers stand in the line of John the Baptist, but one gets hints moreover that Grundtvig saw his own work in translating "the ancient chronicles and *Beowulf*" in this light.[6] Grundtvig might well have echoed Sittler's comment thusly: "A Christian theology cannot go from grace to folk-life; the incarnation demands that it so relate grace to folk-life that the presence of God as grace in folk-life is not in principle excluded."

Joseph Sittler believed that the recognition of the changing contours of God's presence as grace was at the top of the theological agenda in his time. He also recognized that most mainstream theologians did not appreciate this challenge with the urgency that he thought necessary. In the essay I am focus-ing upon, he makes the point several times that "theology as a realm of dis-course is literally fighting for its life as an intelligible and thereby legitimate field of human activity."[7] And the neuralgic point in this fight for survival is that theologians tend to consider their task too much in terms of custodial re-sponsibility with respect to the past traditions. Let me quote his opening paragraph:

… one must try to go beyond the venerable tradition of theological work as that tradi-tion understood its task as preservation, clarification, transmission. For so powerful have been the reassessing necessities laid upon us by historical and critical studies in all areas, and so disintegrative and reconstructive have been the shifts in center and in effective force of the components of modern culture, that the theologian is forced to re-gard the past, not as a place to stand, but rather as a place from which to work toward shaping-the-possible in Christian theology.[8]

He chided the Lutheran tradition with particular sharpness. "I am aware that in such an exercise of creative imagination one is certain to be accused of theologizing beyond the generally accredited rules … How strange indeed that theological practice in the tradition of Luther should have become suspi-cious of creative theological imagination!"[9]

5.   Grundtvig, "Rudelbach," p. 45. See also Grundtvig, "Folk-Life and Christianity" in *Selected Writings*, p. 42. Hereafter referred to as "Folk-Life."
6.   Grundtvig, "Folk-Life," p. 43.
7.   Sittler, "Presence," p. 90.
8.   Sittler, "Presence," p. 90.
9.   Sittler, "Presence," p. 92.

The locus of this call for and defense of theological imagination was the recognition that the place in which we exist, and in which God's presence as grace is real, is a changing order. When he asserted this in his 1961 New Delhi address at the World Council of Churches Assembly,[10] to the effect that nature is now a central category for human self-understanding he was accused of selling out to the Hindu culture in which that address was delivered. When he took recourse to *Colossians* and *Ephesians* as grounds for his ideas, he was charged with neo-Gnosticism and failing to understand rightly that grace pertains to humans and to the context of Christ's forgiving sins and not to nature. From his earliest writings until his last, he pleaded with Lutherans to recognize that grace is relevant to more than the forgiveness of our sins and that it did not originate in the appearance of Jesus of Nazareth in the first century.[11] If our tradition does not face up to this urging, he believed, it will prove itself to be unintelligible and thereby illegitimate because it will have failed to understand that where we live today is not encompassed by a conviction that we are sinners and a confidence that those sins are atoned for by Jesus Christ. Our human situation is larger than the categories of sin and forgiveness can be made to cover. So is God's grace. The terrain in which we live defines the minimum dimensions into which God's grace can and does reach. This being so, our comprehension and proclamation of grace must attain at least those same minimum dimensions. Although the context of Sittler's insistence is markedly different from that of Grundtvig a century earlier, I would suggest that the Dane's concern for folk-life as the ambience for Christian renewal requires the same kind of judgments about sin, nature, and grace that Sittler called for.

The issue at stake in the revaluing of "things that are" was the doctrine of Creation out-of-nothing. The issue that underlies the embodiment of grace on the terrain of change is also the doctrine of Creation, but in this case in its classic form of *continuing Creation*, since it is this doctrine that articulates our Christian faith that every moment in the process of creation is related to God in the very same terms that are affirmed in the Creation out-of-nothing: The mind-blowing versatility, surprise, and change that we experience in the created order is grounded in God the Creator and in nothing else.

Grace is the work of the Triune God
There is a central theological issue that Sittler moved toward in his last decade of theological activity that I wish to elaborate, and I believe it to be an is-

10. Joseph Sittler, "Called to Unity" reprinted (from *Ecumenical Review*, 1962) in *Currents in Theology and Mission*, 16:1 (February 1989), pp. 5-13.
11. Joseph Sittler, *Essays on Nature and Grace* (Minneapolis, Fortress Press, 1972), p. 88. Hereafter referred to as *Essays*.

sue that flows from Grundtvig's thinking as well. At least it flows from Grundtvig's thought when we read him and take him seriously in our own situation, and we have no alternative today but to read him as our contemporary, even if our interest is primarily historical.

The issue here is simply stated: *Wherever we encounter in our experience that which we believe to be the deepest, the highest, and the holiest in forms that we call gracious, we are obliged by our faith to say that we have encountered the Triune God in that place.* This assertion is complex and rich; its elaboration could easily fill a large volume. Even though it may seem out of place in a brief essay like the present one, it nevertheless must be stated because it clarifies just what is at stake in the Grundtvig-Sittler proposal. This mammoth issue makes us aware of how high these two theologians have upped the ante for our understanding the Christian faith and our preaching and teaching that faith.

Let me elaborate briefly from Sittler's writings. His point is simple and direct. He insists that the risk of faith includes what he calls the risk of "the act of investiture." By investiture, he means that in any and every instance in which human experience engenders the sense of redemptive grace, that experience must be invested with the meaning and significance that attaches to the idea which we have of the God who works that grace. For Christians, that God is the Triune God, Creator, Redeemer, and Sanctifier. This means, on the one hand, that any occasion of God's presence is an occasion of the presence of the fullness of God. We dare not describe any encounter with God in terms so small that our description in fact betrays – that is, actually commits treason against – the richness of what we actually believe about God! On the other hand, our understanding of the natural occasion in which God's presence is known is also transformed into terms that are commensurate with what we believe about God. In the framework of the Triune concept of God, this means that the situation in which we meet God is the creation of God, that it has been created for redemption, and that the ongoing presence of God as Spirit aims at making actual for us the redemption of the creation in which our lives participate. In other words, our concept of the God who is present in our situations requires that we do not settle for too low a concept of the situation which has been the medium of God's presence as grace. Strangely, we most often do settle, in our ordinary lives, for too small a concept of God and also too small a concept of our situation. The situation in which we meet God's grace is not only an occasion of redemption, it is also the creation of God, and redemption constitutes the meaning of the created situation. This is very heavy stuff! In the concluding section of this paper, I will call attention to the explosive implications of this Trinitarian perspective for suggesting that all of the creation, including the non-human sector, must be considered as a realm governed by the love that is associated with the Triune God.

Sittler writes:

For what the doctrine of the trinity affirms and labors to protect against misunderstanding and diminishment, is that creation, redemption, and sanctification have their source in God, that this God is not identical with but is present in what he creates, is present in the redemption of what he creates and is present in all restoration, uniting, and upholding of his redeemed creation.[12]

We most often do not view ourselves and the conditions of our ordinary life in these terms. We do not think of these as the creation of the God whose aim is to be present in grace for the redemption of who we are and where we live. Nor do we often enough understand the presence of grace in our lives as the presence of the Creator God whose intention is the redemption of the creation within the ongoing care of the sanctifying Spirit. We do not, in other words, understand the meaning of our lives and the situations in which we carry out our lives to be found in the creating and redeeming work of God.

This is, however, exactly the significance of what Grundtvig and Sittler proposed – at least that is the way I read them. For Grundtvig, this is expressed in terms of "Man first and then Christian/ Therefore every man on this earth/Must strive to be a true person."[13] It was also expressed in his insistence that the Danish people must come alive in their Danish folk-life if they are to receive the fulfillment that comes in Christ. He rejected the notion that humanity lives "a life in heaven or in the sky, never on earth. On earth you never find humanity without folk-life, whether folk-life encompasses humanity or, as in the case of Jesus Christ, humanity encompasses folk-life."[14] He also wrote, "If the people really are to see, hear, and find what the spirit of the Lord, as a foreign guest, has to give, and what the essentials are, they must have a living participation through their natural imagery, for this is where the living proclamation of Christianity of necessity must begin."[15]

What are we to conclude from such notions but that Grundtvig believes that our basic humanity, as well as our folk culture and mores, are God's creation and as such constitute who and what we are and the form of creation which God intends to fulfill in redemption? And what are we to conclude of the occasions of grace that meet us in our basic humanity and culture except that they are the presence of the God who intends to redeem what has been created under the illumination of the Spirit? *This, then, is the fundamental meaning of our humanity and our culture, that they are the creation of God, governed*

---

12. Sittler, "Presence," p. 91.
13. Grundtvig, *Selected Writings*, pp. 140-41. For a fuller discussion of this theme in Grundtvig's thought, see Johannes Knudsen, *Danish Rebel: A Study of N.F.S. Grundtvig* (Philadelphia, Muhlenberg Press, 1955), especially chapters V and XII.
14. Grundtvig, "Folk-Life," pp. 41-42.
15. Grundtvig, "Rudelbach," pp. 47-48.

by God's intention to redeem them. Grundtvig put this, in Sittler's own words, in the epigram: Human beings are "a divine experiment, which demonstrates how spirit and dust can interpenetrate one with another and be transfigured in a common, divine consciousness."[16]

For Sittler, the force of this insight extended from human life to the entire non-human natural world. In his view, the critical change in outlook of the past century was the recognition that world-as-history has to take the measure of world-as-nature; the explosive change in our worldview is that our human history transpires within the larger processes of nature's history. He understood that our self-consciousness is being reshaped by this worldview change.We define ourselves as *Homo operator*, Operational Man, that is, as persons who are what we are by virtue of our intercourse with the non-human natural world, according to how nature shapes us and how we in turn reshape nature.[17]

Faith takes a risk when it rejects too small an understanding of either the moments of grace experienced within the ambience of the natural world or the natural occasions that bear those moments. Conventional wisdom does in fact view reality in terms that are too small. The risk of investiture that faith undergoes is to conceive of nature "as a field of grace" undergirded by a God who is creator and incarnate redeemer. *The fundamental meaning of the natural order, consequently, is informed by its status as creation-intended-for-redemption.* In Sittler's own words,

Faith, that is to say, when it becomes maturely conscious of the risk-character of its demand, is always an act of investiture of total reality with that vision, value, and meaning which has been granted to us in our encounters with the deepest, highest, and holiest. When that deepest, highest, and holiest is the presence and power of grace, and when the occasions of its life-sustaining gift are granted us within our residency within the non-human world-theatre of our existence, the place and scope for the ethical is given along with the realm of the gracious.[18]

Note that Sittler introduces the ethical dimension to the discussion. The presence of the Triune God as grace encompasses the Sanctifier Spirit informing the behavioral direction of our lives. If nature is the theater of creation and redemption, then it follows that our behavior is called to take the shape that is appropriate to such a theater, and that shape includes an appropriate ethic.

16. Quoted in Theodor Jørgensen, "Grundtvig's *The Church's Retort* - in a Modern Perspective," in A.M. Allchin et al. (eds.), *Heritage and Prophecy. Grundtvig and the English-Speaking World* (Aarhus, 1993), p. 176.
17. Sittler, "Presence," p. 124.
18. Sittler, *Essays*, p. 116.

When we look at nature from this center, then we learn that "the grace of the Creator is a principle of the creation,"[19] and this changes our total outlook both on the world of nature and on ourselves. We are to assess the world and use it in ways that are consistent with the revelation that it is of God and a place of divine grace. When we do this, then we have had the truth revealed to us, and we know how to act in obedience to the truth. Sittler writes:

If, for instance, Lake Michigan is assessed according to its given ecological structure as a place for multiple forms of life, by nature self-sustaining and clean, available for right use and delight, then in a blunt and verifiable way, we are "justified" by grace even in our relation to the things of nature. The opposite of justification is condemnation … If a lake becomes a disposal-resource, or a dump, or a source for water to cool ingots with, or a bath to flush out oil-bunkers then a repudiated grace that "justifies" becomes the silent agent of condemnation.[20]

Instinctively, a Lutheran recognizes that Sittler is touching upon the rhetoric of Law and Gospel. "The Law always accuses." In Lake Michigan as garbage dump, we encounter the hidden God, whose wrath is known in the accusation leveled by the silent agent of condemnation. Sittler believed that such an understanding constitutes a major instance of revelation, especially for the heirs of the Reformation, who are inclined to restrict both Law and Gospel to the privacy of individual sin and its forgiveness. Nature is not the source of justification, nor of Gospel, but our transactions with Lake Michigan are the place in which the Gospel's justification is either present or not present. If it is not present there, then it is really absent; if it is present, it is really present. The revelation is not complete, however, until we understand our lives in the natural world to be fully incorporated within the central Christian vision of the Trinity.

III. Variations within the theme

Since Grundtvig and Sittler lived and worked in such different settings, a century apart, it would be inappropriate to make too meticulous a comparison of their convergences and differences. There are, however, some interesting comparisons to be made, within a loosely fitting interpretive framework that aims at heuristic suggestions rather than definitive judgments.

19. Sittler, *Essays*, p. 121.
20. Sittler, *Essays*, pp. 121-22.

Some converging moves

One of the most interesting impressions I have gained from this comparative study is that these two theologians seemed obliged to make some of the same conceptual moves as they attempted to establish their fundamental notions concerning the created order of nature and culture. I note four such moves.

1. Sin and the Fall. I have already indicated that Grundtvig and Sittler each carried on a polemic against conventional concepts of sin and the Fall. Even though they share a great deal in their interpretation of these concepts, they also make their moves from somewhat different positions. For both, it was a matter of some urgency to insist that whatever sin and Fall mean, they cannot destroy the integrity of God's will and work at creation. Sin and Fall cannot be allowed to dig a chasm between creation and redemption so deep that the New Testament image of "new creation" could be interpreted as a creation *different* from God's original creation, rather than as the more acceptable idea of a *renewed* creation.

Within this general framework, for Grundtvig, it is specifically a priority to defend the viability of the concept of the "image of God," in which humans were created. If the image of God in humans is substantially obliterated by the Fall, then he is unable to defend his basic thesis that reborn Christian humanity is the fulfillment of the innate humanity and folk-life in which we find ourselves. Sittler's proposals require, in a somewhat different vein, that sin and the Fall not be considered as the sole target of God's gracious intention. This would result in a moralistic and anthropocentric reductionism of grace, what *Wolfhart Pannenberg* terms "soteriological reductionism," and one of Sittler's principal aims was to nullify such a reductionism.

2. The Incarnation. Both theologians consider the Incarnation of Christ to be the cardinal validation of their proposals for interpreting the natural created order. The Incarnation establishes both that the fleshly order of human nature was not rendered by its finitude unfit as vehicle of God's presence in redemptive grace and that God's intention is to redeem created nature and not to destroy or replace it.

3. Eastern Christian traditions. Both Sittler and Grundtvig take recourse to Eastern tradition in order to substantiate their theological hypotheses. Grundtvig made direct use of Irenaeus and received indirect influences, in the course of his visits to England, from his contacts with members of the Oxford movement. Sittler encountered the East chiefly through his long tenure on the Faith and Order Commission, which brought important friendships with such Eastern theologians as Nikos Nissiotis, John Meyendorf, and Alexander Schmeman, as well as with scholars of Eastern thought, such as Charles Moeller and Geoffrey Lampe. His work abounds with references to the work of Gregory of Nyssa, Irenaeus, Gregory Palamas, and others.

The Eastern traditions furnished a number of resources for their proposals: a congenial interpretation of sin and the Fall; a view of grace that focused upon transformation, presence, and theosis, rather than sin, guilt, and moral defect; and a cosmic Christology that Sittler found especially fruitful.

4. Language. Both men were unusually sensitive to the function of language as an essential dimension of human nature and of the human quest for meaning. Their views are not identical, but one might guess that they would have enjoyed each other's company for reflection on language and faith and also for the love of poetry that they both shared.

Some differences worth probing
There are many differences between these two theologians that are not worth pursuing because they throw no light on the common project that Grundtvig and Sittler shared. Two differences are fruitful for elaboration, however.

1. Creation as nature and as culture. It is likely that both men would want to affirm that both non-human nature and human culture qualify as dimensions of God's creation, but their respective situations and intentions led them to focus upon these dimensions from different perspectives. My understanding is that Grundtvig dealt with non-human nature more extensively in works that are inaccessible to me. Be this as it may, it seems to me that the cutting edge of his theological and social proposals required more attention to creation as human culture. His concern with Nordic literature and religion, his insistence that community is as central to human nature as individuality, and his belief that Christian renewal of human existence fulfills indigenous culture – all of these moved creation as culture to the fore of his constructive thinking. Sittler, on the other hand, believed that it was precisely the pressing new awareness that human history is an event within the history of non-human nature that must be recognized to be the engine of the imaginative theological construction that is required if theology is to survive as an intelligible and legitimate enterprise.

Sittler recognized that human and non-human nature are intimately and dialectically related, and he also understood that both are grounded in God's work of creation and redemption. I have no knowledge that Grundtvig gave attention to the dialectic that conjoins human and non-human nature. In any case, whether the difference between the two thinkers is real or only apparent, this is an issue that requires further reflection at some depth. Sittler did clearly recognize this need, but he did not enter into extensive discussion of it, apart from his insight into the intimacy and ethical implications of the relationship between humans and the rest of nature. Whether it be viewed as part of the Grundtvig-Sittler legacy or as an item of their unfinished business, this is an important issue for theology to reflect upon today.

2. Attitude toward the past. My reading of these two theologians leads me to believe that although both were innovative and both found it necessary to construct impressive conceptual theological scaffolding to protect their innovations, they reflected differently on how they related to the past traditions that were at hand for their work. Both men honored the traditions of Christian faith and thought, and they were both learned in those traditions. Since both of them were eminently "churchly" theologians and concerned with practical parish ministry and preaching, their works are permeated by their appropriation and interpretation of the Bible, theological traditions, and traditions of worship, church structure, and catechesis.

Grundtvig, however, although he is clearly an innovative thinker, appears to understand himself in churchly circles as a defender of the past tradition. However sound its argumentation may be, the critical work that early on brought upon him the verdict of censorship and exile, *The Church's Retort*, as well as the writings that are translated into English by Ernest Nielsen under the title, *What Constitutes Authentic Christianity?*,[21] seem to be an attempt to turn back the tide of critical biblical scholarship that Sittler, a century later, would simply acknowledge as the beginning of a fundamental deconstruction of tradition that cannot be gainsaid. Sittler appreciated the traditions of the Church as much as Grundtvig did, but he believed that as an obedient theologian, he was compelled by the tide of critical thought and the rearrangement of human experience of which such thought is a symptom to render that tradition in a radically new way. His sharpest jabs are not at the critical thinkers and movements that have deconstructed the past traditions, but rather at the custodians of tradition who refuse to acknowledge the deconstruction and to act upon that acknowledgment.

If I am correct in my hunches at this point, then we have here another item that deserves further reflection. Is the difference between the two attitudes toward the past fully explained by taking into account the difference in their historical and cultural placement? Or do we encounter here two diverging options for those who see their vocations in terms of churchly and theological innovation?

IV. A legacy worth claiming

I am reading Grundtvig and Sittler, not primarily as figures from the past that deserve historical interpretation (although that dimension is contained in what I have presented), but rather as conversation partners in the theological

21. N.F.S. Grundtvig, *What Constitutes Authentic Christianity?*, tr. Ernest D. Nielsen (Minneapolis, Fortress Press, 1985).

task that faces us today. I have deliberately described their project in terms that are interesting in relation to my own, thereby perhaps following Rudolf Bultmann's insight that the truest objectivity with respect to the past is to pose to it, in a self-aware manner, our own questions, in the hope that we can receive its wisdom for what concerns us most, rather than pretending that we can insert ourselves into the projects of the past apart from our own interests.

I have interpreted the two men's projects under the rubric of Creation. I conclude my discussion by highlighting four sets of issues that seem to me to be part of their legacy to us as we reflect upon Creation. I consider these issues to be live ones today, and I am grateful to Grundtvig and Sittler, if for nothing else, for having reminded me that these issues are both urgent and inescapable for theology and the Church today and, in particular, for the Lutheran Church and its theology.

1. East and West. Grundtvig and Sittler compel us to ask whether it is possible for us to reflect with adequacy upon Creation unless we bring both Eastern and Western traditions to bear in equal measure upon this task. Heirs of Augustine, we continue to write books, preach sermons, and prepare candidates for ordination as if Augustine's judgment concerning the Pelagians were the only viable judgment, as if his interpretations of the Fall and Original Sin were not themselves considered to be heterodox by his peers in the East – I think of Gregory of Nyssa. Even more questionable is our neglect of the profound alternative readings of the Christian theology of Creation, sin, freedom, grace, and sanctification that are offered to us by Eastern traditions.

2. Human and non-human nature. These two theologians remind us forcefully that nature is both human and non-human, and so is Creation. Although both of them recognized that how these two facets of nature/Creation interrelate, both in their origins and in their contemporary unfolding, is of cardinal importance for us to understand, neither of them provided for us the insights and the concepts that can undergird such an understanding. Despite the massive amount of reflection that has taken place since Grundtvig wrote and even since Sittler was in his prime, the Church and its theological community still have not taken the measure of these issues. The recent excitement concerning the patenting of biological processes, in which several hundred church leaders in the United States allowed themselves to be coopted by a secular activist who opposes technology, reveals, regardless of our particular opinions, that these leaders were virtually helpless and defenseless when faced with the challenge to understand how humans are related to the rest of the natural world and what action such an understanding requires. Environment, technology, medicine, reproduction, and death – these are but a few of the urgent contemporary questions that require of us a sense of Creation that encompasses the interrelationship between human and non-human nature. One might say that the challenge facing the Church and its theology today is to take the measure, Christianly, of contemporary understandings of the world, and that includes interpreting the world's meaning within the life of the Triune God. No single issue is more central to this task than that of understanding how human and non-human nature are to be interrelated.

3. *Nature and Grace.* Grundtvig and Sittler remind us that the rubric of Creation is *ipso facto* also the rubric of how nature and grace are related. This issue is interwoven with the two previously cited issues. The challenge here is the same as I have just described: to take the measure of nature within our Gospel of grace. In Sittler's terms, we are obliged to conceive of God's presence as grace in terms that are commensurate with the dimensions of the field in which that grace is active and experienced. We have made remarkably little advance in our theological understanding of these issues in the century and a half since Grundtvig began writing.

One of the most difficult and exciting aspects of this set of issues is Christology. Grundtvig pressed us to understand how Christ relates to indigenous cultures, whereas Sittler seeks a Christology of "cosmic extension," encompassing the non-human natural order. I find it curious that, with respect to Grundtvig's concerns, we are quite in agreement that Christ must be related constructively to the non-Western and so-called "marginalized" cultures in which Christianity is taking hold – Third World, African American, Latino, Women – while we give little or no attention in a theologically constructive way to the mainstream Western cultures in which Christendom has expressed itself. Lutheran seminaries in the United States, for example, give virtually no attention to the philosophical or literary or social-scientific or social-political traditions of U.S. culture, except as those traditions have emerged from marginalized groups. Except for a few leaders, like Samuel Simon Schmucker, there has been no effort to take American culture seriously in the Lutheran churches in the way that marginalized groups are doing. We have virtually no sense whatsoever of "Human first and then Christian" with respect to the humans who comprise what is often called "Christendom," particularly not in the Grundtvigian sense that takes indigenous national cultures into account. We give virtually no attention, among "non-marginalized" groups to his words, "If the people really are to see, hear, and find what the spirit of the Lord, as a foreign guest, has to give, and what the essentials are, they must have a living participation through their natural imagery, for this is where the living proclamation of Christianity of necessity must begin."[22] We are strong on a Christology of critique with respect to Western cultures, but very weak on constructive Christology. This is an unpopular message in a time when so many theologians consider the task of theology to be deconstruction plain and simple. I am calling for a post-deconstructionist

22. Grundtvig, "Rudelbach," pp. 47-48.

constructive Christology that can encompass both the insights of the decon-
structionists and the Grundtvigian criteria.

The tradition of Cosmic Christology, of which Sittler was one of the two
principal 20th-century expounders,[23] is also vastly underdeveloped in our
time. One is more likely to find New Age thinkers appropriating this tradition, and often in seriously inadequate ways. Sittler's insight holds, however,
that the only fully adequate theological understanding of nature as Creation
is a Christological understanding.

4. Grace as the principle of Creation. The bottom line in the Grundtvigian
dictum, "Human first, then Christian/Therefore everyone on this earth/
Must strive to be a true person," as well as in the Sittlerian premises of cosmic
Christology and the presence of the Triune God in Creation, is a clear and difficult one: *that all of Creation, both in its human and non-human nature, is governed by the grace, or love, that we ascribe to God.* This bottom line is disturbing to
a theological tradition that often has shared both in a dualistic understanding
of humans and the non-human world, and also in concepts of Two Kingdoms
and Law/Gospel that often establish a discontinuity between grace/love and
the created order. The gut-level intention of the Lutheran tradition is to use
the Two Kingdoms and the Law/Gospel concepts to affirm that all of Creation is in the hands of a loving God, but the concepts have often betrayed the
intentions. The Two Kingdoms doctrine could be interpreted in such a way as
to parallel Grundtvig's understanding of the relation between innate and reborn humanity, and both the first and the second uses of the Law put it in the
larger service of the Gospel. This means that, when all is said and done, both
the Left-Hand Kingdom and the Law are driven fundamentally by love. Even
though this interpretation could be defended (despite its being vulnerable to
sadistic distortions – for example, "I am only spanking you because I love
you so much"), it does cloud the vision of grace as the determinative principle of Creation. The power of these traditional Lutheran doctrines lies in the
apparent mountain of empirical evidence that suggests that love and grace
are not the principle of Creation. Sittler and Grundtvig are challenging us to
recognize that Christian faith asserts a picture of the world that is often, like
quantum physics and genetic science, *counter-intuitive*, that flies in the face of
conventional empirically-based wisdom. The issue here is that the character
we ascribe to God, particularly in God's relationship to Creation, and specifi-

23. See the discussion in J.A. Lyons, *The Cosmic Christ in Origen and Teilhard de Chardin: A
Comparative Study* (Oxford, Oxford Univ. Press, 1982), where he sets forth the thesis
that Sittler and Teilhard are the two primary proponents of Cosmic Christ traditions
in the 20th century. Sittler's role stems from his New Delhi address, according to Lyons. This book also documents the worldwide reaction to the address, including the
scholarly opinions that accused Sittler of romanticism and pantheism.

cally to humans, no longer makes sense unless we can relate that character of God meaningfully to the totality of the created order. It must be related to our culture because, as Grundtvig said, we must avoid speaking of human beings as if they inhabit "a life in heaven or in the sky, never on earth. On earth you never find humanity without folk-life".[24] The character of God must be related to non-human nature, because we now know that God created us humans, even in the inner sanctum of our personhood, from the stuff of non-human nature. We live on earth, not in the sky, and on earth you never find a humanity without physics, geology, biology, and neurobiology.

V. Coda

By coincidence, the copy of the Grundtvig writings published as *What Constitutes Authentic Christianity?* that I took from my shelf to prepare for this paper turned out to be Joseph Sittler's copy originally, which he had given me. In the back, I found two pages of notes that he must have dictated to be written there, since by the time it appeared in 1985, his eyesight was so poor that his access to books was dependent upon having them read to him by students and friends. In the notes, I found these words: "This knowledgeable selection of Grundtvig's writings by a skilled translator is important for two reasons: (1) It makes vintage Grundtvig available in English, and (2) it documents and underlines a rich and little known strand in the ethos of Lutheranism."

"A rich and little known strand in the ethos of Lutheranism." That statement could apply to both Grundtvig and Sittler, even though this volume is an attempt to remedy that situation. Virtually none of Sittler's writings is in print, including all of those that I have cited here, and there is not much of Grundtvig available outside Denmark. The mainstream of Lutheran theology and church life, at least in the West, does not subscribe to Grundtvig's views of the Bible, the Creed, the Church, worship, or culture, just as it does not subscribe to Sittler's Christology, his concepts of nature and grace or his understanding of the Triune God. I find this very frustrating because I believe that it is correct to say that unless theology and church life can relate to the kinds of issues that both the Dane and the native Ohioan focused upon, theology and church life will finally risk being unintelligible to men and women today. And since we believe that it is the intention of God to be present as grace in our world in an intelligible manner, an unintelligible theology is an illegitimate theology, and a stumbling-block to the Church.

We owe a great debt to these two theologians because they were so unflinching in laying out the demands of the Gospel for us, and because they

24. Grundtvig, "Folk-Life," p. 41.

did so with an unambiguous concern for the Church and its parish ministries of preaching, teaching, and conducting worship services. To take them seriously is to take their project seriously, for the Church and its theology.

Generous Orthodoxy:
Regin Prenter's Appropriation of Grundtvig

By Michael Root

Editors of a *Festschrift* have the problem of deciding which younger students and followers of the honored professor to invite as contributors. The editors of the 1936 *Festschrift* for Karl Barth's 50th birthday "overlooked" the young Dietrich Bonhoeffer but included one of Barth's even younger former students, Regin Prenter, a Danish priest, then not yet 30, who had studied with Barth in Bonn during the fateful years 1933-34.[1] Prenter's contribution like the article he had published the year before in the first volume of the journal *Evangelische Theologie* represented what may seem an odd enterprise, the interpretation of N.F.S. Grundtvig within an outlook on modern theology strongly influenced by Karl Barth.[2] Nevertheless, these essays were not a passing phase in Prenter's theological development but laid foundations that would remain determinative for his theology until his death in 1990. The aspects of Grundtvig emphasized and analyzed in these essays, the "kirkelige Anskuelse" (the churchly viewpoint) and the interrelation of created and redeemed humanity crystallized in Grundtvig's phrase "Menneske først og Kristen saa" (human first and then Christian) formed the most important methodological and substantive compass points for his theology. When in the 1970s he addressed the newer political theology from a Grundtvigian perspective, he made his arguments again by elaborating these two aspects of Grundtvig's outlook.[3]

In this short essay, I will summarize Prenter's interpretation and theological use of these two central Grundtvigian themes. On the one hand, Regin Prenter was one of the most important Danish theologians of the 20th century, professor at Aarhus from 1945 until 1972.[4] His dogmatics text, *Skabelse og Genløsning*, was translated into English, German, French, and Japanese and was widely read in the 1950s and 1960s.[5] His interpretation of Grundtvig, with whom he closely identified,[6] is thus in itself worth noting.[7] On the other

---

1. On the *Festschrift* and the omission of Bonhoeffer, see E. Busch, *Karl Barth: His Life from Letters and Autobiographical Texts*, tr. J. Bowden (Philadelphia, 1976), p. 276.
2. See R. Prenter, "Die Frage nach einer theologischen Grundtvig-Interpretation" in *Theologische Aufsätze: Karl Barth Zum 50. Geburtstag* (Munich, 1936), pp. 505-13; and R. Prenter, "Die sogenannte 'kirchliche Anschauung' N.F.S. Grundtvigs als Frage an die evangelische Theologie von Heute" in *Evangelische Theologie*, vol. 1 (1935), pp. 278-88.

hand, my interest in Prenter's interpretation of Grundtvig is not simply historical. Especially in these areas where he appropriates ideas from Grundtvig, Prenter represents a fundamental theological option well worth continued attention. Prenter's works have found few readers in the last 20 years in the German- and English-speaking worlds. Their language, style, and concerns are very much those of the post-war period and can seem dated. Nevertheless, these works still contain lessons for theology at the turn of the century, especially for theology in the post-liberal mode explored by Hans Frei and George Lindbeck. Prenter's appropriation of the "kirkelige Anskuelse," in close connection with Karl Barth's rejection of the dominant theological method of Neo-Protestant liberalism and Prenter's theological clarification and assertion of what Grundtvig at least might have meant by the priority of creation, point toward a more relaxed and open form of theology in the tradition of Barth and Luther.[8]

3. See R. Prenter, "Grundtvigs udfordring til moderne theologi" in *Grundtvig Studier* (1973), pp. 11-29.
4. Biographical information and appreciations of Prenter's work can be found in eulogies written upon his death; see S. Kjeldgaard-Pedersen, "In memoriam Regin Prenter" in *Lutherjahrbuch,* vol. 60 (1993), pp. 13-16; J.H. Schjørring, "Regin Prenter im memoriam" in *Grundtvig Studier,* vol. 42 (1991), pp. 7-19; A.M. Allchin, "Regin Prenter, A Personal Tribute" in *Grundtvig Studier* (1991), pp. 20-22.
5. R. Prenter, *Skabelse Og Genløsning: Dogmatik,* 4th ed. (Copenhagen, 1967).
6. Prenter rarely finds fault with Grundtvig. In "Die sogenannte 'kirchliche Anschauung'," Prenter did grant that Grundtvig seems to have undervalued preaching, but this criticism is absent from his later detailed discussion of this topic in R. Prenter, "Grundtvigs Syn på Forkyndelsen" in *Grundtvig Studier* (1948), pp. 63-78. N. H. Søe criticized Prenter for being more willing to bend Grundtvig (and Luther) to make them mean what he thginks they ought to mean, than to admit they might be wrong (see N.H. Søe, *Dansk Teologi Siden 1900* (Copenhagen, 1965), p. 190). The term "Grundtvigianism" seems, however, to have been a rather negative term for Prenter (see R. Prenter, " Karl Barths Møde med Grundtvigianisme og Indre Mission" in *Dansk Kirkeliv,* vol. 16 (1939), p. 41; Prenter, "Grundtvigs Syn," p. 66).
7. I will here only deal with Prenter's Grundtvig studies during the period of his most important work as a theologian prior to his retirement from Aarhus in 1972. I will make no attempt to argue that Prenter represents the best or most accurate interpretation of Grundtvig, a dangerous enterprise and one that would require far more space than this essay allows.
8. Most of what will be said in this essay was developed at much greater length in my doctoral dissertation (M. Root, Creation and Redemption: A Study of Their Interrelation, with Special Reference to the Theology of Regin Prenter. Ph.D. Diss. (New Haven, 1979) and in a short article on the relation between creation and redemption in Prenter's theology (M. Root, "Creation, Redemption, and the Limits of System: A Study of Regin Prenter" in *Creation and Method: Critical Essays on Christocentric Theology,* ed. H. Vander Goot (Washington, DC, 1981), pp. 13-28.

I. The "kirkelige Anskuelse"

The genre and style of Prenter's writings were quite different from those of Grundtvig. Like Grundtvig, Prenter was a churchman, but unlike Grundtvig, his writings, especially the larger ones, are academic and dogmatic in the best sense of those abused words. They were academic in their concern for the scholarly and analytic standards of the academy and dogmatic in their engagement with the church's dogma, the normative teaching of the Christian community, rooted in the teaching tradition reaching back to Nicea and Chalcedon. Prenter himself did not write the wide-ranging mythological, historical, and cultural works that are prominent in Grundtvig's production, although he defended the character of these books as "secondary theology."[9]

Despite these differences, the fundamental location and concerns of Prenter's theology were shaped by his commitment to Grundtvig's "kirkelige Anskuelse," the viewpoint of the church. Prenter presented a paper on this topic to Barth's theology seminar in Bonn in 1933-34, and this paper formed the basis for the essay that appeared the following year in *Evangelische Theologie*.[10] For Prenter, the "kirkelige Anskuelse" meant the rejection of the model of the creative, virtuoso theologian and a commitment to a kind of theological modesty. It is not the task of the theologian creatively to determine the subject matter of theology, the Christian message which is to be interpreted. Nor is the subject matter simply Scripture, the diversity and difficulty of which might then require the theologian to construct an hermeneutical framework to guide (or control?) its interpretation. "The rule of faith which is to guide all understanding of Scripture is neither autonomous reason nor a doctrinal statement drawn up by man, but *the confession of faith which constitutes existence in the church*. The new thing that is seen here [in Grundtvig's *The Church's Response*] is that existence within the church, in the perceivable, true Christian church, is the presupposition for having a Holy Scripture and thus also for the ability to understand and interpret this scripture."[11]

The confession of faith in the sacraments can play this role because "the confession of faith is not some human construct set up in the church, but sim-

---

9. Prenter, "Die Frage," pp. 505-13.
10. Especially in his rejection of the Grundtvig interpretation of Kaj Thaning, Prenter made clear that he saw the "kirkelige Anskuelse" and the shift in Grundtvig's outlook in 1825, expressed in *Kirkens Gjenmæle*, as decisive and of lifelong significance for Grundtvig (see R. Prenter, "K. Thanings Grundtvigbog" in *Dansk Teologisk Tidskrift* (1964), pp. 193-210).
11. See Prenter, "Die sogenannte," p. 281. Translations of texts which have been published only in German or Danish are my own. When a published English translation exists, it is cited, and I have used the published translation without correction or alteration to meet contemporary standards of inclusive language.

ply the two sacraments instituted by the Lord of the church himself: baptism and the Lord's Supper."[12] Crucial for Prenter's appropriation of Grundtvig in this early essay was his rejection of any merely empirical argument for the hermeneutical authority of the baptismal creed. Such an empirical argument would take the form: we know what the church teaches; the church makes this clear at the decisive moment when it asks the candidate to confess the faith; since this baptismal creed has changed little since the first centuries of the church, this teaching is to be seen as stable and definite. Such an empirical approach would be problematic for Prenter because it would weaken the distinction he wishes to draw between this confession and any merely human doctrinal statement. He needs to go a step further and base the authority of the baptismal creed in Christ and the Spirit, but how is this to be done without the historically dubious arguments about the apostolic source of the Creed to which Grundtvig became committed?[13]

Prenter's argument is complex. As the above quotation indicates, the decisive link is the character of the sacraments as divine in a double sense: They are instituted by Christ and within them God is acting today. Both sacraments involve a saving inclusion of the recipient in the history of God's engagement with the world and humanity. Both sacraments thus involve as essential elements a recitation of the events of this history into which the recipient is being taken up. In the Eucharist, this recitation occurs typically both in the prayer and in the creed. In baptism, the focus on the creed is even sharper and its centrality more pronounced. In his later dogmatics *Skabelse og Genløsning* (English translation, *Creation and Redemption*), Prenter interprets baptism in terms of covenant and the creed is the word by which the covenant is established. "The creed as confessed by the congregation is a covenant word, which is especially apparent in its use at baptism – in fact Grundtvig recognized the creed only as baptismal confession. In the divine history, to which the articles of the creed point, God establishes his covenant with us. And in the confession of the creed at baptism God, through the covenant history, personally confronts each individual with the question: 'Will you accept this covenant which I now offer you?'"[14]

If baptism is the foundational event of the Christian life, and *if* the Christian life is a gift of God, and *if* the covenant word, narrating and interpreting the larger history which defines the Christian life, is essential to and definitive of the character of baptism, *then* the creed cannot be a mere human doctrinal construction but must itself be a word through which God speaks to

---

12. See Prenter, "Die sogenannte," p. 281.
13. On these arguments, see P.G. Lindhardt, *Grundtvig: An Introduction* (London, 1951), p. 86.
14. R. Prenter, *Creation and Redemption*, tr. T.I. Jensen (Philadelphia, 1967), p. 57.

humanity. If the baptismal creed were anything less, then baptism could not be the secure foundation of the Christian life. Prenter is careful to root the creed in Scripture so that he can continue to confess the Reformation *sola scriptura*.[15] Nevertheless, the existentially decisive character of the baptismal word, even in distinction from Scripture, is clearly stated.

Grundtvig's assertion – often condemned and misused – that it is only in baptism and the Lord's Supper that we hear God's word to us is in reality a superb expression for the connection between historical revelation and the present transmission of that revelation … God's word in which he himself establishes his covenant with us, is heard only at baptism and the Lord's Supper. We are not born again nor nurtured in the new life with the gifts of the body and blood of Jesus Christ by forsaking the congregation and sitting down to read the Scriptures in order, by ourselves, to appropriate its "truths." … The Bible's true authority addresses our day through the confession.[16]

While Prenter rejects any use of the content of the creed as a juridical norm, he acknowledges that the creed "speaks with definiteness" and "expresses a definite position which excludes every other position." The theologian is thus provided with a definite orientation, an orientation which Prenter was himself to follow.

Two further comments should be made here on Prenter's appropriation of the "kirkelige Anskuelse." First, as the above argument indicates, Prenter's argument for the normative character of the baptismal creed rests on an indwelling of divine action in human action. Here Prenter finds what he calls the heart of the "kirkelige Anskuelse." "This entire way of thinking is borne by the idea of the Christian life as Christ's own life. This way of thinking is at the heart of Grundtvig's "kirkelige Anskuelse": the thought of the living Christ who lives his life now in the community in the word, in which he himself is life and gives life."[17] Like Luther, Grundtvig and Prenter understand the Christian life as union with Christ."This mysterious unity between the fallen person and the God-man, between Christ and his bride, turns a human life into a Christian life. This is pregnantly expressed by the term 'Christ-like,' for it is a participation in Christ's own life."[18]

Prenter has no wish to set up human norms and ceremonies as divine institutions. Nevertheless, unlike some strands of modern Lutheran theology, his ecclesiology is not controlled by a rigid separation of divine act and human act. The insistence that the indwelling of Christ in the Christian is medi-

15. Prenter, *Creation and Redemption*, see esp. #7, "The Bible and the Confession of Faith."
16. Prenter, *Creation and Redemption*, p. 121.
17. Prenter, "Grundtvigs Syn," p. 65.
18. R. Prenter, "Grundtvigs Ansicht vom Menschen" in *Evangelische Theologie*, vol. 9 (1950), p. 395.

ated communally and, more specifically, ecclesially leads to a different valuation of the church and its traditions. Popes, bishops, and councils may err, but if the church in its sacraments is regularly locus of the Spirit's presence, then an essential trustworthiness should characterize the church. Herein lies, I believe, the central root of the "catholic" character of Prenter's theology. Prenter is by no means uncritical of the wider, catholic ecclesial and theological tradition, but his writings exude (at least to me) a fundamental trust in that tradition, an at-home-ness there.

Second, Prenter's form of the "kirkelige Anskuelse" combined easily with certain methodological commitments that could be called generally Barthian, although the "kirkelige Anskuelse" itself did not require these commitments. P.G. Lindhardt refers to Prenter as one of a group of "churchly Barthians" in the Danish Church of the late 1930s.[19] While Prenter came to disagree strongly with Barth on a series of issues, his theological method continued to display Barthian traits, both negatively and positively. On the one hand, he agreed negatively with Barth in the rejection of the most important foundational moves of neo-Protestant liberal theology. He explicitly rejected the need for independent epistemological prolegomena to theology.[20] In addition, he rejected the use of a general category "religion" which might be used to interpret the meaning of Christian faith.[21] Most fundamentally, Prenter gives no sign of sharing what seems to me the deepest conviction that has driven neo-Protestant liberal theology since its first statement in Schleiermacher's *Reden*: the conviction that in their respective depths Christian faith and modernity are mutually complementary, so that the correction of each by the other will allow both Christian faith and modernity to appear in their essential (and essentially congruent, if not identical) natures. This conviction, shared by Schleiermacher, Hegel, Ritschl, Bultmann, Tillich, and the early David Tracy, determines the typical method of academic liberal theology, in which an apologetically conceived anthropology provides the systematic hermeneutic for interpreting Christian faith. It also propels the "apologetic pathos" that typifies so much of 19th- and 20th-century theology. Of all this, Prenter shows very little sign.

On the other hand, he seems to agree also positively with Barth in insisting that all theology is ultimately Christology.

---

19. P.G. Lindhardt, *Den Danske Kirkes Historie*, vol. 8 (Copenhagen, 1966), p. 208. He also lists N.H. Søe, K.E. Skydsgaard, and Hal Koch as representatives of this outlook.
20. Prenter, *Creation and Redemption*, pp. 12, 184.
21. In both of these cases, he explicitly distances himself from both Schleiermacher and the Swedish Lund school of Anders Nygren et al. (see Prenter, *Creation and Redemption*, pp. 26-32).

Christology is not merely theology, that is, it is not only a particular section or phase of theology; but theology is Christology, that is, Christology is the center of all theology as the voice which defines (*medbestemmer*) every statement in theology. In this sense, Christology is the proclamation, not only of the God of redemption, but also of the God of creation. Christology is not only an understanding of the new man of redemption through the proclamation of the God of redemption; it is also an understanding of the old man of creation through the proclamation of the God in creation.[22]

As will be noted below, this statement, especially if one attends to the original Danish, is less Barthian than it appears at first sight. Nevertheless, Prenter is committed to a kind of noetic Christocentricity that places his theology much closer to Barth than to most other trends in modern theology.

While these similarities to Barth should be noted, it should also be remarked that Prenter justifies such aspects of his theology in rather un-Barthian ways. As will be detailed below, he explicitly rejected the way Barth sought to derive all theology from Christology by means of supralapsarian unification of all God does, ad intra and ad extra, in a primal election. Prenter instead provided a more complex, less integrated form of Christocentricity. In addition, he denied the need for independent epistemological prolegomena on grounds internal to philosophy.[23] His refusal to use a general category "religion" to interpret Christian faith was justified by a general argument that the interpretation of no significant human phenomenon should be controlled by a general interpretive category established independently of a consideration of the phenomenon to be interpreted.[24] Prenter thus reaches methodological conclusions similar to Barth, but in a more diffuse, one might say more relaxed, way. Here he is similar to recent "post-liberal" theologians such as Frei and Lindbeck.[25]

Prenter's theology can be understood as an academic, dogmatic theology within a "kirkelige Anskuelse." The particular way he carried out this development shows how it can be combined with developments set in motion by Karl Barth. But, the question would be asked by anyone familiar with Grundtvig, did not Grundtvig's vision of the integrity of creation and of everyday human life in distinction from redemption mark a fundamental contrast from any theology responsive to Barth? Strikingly, Prenter combined a Barthian-colored version of

22. Prenter, *Creation and Redemption*, pp. 295f.
23. Prenter, *Creation and Redemption*, p. 184.
24. Prenter, *Creation and Redemption*, p. 28.
25. In *The Eclipse of Biblical Narrative: A Study in Eighteenth and Nineteenth Century Hermeneutics* , H.W. Frei noted he was justifying a biblical hermeneutic of a Barthian sort in an "external" way that "Barth might well have rejected out of hand" (New Haven, 1974), p. viii. See also G.A. Lindbeck, *The Nature of Doctrine: Religion and Theology in a Post-liberal Age* (Philadelphia, 1984).

the "kirkelige Anskuelse" with an emphasis on the priority of creation expressed in Grundtvig's poem "Menneske først og Kristen saa." How he did this will be the subject of the second section of this essay.

II. "Menneske først og Kristen saa"

In 1946, Prenter reviewed Volume III, part 1, of Barth's *Church Dogmatics*, the first section of Barth's doctrine of creation. He expressed admiration for the skill and even beauty of Barth's integration of creation into the covenant realized in Christ. "But – when the first enthusiasm has worn off, one asks oneself: is there not too much beauty here?" Between creation and the triumph of Christ stands the cross. "And where the cross is, there is not just beauty. This is true also for exegesis, that there must also be a cross, even if only in the banal form of the 'crux interpretationis,' the exegetical aporia, the unsolvable riddle. An exegesis in which everything goes *completely* smoothly and everything is *conclusively* dealt with and which precisely in this smoothness and conclusiveness is so *beautiful* has finished off the cross too quickly."[26] Prenter does not deny a strong connection between creation and Christ. After all, Christ is the Word through which all things come to be. But to achieve such a smooth, complete, and beautiful integration of creation and redemption requires a grasp of *how* Christ in his death and resurrection realizes and demonstrates his Lordship over creation.

For Prenter, such a grasp is simply impossible. In the light of glory, we will see, but now we stand under the cross and live by faith rather than sight. What stands between theology and a full understanding of the unity of creation and redemption is an essential contradiction between life and death. To understand the unity of God's *opus alienum* and *opus proprium* would be to understand how Jesus overcomes death by death.

The final inability of theology fully to integrate creation and redemption forms one of the most important structuring themes of Prenter's theology and cannot be fully discussed or justified here.[27] What should be noted is that while in such discussions Prenter predictably calls most often on Luther, he understands himself to be in full agreement with Grundtvig. After all, Grundtvig had insisted on the opposition of life and death which could be subsumed in

---

26. R. Prenter, "Die Einheit von Schöpfung und Erlösung. Zur Schöpfungslehre Karl Barths" in *Theologische Zeitschrift*, vol. 2 (1946), pp. 167.
27. This theme in Prenter's works is explored in detail in Root (*Creation and Redemption*). It should be noted that Prenter's argument is against *any* smooth transition between creation and redemption. It would also apply to such systematic theological structures as that of Schleiermacher or, despite its dialectical subtlety, that of Hegel.

no dialectical synthesis.[28] In his article of 1950 on Grundtvig's anthropology, Prenter insists that for Grundtvig the created and the redeemed life of humanity are one, but this oneness always contains an indissoluble tension. "Creation in time and redemption in eternity belong together in Christianity within a strong tension which can never be rationally mastered. All dogmatic systems break down under this tension. Grundtvig's conception of humanity expresses this tension through the dialectic in his view of temporal human life and eternal Christian life, of the earthly life of the nation or people and the spiritual life of the Christian community, of the universal, God-created human existence, through which runs the great chasm of renewal and rebirth in Christ."[29] For Prenter, Grundtvig is no less a theologian of the cross than Luther.

If one insists on the unity of creation and redemption under the Lordship of Christ who is both the creating and redeeming word and also on the theologian's inability to take up the supralapsarian viewpoint from which the final unity becomes fully comprehensible, then the categories which are available to the theologian for understanding that unity must remain dramatic and narrative. The categories by which one understands the unity of created, sinful, and redeemed humanity must be those of a story in which various events relate to one another in the meaningful but not strictly necessary or deductive form typical of narratives. (Unlike Grundtvig, Prenter's prose style is not dramatic, but the logic of his theology fully supports the dramatic mode in which one might say Grundtvig thought and wrote.)

The crucial narrative category for Prenter's interpretation of the relation between creation and redemption is that of restoration (*genoprettelse*). Redemption is restoration and not replacement. Replacement would presuppose only sin, which it would eliminate and replace with a new humanity. Restoration must presuppose both sin and creation. Restoration presupposes that human nature as created still exists, however corrupted by sin. This created nature is restored in Christ. If redemption is restoration, then the logical ordering "humanity – redeemed humanity" is irreversible. Here Prenter finds the dogmatic heart of the Grundtvigian theme: "Menneske først og Kristen saa."[30]

---

28. H. Koch, *Grundtvig*, tr. L. Jones (Yellow Springs, 1952), pp. 25, 31.
29. Prenter, "Grundtvigs Ansicht," p. 405.
30. The fullest discussion of this theme is in R. Prenter, *Skabelse Og Genløsning: Dogmatik*, 4th ed. (Copenhagen, 1967), pp. 276ff. The English translation of Prenter's dogmatics eliminates the phrase "Menneske først og Kristen saa" as the subtitle to this section on "The Original State and the State of Grace." In addition, it shortens the excursus at the end of this section (see the Danish original, Prenter, *Skabelse Og Genløsning*, pp. 296-308), which ended with an extended discussion of Grundtvig's poem that begins with this phrase. The German translation eliminated the excursus totally.

This theme is most fully explored in relation to the humanity existing as the image of God. For Prenter, drawing on Grundtvig, the image of God is not an indwelling quality (*hvilende kvalitet*) in the human which could be grasped by looking at humanity alone. The image is rather bound up with humanity's relation to God, a relation that is paradigmatically mediated by language. In the creation narratives, God speaks a word not only about (*over*) humanity, but also a word to (*til*) humanity, a word that calls for a response, an echo in which humanity accepts its created nature. "The fundamental thought in Grundtvig's discussion of the image of God is that God's image is God's word itself, and human persons take on the image of God by hearing God's word and echoing it in their own voice."[31]

This word is spoken to us in the "covenants of creation," which are the living forms by and in which we encounter our neighbor and by which God continues to create and preserve our humanity.[32] Sin is the human attempt to speak some other word about God, the world, and ourselves, and thus the attempt not to echo God's creative word. God's creative word in this situation becomes law. As law, it coerces us into a minimal, even if grudging, care for the neighbor and the world. God's creative word is echoed, but in a twisted, deformed manner. The sovereignty of the Creator and humanity's dependence on God implies that humanity cannot truly be other than what is was created to be. Sin can be destructive, but it cannot be truly creative. Sin is existence in self-contradiction between what humanity cannot but be (the creature God created) and what humanity seeks but must fail to be (a being of its own disobedient choosing).

This summary of Prenter's rich discussion of creation, image, and sin is exceedingly condensed, but I hope it suffices to indicate two conclusions. First, Prenter's appropriation of Grundtvig's "Menneske først" does not imply an optimistic anthropology at odds with the Reformation. Here Prenter (and Grundtvig) are repeating the classical Lutheran rejection of the contention of Mathias Flacius that the sinner no longer exists as the image of God but as the image of the devil (Formula of Concord, SD, I). Prenter means to do no more than indicate that redemption as restoration implies that the human to be redeemed in fact still exists, even if in need of redemption. In his interpretation of Grundtvig's anthropology, Prenter contends that a parallel to Grundtvig's thought can be found in Luther's *De servo arbitrio* when Luther pronounces himself willing to accept a power of free choice if that concept refers only to an *aptitudo passiva*, "that by which a man is capable of being taken hold of by the Spirit and imbued with the grace of God, as a being created for

31. Prenter, *Skabelse Og Genløsning*, pp. 304.
32. R. Prenter, *Creation and Redemption*, pp. 204, 255.

eternal life or death. … For heaven, as the saying is, was not made for geese."[33]

Second, Prenter's understanding of the creative word of God mediated through the structures of creation implies that these structures are and remain the locus within which we live out our humanity. The redemptive word of the gospel does not replace or render superfluous the creative word. Since the redemptive word always comes to me through particular persons (and thus always shaped by particular interpersonal relations) and in a particular language, any simple separation of the redemptive word from the creative word is impossible. The church also exists within and is permeated by the structures of creation. The creative word, mediated by the structures and covenants of creation (including, importantly for Grundtvig, national structures), continues to shape the identity in which persons are the concrete individuals they are. Christian life is born in baptism and nourished in the Eucharist, but the "everyday" forms the context of its unfolding. Thus, Prenter said that Grundtvig stood in the middle between the holy-day and the everyday.[34]

The unbridgeable gap represented by the cross which blocks any thorough integration of creation and redemption blocks also any reduction of the significance of the structures of creation to their significance for redemption. They retain a certain opacity, resisting an interpretation which reduces their significance to their relation to Christ. (In his review of vol. III/1 of Barth's *Church Dogmatics*, Prenter accuses Barth of precisely such a reduction by means of the consistent use of Christological analogy to interpret various aspects of creation. As a result, "the reality of the created world dissolves and the understanding of created human life becomes docetic").[35] The Christian has faith that the creative Word that calls all into being and the redemptive Word incarnate as Jesus Christ are one Word, but that faith cannot become an interpretive tool by which we master creation. We remain here also under the cross.

Here we must return to questions of theological method. If this limit to Christological interpretation exists, then how can all theology be Christology, as was said above? An answer comes in attending closely to exactly what Prenter says. While the English translation states that Christology *defines* every statement in theology, the Danish verb is *medbestemmer*. The prefix *med-* would indicate "co-defines" as a more precise translation. With this correction and the context of the sentences leading up to this statement, Prenter's point becomes clearer. "Because the divine sovereignty is attributed to the historical Jesus under the name of Christ, every word concerning

33. Prenter, "Grundtvigs Ansicht," p. 401, citing Luther in WA 18:636.
34. R. Prenter, *Protestantismen i vor Tid* (Copenhagen, 1957), p. 136.
35. Prenter, "Die Einheit," p. 175.

God and every thought concerning God, which such words presuppose, is subject to Christ's sovereignty. Therefore, Christology is not merely theology, that is, it is not only a particular section of phase of theology; but theology is Christology, that is Christology is the center of all theology as the voice which co-defines every statement in theology."[36] The light of Christ illumines all, and theology must permit that illumination to reshape our understanding of whatever is under discussion. Anything less would be a denial of the incarnation of the *creative* Word in Christ. But illumination does not imply either that we can then *derive* everything in theology from its Christological center or that we then should seek an exhaustive Christological understanding of the world and culture beyond the church.

As a result, there is room within dogmatics for a kind of "method of correlation," but of a quite different sort than that represented by Paul Tillich.[37] If theology remains true to the foundational claim that the Word in Christ is the Logos in which all things cohere, then it must make some attempt, however provisional, to relate that claim to our sense of "all things."[38] The relation of revelation to reason is "inclusive. In revelation, reason is not de-throned but rather is included. Its own most central concerns are fulfilled in a way which could not have been expected within the framework of its own innate possibilities."[39] This inclusivity does not imply a "monistic-speculative" unification of philosophy and theology by means of a Logos-Christology. This enterprise always fails and theologically leads to a "positivism of revelation" in which theology is cut off from wider human life and reflection.[40] Rather, theology should respect its own limits, making use of philosophical categories and results when they aid in its own task and, when possible, pointing to the fulfillment of the deepest concern of philosophy in Christ. Here Prenter is recommending something similar to what William Werpehowski, a student of Frei and Lindbeck, has proposed under the title "ad hoc apologetics." Parallel to Grundtvig, Werpehowski works from the assumption that the non-Christian is already "one whose own characteristic patterns of action and purpose bear some uneradicable relation to an origin in God." Apologetics seeks those points where the non-Christian's "projects and purposes

---

36. Prenter, *Creation and Redemption*, p. 295.
37. Prenter was willing to grant a legitimacy to Tillich's enterprise, but as philosophical theology, not as dogmatics (see R. Prenter, "Philosophical Theology" in *The Encyclopedia of the Lutheran Church*, ed. J. Bodensieck, s.v. (Minneapolis, 1965), p. 1891).
38. R. Prenter, "Die Beziehung zwischen Theologie und Philosophie als dogmatisches Problem. Einige Thesen zu dem oft diskutierten Problem des gegenseitigen Verhältnisses von Theologie und Philosophie" in *Solange es "Heute" Heißt*, Festgabe für Rudolf Hermann zum 70. Geburtstag (Berlin, 1957), pp. 219.
39. Prenter, "Die Beziehung," pp. 221.
40. Prenter, "Die Beziehung," pp. 222ff.

would be advanced and would make more sense with the introduction of the theological factor," that is, it seeks those points at which the deepest concern of the non-Christian might be illumined, transformed, but in the process also recognizably fulfilled by inclusion in the larger context of Christian faith.[41] Such an apologetics is inevitably ad hoc, for it relies on the contingencies of where such demonstrations are feasible. But it is part of the openness to life that Grundtvig saw as intrinsic to Christian faith and theology.

III. A "generous orthodoxy"

Prenter's appropriation of the Grundtvigian themes of the "kirkelige Anskuelse" and "Menneske først" points to one form that might be taken by what the late Hans Frei called a "generous orthodoxy."[42] The "kirkelige Anskuelse" means that theology remains true to its own content, its own location, and its own task. It thus remains "orthodox." But the understanding of the relation between creation and redemption crystallized in the phrase "Menneske først" implies an openness toward and interest in the wider world that too often is missing from the usual connotations of "orthodox." In addition, the understanding of creation and redemption which Prenter appropriated from Grundtvig also implies a confidence in the Christian approach to the wider world, a confidence which need not be dominated by the apologetic pathos that has so dominated much of 19th- and 20th-century theology.

If this distinction [between creation and redemption] is maintained clearly and honestly, then Christianity remains authentic (orthodox, churchly) Christianity … But human life then also, in a corresponding way, remains authentic human life, all-embracing, common to both Christian and non-Christian. … If the distinction is rightly maintained, the way is opened for a human Christianity, i.e., a Christian faith, hope, and love which is a truly free matter, borne only by the power of the truth of the word. … and for a Christian humanity, that is to say, a human life which remains human and therefore can freely open itself to Christianity and freely refuse it, when the gospel is freely preached.[43]

41. W. Werpehowski, "Ad Hoc Apologetics" in *Journal of Religion*, vol. 66 (1986), pp. 287.
42. H.W. Frei, *Theology and Narrative: Selected Essays* (New York, 1993), p. 208. See the sensitive development of this theme by George Hunsinger in the Afterword to this same volume, pp. 256f.
43. Prenter, "Grundtvigs udfordring," p. 29.

The Christian trusts that the redemptive word is the same as the creative word already at work in all things. Thus, with Grundtvig, one can believe that "As Christianity then is the truth, even if he [the seeker for truth] is not a Christian today, he will be one tomorrow."[44]

By the time of his death in 1990, even perhaps by the time of his retirement in 1972, Prenter had come to seem a man of the past, shaped by the concerns and conflicts of the years that surrounded World War II. And yet his suspicion of the too easily systematic can be read as a foreshadowing of typically postmodern concerns and, as I have suggested, his generous orthodoxy can be understood as hinting at a postliberal outlook. His interpretation and appropriation of Grundtvig also might have looked old-fashioned at one time, but they are not all that far from the understanding of Grundtvig recently portrayed with such attractiveness by A.M. Allchin.[45] The heritage of Grundtvig is so diverse that there are various ways of appropriating aspects of Grundtvig's outlook into a contemporary theological perspective. The work of Regin Prenter presents one such appropriation that merits continuing appreciation.

44. N.F.S. Grundtvig, *Selected Writings*, ed. J. Knudsen (Philadelphia, 1976), p. 141.
45. Prenter and Allchin are alike in seeing the churchly turn of Grundtvig in 1825 as of permanent significance and not erased by the insights of 1832 (see A.M. Allchin, *N.F.S. Grundtvig; An Introduction to His Life and Work* (Aarhus, 1997), pp. 60f.).

Danish Grundtvigians in the United States: Challenges Past and Present

By Axel C. Kildegaard

Challenges change. Those that confronted my grandfather, who emigrated from Jutland to mid-America some 125 years ago, were radically different from those of our day. His identity, as ours, was rooted in history as he perceived it. The context in which he was to forge a new life constituted a new history to integrate with the old. That presented challenge. A new self-understanding, a new identity, emerged.

The thread of continuity is discernible and cherished, but it will also differ widely for a people fragmented by space and time. Challenges grow out of questions raised by new circumstances that differ radically from those known in the past. To address the challenges met by those who carried with them to America an awareness and remembrance of N.F.S. Grundtvig requires a review of their history in the new land in which their lives were shaped. Particular aspects of the Grundtvigian tradition took on a life of their own, through the uniquely American dialogue, the institutions formed, the songs and the hymns translated, the folk culture that developed, and the self-understanding of the new church. In all these matters, Grundtvigians in Denmark may recognize some aspects of the poet's thoughts and also recognize that these have survived and developed in different ways in the new world.

The Spirit continuously gives birth to the Word in new incarnations as historical contexts and realities change. A change in the perception of either the heritage or the context rewrites the challenge. The heritage perceived by my grandfather and his peers was wedded to the ethnic marks of language and history. The challenge of preserving that memory linguistically persisted into the second and even third generation. But cultural, sociological, economic, and theological evolutions and revolutions over the past century have all contributed to a new context. On the threshhold of a new century, new assessments of the old heritage are being made and new challenges are to be identified. These have changed dramatically and are in sharp contrast to the understandings and challenges named at the outset of the 20th century.

Danish emigration to America was at its peak 100 years ago. Traceable in part to the new industrialization that had drawn farm folk to the cities, a new secularism chasing the thoughts of Georg Brandes, a rather rigid social structure, and an economic depression, they left more than simple geography when they left Denmark. Far fewer in numbers than the immigrants from Norway and Sweden, they were also widely dispersed in the new world. Perhaps a lower percentage of Danes affiliated with their own ethnic organizations than did the immigrants of any other culture.

But many of them, those who came from rural areas seeking the cheap but rich farmlands of the Midwest, brought with them the faith of their fathers. In the early years, they sought spiritual nurture with other Scandinavians, primarily Norwegians. But two factors militated against that relationship. First, although the Lutheran faith was a common bond, the Norwegians leaned toward a pietistic orthodoxy which was suspicious of any taints of Danish Grundtvigianism. Second, the by far outnumbered Danes soon felt that their primary challenge was to keep and preserve their ethnic identity. Both of these factors were reinforced by their ties to their homeland. Early on the more independent Norwegians established their own schools and seminary in the new world. The Danes were closer to their mother church. By the early 1870s, a number of Danes had broken away from those relationships and established a Danish Church. According to Enok Mortensen, historian of the Danish Church in America,[1] Grundtvig was not the rallying cry of this new effort. Only one of the four pastors who pioneered the new church was a follower of Grundtvig. They considered themselves to be orthodox, evangelical Lutherans whose home church in Denmark (to which they continued to give their allegiance) gave room for a variety of viewpoints. Within the next quarter of a century, the issue of Grundtvigianism was to become dominant within the Danish-American communities and in their relationships with other Scandinavians.

The Danes had joined a nation just beginning to flex its muscles in the world. The United States had become involved in what has been called a "convenient little war" to the joy of William Randolph Hearst, whose newspapers prospered from the resulting growth in circulation. That may have been the mustard seed of the cynicism later to appear in the American psyche, one that grew to mature dominance in the later decades of the 20th century.

However, most of America reflected an opposite mood. The frontier and the lavish promises of the West were still alive and healthy. They continued to invite the adventurous and the ambitious to go west. Immigration from Europe was hitting new peaks. New communities, with new enterprises, new schools, and new churches faced the future with optimism. America had survived a great civil war which had put dreams in jeopardy. The expanse of

---

1.   Enok Mortensen, *The Danish Lutheran Church in America* (Philadelphia, Board of Publication, Lutheran Church in America, 1967).

a great land was being conquered with the highest technology: the Winchester rifle, the steel-faced plow, the railroad, and the telegraph. These helped to shape the context in which challenges were defined. Nothing could stop us now.

Church leaders were similarly optimistic. A new wave of missionary activity prompted church leaders to speak confidently of winning the world for Christ in their own lifetime. A blossoming of imperialism marked the day. A new weekly magazine, not officially related to any church body but reflecting the general Protestant orientation, reflected that confidence in its title: *The Christian Century*. Although that journal continues to publish, the claims today are less audacious, more ambiguous. The premise that we are a Christian nation is no longer tenable, and the challenges which that premise assumed are muddled.

As immigrants streamed into the new promised land during the last decades of the 19th century and the beginnings of the 20th, they brought with them their own personal and communal challenges. But they also bought into what was known as the "American dream." For some, that meant the abandonment of their own history. I have been told of immigrants who vowed never to speak a word of their mother tongue once they set foot on western shores. They subscribed to what became known as the "melting pot" concept of the new America.

Others continued to define themselves in terms of their origins. My father's father migrated in the late 1870s after completing a short course of theological studies at Askov (see below). He never became an American citizen although he served the Danish Church in America for more than three decades. He considered himself a Dane and the churches that he served to be Danish. His challenge was to cling to and nurture the identity which he knew as Danish.

Economic growth raced unbridled in the expansionism of a country occupied with empire building. Social, political, and economic corruption paralleled a religious dogmatism and escape into subjective pietism. In the church, biblical literalism and doctrinal conservatism ruled. It was also a time of schism and division. Denominations and sects grew in numbers as they grew in competition and intolerance. The separation between the holy and the profane was sharply drawn and exploited. Post-Civil War churches often subscribed to a transcendental belief structure that justified the neglect and avoidance of many human concerns. At the same time, a folk religion reigned that expressed itself in subjective sentimentalities. It was hardly a receptive climate for the Danes, especially those attracted to Grundtvig, who valued a cultural development as the historical deposit of the spirit, the wealth of the human experience, and an incarnational theology which celebrated the involvement of God in history.

The designation of "Grundtvigian" was neither chosen nor sought by the early leaders of the Danish Church. It was a name of derision that carried with it the implications of heresy and falsehood. Grundtvig was for them a revered hymnwriter and spiritual leader within their home Church in Denmark. He was a voice which participated in that constant, lively dialogue in which Christians take part. The church was big enough to hold a number of viewpoints, even as disparate as those forwarded by Vilhelm Beck, the leader of the pietistic Inner Mission movement, and by N.F.S. Grundtvig. The broad church view reigned in Denmark and persisted for some time in America.

But another view of the church was spawned by 1) separation from a political and a people's base, and 2) an American climate of sectarianism and division that demanded a uniformity of doctrine before fellowship could be celebrated. Agreement of pure and unadulterated doctrine was considered essential.

By 1900, there were many communities, easily reaching into the hundreds, where Danes clustered and built their churches, social halls, and lodges with the challenge of preservation foremost in their minds. Most were in rural areas, some established intentionally as Danish communities. But there were also gatherings in the cities: New York, Detroit, Chicago, Omaha, and Minneapolis to mention a few. In Racine, Wisconsin, there were so many Danes that they sometimes forgot they were a minority. On the main street of the city, some merchants placed signs in their windows, "English spoken here." Danish fluency was assumed.

More often these small enclaves knew themselves to be minorities and clung to the Danish language in their homes and churches. Saturday schools and extended summer sessions were held for the children. The purpose was to teach the Danish songs and stories and most importantly to keep alive the language. This pattern continued through the first quarter of the century and, in a few places, beyond that. But stories generic to the new world were also told, and portraits of Washington and Lincoln often adorned the walls.

In desperate need for pastors, the fledgling Danish Church appealed to the Church of the homeland. A Commission for the Propagation of the Gospel among the Danes in America (commonly referred to as "Udvalget," in English "the Commission") was established in 1869 and sought to meet those needs. A school for the preparation of pastors to serve in America was established at Askov Folk High School, and beginning in 1874 men were sent from that school to be ordained in the United States. Over the next few years, 24 men received all or part of their theological education at Askov (including, incidentally, both my own and my wife's grandfathers). Their education in the shadow of the preeminent folk high school in the heartland of Grundtvigian influence also contributed to the growing resistance which the orthodox Norwegian-Danish contingencies felt toward this offending point of view.

Immigrants pursued their own ethnic dreams in the context of the American dream. There was, of course, interaction. Sometimes the dreams competed, but often they were perceived to be complementary. Many rejected the melting pot and pictured the culture of the new world as a fabric into which the threads of many heritages were woven. Some of the new songs sung by the transplanted Danes were songs of the new land whose flag was the red, white, and blue. Old Glory was raised beside Dannebrog.

One who stood astride that divide between the Danish and the American dream was Frederik Lange Grundtvig, the youngest son of N.F.S. Grundtvig. He came to America not as a pastor or a theologian but as an ornithologist. He pursued his studies and research in Wisconsin, but in his personal life he sought more. After an encounter with Pastor Thorvald Helveg, his life found new directions. He began the study of theology and was ordained to a pastorate at Clinton, Iowa, where he served for 17 years before returning to Denmark.

As his father, Frederik Lange was a poet and an author. His songs and hymns became widely known and sung among the Danish people in America. In 1889 he collected and published a songbook for the Danes.[2] That book was perhaps the most significant and influential book in the Danish Church and communities. It went through six enlarged editions, the last appearing in 1931 with an English supplement added. It is still used at a number of annual folk meetings. The book also spawned translations and the publication of an English songbook entitled *World of Song* (1941). A number of mutations of that have appeared since and are still in use. Many consider this book a major contribution to this heritage.

The songbooks are not hymnbooks, although a number of hymns were included. They parallel and resemble the *Højskole Sangbog* in Denmark and were and are used in much the same manner at folk high schools and gatherings other than worship services. They also epitomized that which the opponents of Grundtvig deplored and scorned. Although rooted in the common celebrative faith of a people who were children of the church, the songs were dismissed as "worldly."

For most Scandinavian Lutherans, the hymns of Grundtvig were contaminated on two opposite grounds. His own orientation to Word and Sacrament – the Word alive at the font and the altar – was rejected as the "church view". Other Lutherans of the frontier were much more inclined to a biblicism that identified the Word with Scripture. His hymns and songs, on the other hand, were considered to be culture-reflective and earthbound. The Scandinavian Lutheran hymnal printed in English a little over a century ago had no hymns by Grundtvig. These were all omitted, as he was considered a heretic and one of Lutheranism's destroyers.

2. *Sangbog for Det Danske Folk i Amerika* (Cedar Falls, 1889-1931).

While the Danes may not have known much of Grundtvig's sermonizing or his historical writings, they did know his hymns and sang them on all occasions. Their folk theology was defined by these. This is the day of salvation, the day the Lord has made. And so we will keep the festival, the festival of the Spirit which grows out of Christmas and Easter. All of creation knows that and expresses its joy in the life-giving sunshine, the songs of the nightingale, the bloom of the lilies and the promise of a golden harvest. There are 40 hymns under the section called the "Holy Spirit" in the 1953 edition of the *Danish Hymnal*. Grundtvig wrote or revised 36. In the current Lutheran Book of Worship in America, five hymns are included in the corresponding section; one of these is by Grundtvig. Another of his Pentecost hymns is included in another section. A total of eight hymns by Grundtvig are included.[3] Many more have of course been translated. Some were poorly done, attractive only to those who remembered and revered the original. Much of Grundtvig's poetry is so steeped in Danish folklore and rooted in Danish history that it defies literal translation. Even if this barrier should be breached, the rejection of his hymns was likely because of the worldly imagery and the supposed theological deviation.

Frederik Lange Grundtvig was also instrumental in establishing the Danish Folk Society (Dansk Folkesamfund/D.F.S.). In an invitation to join this, he envisioned a new society which would preserve, cultivate, and pursue the spiritual and cultural heritage received from the fatherland. The younger Grundtvig spoke of America as an arena where people from all over the world could share their treasures. He was also convinced that ethnic groups should retain their mother tongues and continue to be nurtured by their roots.

D.F.S. societies sprang up throughout the country. They served as reading circles, song societies, and fellowship centers; and they officially related to the church.

The primary task of the societies was to define and explore the identity of their members as a new people, Danish-Americans. At its base, this was a Grundtvigian concern and task. Questions of church life and doctrine were discussed freely and often polemically; accusations abounded and derogatory name-calling was common. At times appeals were made for more moderate or reasonable discourse, but wild discussions continued. Some argued

---

3.   The eight hymns included are: *Det kimer nu til Julefest* (The Bells of Christmas); *Dejlig er den Himmel Blaa* (Bright and Glorious is the Sky); *Den Signede Dag* (O Day full of Grace); *Herren strækker ud Sin Arm* (Cradling Children in His Arm); *Guds Ord det er Vort Arvegods* (God's Word is our Great Heritage); *Du som Gaar Ud* (Spirit of God, Sent from Heaven (for Pentecost)); *Fred til Bod* (Peace to Soothe Our Bitter Woes); *Kirken den er et Gammel Hus* (Built on a Rock).

that these discussions were harmful to the peace of the community, but others felt that free and spirited exchange was necessary. A lively forum was evidence of the Spirit at work. Such discussions were a common heritage from the public discussions in Denmark and indeed might be a mark of the Danish heritage!

Annual folk meetings and conventions drew participants from all over the country and similar annual meetings were held in nine geographic districts. Reading circles circulated the latest books from Denmark by mail. Locally, congregations built halls adjoining the churches. These were often equipped with stall bars for gymnastics and stages for amateur dramatics, and had ample room for folk dancing and their primary purpose: a gathering place for singing and lectures.

Other groups, as I recall them from my childhood, regarded all such gatherings and activities as *adiaphora* – not sufficiently religious. They did not gather for folk meetings but rather for what they called mission meetings or Bible conferences. The churches that were aware of and cherished their Grundtvigian traditions are remembered today. But as they prospered, they also served as a major irritant in the dissension growing among Lutherans. Worldly pleasures and entertainments distracted from the spiritual message; interests in mythology and historic writings were considered humanistic. In the 1890s when the division of the Danish Church was imminent, F.L. Grundtvig offered to disband his creation for the sake of peace. However, his dream child refused to follow his lead and continued to flourish for many years. The split did come, as it probably would have even without this irritant.[4]

By the turn of the century, that fractional group of Danes who did look back to the Danish Church and their home country had itself splintered over cultural and theological differences in the ways they chose to define the heritage that they sought to preserve. Now there were two Danish Churches, the smaller of which became the home church of the Grundtvigians. Even among these, there were those who resisted that designation for their church.Yet while few in numbers they did tend to place a higher value on the cultural and theological views associated with Grundtvig and Denmark. As a result they bore the brunt of criticism and even heresy by other American Lutherans for almost half a century.

Despite being scattered across the nation (in 1904, 112 communities in 18 states reaching from Maine to California),[5] an amazing amount of energy marked this small group. A weekly, *Kirkelig Samler* (The Church Gatherer),

4. Thorvald Hansen, *Church Divided* (Des Moines, 1992).
5. 1904 statistics; Aarsberetning for "Den danske evangelisk-Lutherske Kirke i Amerika" (1904).

was established in 1872 by the Danish Church (Fellowship). Soon thereafter, *Danne-Virke* (The Work of the Dane; but also the name of a periodical produced 1816-19 by N.F.S. Grundtvig himself which in turn used the name of the ancient fortified frontier of Denmark below the Jutland peninsula), also a weekly publication, appeared (1880-1950). Although not less for any theological stance on the Word or the Sacraments or God's pervasive presence in the unfolding of history than for the fact that they knew life to be rich and celebrative. A descendant of that tradition would probably be quite content with the common designation of the day. They were the "happy" Danes as opposed to the "holy" or "sombre" Danes. Were they to seek more theological terminology, they would probably have agreed that their churches were less likely to use Augustinian images of sin and redemption. I recall in the early days of my own pastorate that some of the older members were uncomfortable with the liturgical confession of sin. They would much rather view life in all its wealth and blessing. While they did not know the particulars of Grundtvig's theology, they knew and loved his hymns. Their patristic theologian would be Irenaeus as they would echo his statement, "The glory of God is man fully alive."

Shortly after the division of the church, in a time of national recession, this remnant founded what they talked of as the Danish University of America. There already were a number of folk high schools[6] and these continued to flourish for the first two to three decades of the century. Some of the methodology of the folk high school and much of the spirit was to live on at Grand View College. However, the new venture in Des Moines, Iowa, was to be an academic institution for the education of pastors and the advanced study of the young people. For the first half-century of its life, the college was the one institution which more than any other bonded second and third generation Danish-Americans. Over the course of time, it has become a fully accredited institution of higher learning whose students now have little genetic connection with Denmark.

But there does remain at Grand View a vestigial memory and an intentional pursuit of the ideals and the life of its founders. In 1995, the drama department presented a musical saga in which one of the characters was N.F.S. Grundtvig. The play was an attempt by contemporary students to explain to their visitor from the past their current life and study. The students were of various ethnic and racial backgrounds. The visitor from a previous century shared some of his views of "education for life." The presentation was done

6.   Namely, at Elkhorn (Iowa), Danebod (Minnesota), Ashland, Grant (Michigan),
      Nysted (Nebraska), Atterdag, Solvang (California), and Dalum, (Alberta, Canada).

with humor and a light touch but nonetheless with content. It drew considerable interest.

After the First World War, immigration slackened considerably and much of America moved from farm to city. A number of pastors of the Danish Church returned to Denmark and the language question became more and more pressing. We now began to think of ourselves as Americans of Danish descent and tended to coast on our past achievements and lives.

Considering the challenges of the past involved remembering those who initially valued this heritage and their times. Present challenges require a similar review. Who remembers and still carries some degree of the same commitment to that history, those values? How is that inheritance perceived today; and how can those values be related to our times? Challenges, again, grow out of a convergence of perceived values and present context.

Political, technological, economic, and social changes have pushed any recognition beyond the reach of anyone from my grandfather's day. America became involved in two European wars and emerged proud, powerful, and arrogant. But after a prolonged cold war and two Asiatic conflicts, America's faith in itself was shaken. Common ideals were tarnished. The mood at the 20th century's end is ambivalent, for many cynical. Where idealism ruled, perhaps naively, 100 years ago, there is now a scepticism, a pragmatism. Industrialization has moved us into and through an age where oil has been king and the black gold of empires. But the electronic age will supplant that and the age of cyber space presses upon us. Today's wonders are obsolete before tomorrow dawns.

If such talk would be a mystery to my grandfather, he would have no more comprehension of our economic largesse today. Our homes, the foods we eat, our means of transportation, and all the other realities that reflect our material wealth, which we assume as necessities, describe another life. Finally, sociological changes have likewise developed apace. There are few if any ethnic communities similar to those of a century ago. The New Testament concept that we are members of one another eludes most moderns. It is a strange and curious truth that 100 years ago we addressed all but a handful of people by their surnames. Now when strangers meet, even casually, they expect to be on a first-name basis. Even in Denmark, all must be *dus* with each other.

It has often been said that Grundtvig is difficult to translate not simply because his prose is of another age and style but also due to the richness of an imagery rooted in a shared historical community. By the second half-century in America, as the challenge of translation was emerging, the Danish language itself was losing dominance. Need and praxis were in tension. A few books and biographies appeared together with a number of translated hymns and songs. But Danish was no longer the vehicle of the Word.

As immigration slowed to a trickle, as America moved from a rural to an urban society, as higher education became available and normative, the folk high schools began to close. The great economic depression of the 1930s rang their death knell. They had been the heartbeat of Grundtvigianism in America for half a century. None survived but now awaited a metamorphosis in the middle years of the century. Through the vision of Enok Mortensen, pastor and poet, Danebod, the folk high school in Minnesota was revitalized. A family camp with intentional Grundtvigian overtones in singing, study, and recreation has flourished and grown since the 1940s. Now three such separate weekly camps are held each year. A fall folk meeting attracting almost 200 participants, mostly of Danish descent, has been held regularly for half a century. The only Danish is heard during the two to three hours of singing. Many of the singers no longer understand the words! A Danish worship service is held on Sunday, but the sermon is in English. The last three pastors of the church have not come from a Danish background.

By 1950, the language transition was complete. Insofar as the heritage was remembered, the emerging need was to move beyond nostalgia to definition. Those who remembered faced new challenges without the resources once considered essential. How is a landscape painting to be reproduced with paints that have lost their pigment? For most the final vestiges of language lingered in scattered phrases such as "tak for mad" (thanks for the meal), "Glædelig Jul" (Happy Christmas) and "skaal" (cheers!).

Grand View College continued through World War II to be the central institution and bonding catalyst of the Danish Church. But after the war, an enrollment explosion eroded that connection. Although fewer students of Danish descent came, the numbers enrolled quickly grew tenfold. It had become a regional college, and remembrance of roots now was more theoretical and intentional.

The word Danish was dropped from the name of the church in the same decade. It was a recognition of a reality. The theological school attached to Grand View had become more dependent upon academic relationships with other Lutherans and drew faculty members from them.

In 1960, the school was merged with the Chicago Lutheran Seminary in Illinois. Eight seminary students and one faculty member, myself, were involved in that move. Dr. Johannes Knudsen, Grundtvig scholar and former president of Grand View, had already been a faculty member in Chicago for eight years. Together, Knudsen and I served over 30 years at that school bringing, I believe, some awareness of our heritage to those who studied there.

In 1962, the former Danish Church merged with three other Lutheran bodies,[7] a final recognition that ethnic definitions no longer applied to Lu-

---

7. Namely, the Augustana Lutheran Church (Swedish), the Suomi Lutheran Church (Finnish), and the American Evangelical Lutheran Church (Danish).

theran churches. We were no longer Danes or Swedes or Finns or Germans. We were now the Lutheran Church in America (LCA). We were again challenged to bring to the awareness of others the particular gifts of our heritage. Johannes Knudsen and I were among the delegation that helped design that merger. We did have some impact upon the theological articles of the new constitution. This concerned the doctrine of the Word related now more closely to a living Christ and less to scripture.

A parallel merger took place about the same time to form another large Lutheran body. One of the merging Churches was the former United Danish Church which had separated from the Danish Church 60 years earlier. The two larger churches then merged in 1987 to form the present Evangelical Lutheran Church in America. The descendants of the Danes who had divided so bitterly a century ago were once more in the same church.

No one personally active in the first merger as representative of the Danish Church was involved in the last merger. We had lost our institutional base and with that our institutional voice. The challenge had radically changed. The merger in 1962 marked the end of the Danish Church as an autonomous body. But a sense of identity through a heritage and continued fellowship persisted. The new church established a Danish Interest Conference as a vehicle for fellowship and remembrance. A folk meeting was held annually and a small journal, *Kirke og Folk*, was published. The Danish language portion of both has been minimal. The meetings of the DIC flourished for some years and at times guests from Denmark were invited. But the leadership and clergy in local parishes were no longer Danish and interest waned. Present plans are in limbo. The name of the journal was changed under the editorship of Thorvald Hansen to *Church and Life*, reflecting its readership. It remains one of the last institutional vestiges of the legacy carried from the Danish Church.

Ideas are not contained or limited by human structures, but bereft of institutional homes they are more difficult to assess or describe. Our inquiry becomes far more complex if we are also to consider what new growths or mutations may appear after a century of the celebration of Grundtvig by so small a minority.

Where should we look for Grundtvig's legacy today? In anticipation of this review, I wrote to a number of people who I knew had an interest in Grundtvig. They included clergy, lay people, retired, active, bishops, professors, male, female. All had been significantly touched if not formed by the Grundtvigian ethos. Our communal memory included much nostalgia, but also a deep concern for what our gifts from the past might have for the future. Several who answered wrote movingly in their responses of their spiritual formation – the singing, the fellowship, the reality of a life-giving spirit. The replies carried a strong flavor of nostalgia for what had once been, and for a hunger for its recovery. Several quoted the hymns which they considered central.

Some of their observations indicate how Grundtvig continues to live for them. One remarked that life is received and celebrated with joy for the wealth that it has – not as the ultimate. But neither is it diminished in any way by being penultimate. The view was echoed by others who equate being Grundtvigian with unlimited breadth of interest in all of life. History itself as an unfolding of life ever new is a witness to a living and creative God. Another wrote: "When I encounter a perspective that views history, culture, and language as a heritage of the Spirit, I am also in touch with my Grundtvigian formation."

A common thread was a reference to the centrality of God's creative Spirit. Some despaired at the captivity of much of Christian thought by a sterile literalism of scripture or dogma. They found in Grundtvig a confidence that the Spirit accepts, blesses, and visits our humanness and that its message is one of hope.

A second central theme dealt with their understanding of Grundtvig's anthropology. The phrase "Menneske først og Kristen saa" was interpreted to refer to the priority of the human and a theology that views creation and life in process. We are participants in that process. At its base, the Christian faith is rooted in and only fulfilled within the context of God's creativity and will. Several remarked upon the uniqueness that they envisioned in this view of humankind. Cultural origins and formation are as much testimonials to God's presence and creativity in history as they parallel genetic and DNA evidence of our origin and development. The key to all creation, past and future, is the Word.

One response reflected that Grundtvig was a contemporary and creative man in almost all that he did. He was also a political person who dealt with social, educational, as well as theological issues of the day. Any conference or efforts in his name should evidence the same concern and mission. To be Grundtvigian is to be alive and relevant to one's own day.

However, another respondent argued that Grundtvig's views of life and society are so contradictory to contemporary social values and forces as to be irrelevant. Although his thoughts have been life-giving to many, their vision has little in common with a bourgeois, materialistic culture that has preempted both school and church in our time. Grundtvigianism is almost totally at odds with contemporary mass culture that negates participation and spawns alienation. We who have considered Grundtvig relevant now live lives of accommodation and allow our mentor to become an interesting icon in a museum.

One question that I asked was whether Grundtvig suggested to them primarily a theological position, an educational theory of methodology, a social philosophy, or other. That brought a number of varied responses. Most opted for the first and then wrote concerning the "living word" and the ongoing creative Spirit of God. Only one gave priority to the educator role. She wrote that she really had not been very interested in theology (that supports the contention that theologians and preachers do speak only to each other).

A number resisted and resented the question. Grundtvig in their view was an entity in which such divisions were artificial. Theology embraces education, and education always has a theological premise. Social philosophy is an inescapable, organic consequence of a holistic life view. Daniel Martensen[8] is more broadly involved than anyone I know in conversations with other Christians: Reformed, Anglican, Roman Catholic, and Greek Orthodox. Dr. Martensen made the comment in response to my letter: "The holistic perspective of N.F.S. Grundtvig's integrating anthropology, ecclesiology, and cosmology is a rich resource of church renewal."

Several responders mentioned a number of individuals and groups that have been influenced in some way and have a continued interest in Grundtvig. These include the Campbell Folk High School in North Carolina, Rural Life programs in a number of Midwestern states, and various educational programs. Dennis Bielfeldt, University of South Dakota, made the observation that although Grundtvig's theological position is logically prior to his views on education, most of those whom he knows to be aware of Grundtvig are interested in his educational views and his social philosophy. That comment might also apply to most groups and organizations that Grundtvig has touched.

One such group in the Pacific Northwest publishes a newsletter and a quarterly entitled *The Bridge*. These are dedicated to the remembrance and preservation of the Danish heritage. They also sponsor an annual folk meeting in Oregon. Their roots a generation or two back may have been related to the Church but this relationship has faded and their interest is simply all things Danish. Most places where the name Grundtvig is known it is most often in relationship to his concept: education for life.

An exception to these observations was Walter Capps[9], who was not of Danish descent. Dr. Capps, a professor at the University of California, Santa Barbara, was elected as a representative to the United States Congress not long before his death in October 1997. Over the preceding ten years, he had become very well-known to the Danish-American communities as he had lectured at a number of our folk meetings. As an educator, Dr. Capps was very interested in the implications of Grundtvig's teachings for education,

8. Dr. Daniel Martensen, Department of Evangelical Affairs, Evangelical Lutheran Church in America, Chicago.
9. Dr. Walter Capps died October 1997.

particularly for adults. He was attracted to Grundtvig as a Christian human-ist. Theologically educated himself, he began with theological premises and insights. One of the first times that I met Capps, I asked what the subject of his graduate studies had been. He replied the Church Fathers, particularly Ire-naeus. The answer came as no surprise.

When Walter Capps wrote a brief article for *Church and Life*,[10] concerning his appreciation of Grundtvig, he mentioned four major points: 1. Education is a life-long process. 2. Education is a holistic activity with historical, cul-tural, and social context. 3. Our humanity is the first gift of life – in all its par-ticulars – a premise for fulfillment, and 4. The centrality of the Word. In and through the Word we are aware of and celebrate our Creator, indeed we par-ticipate in the ongoing creation. Capps responds to what he finds in Grundt-vig: a unity and harmony of life. He finds an integral coherence of human life rooted in a spiritual reality.

The 20th century was marked by a consistent and pervasive secularizing of our culture and common life. Now at a new century's beginning there seems to have been a turnaround, perhaps a reversal in contemporary cul-ture. Religion has been rediscovered. However, its reappearance is often in non-traditional forms as many have lost continuity with the past. The Story has been forgotten, and many today who revere the spirit are in search of a story. For some, cyberspace, alien creatures, and strange phenomena from distant unknown worlds fill the void. Creative imaginations fired by dor-mant longings are shaping new stories, new answers. Much of this energy is outside the church and reflects quite esoteric theologies. But they are a strong part of the context that challenges us.

The generic name of "New Age," by which this movement, if indeed it is a movement, is known, speaks more of style than content. It elevates and dwells upon "spirituality" which appears to hold up ethereal, mystical sub-jectivism as the ever present mark and goal. But the whole sense of the incar-nate is endangered. The question must be asked, "Where does the Word be-come flesh and dwell among us?"

This new spirituality has for some led to a rediscovery of Gnosticism, with which indeed it does have considerable kinship. That brings us back once more to Irenaeus, who may be far more contemporary to the current scene than many could imagine. It is in the context of this contemporary wrestling with the spirit that perhaps the most compelling challenge to Grundt-vigians may be heard.

The challenge of the Danish immigrants of 100 years ago was to define and preserve their legacy in a strange and pluralistic society. Some of us

10. Dr. Walter Capps, "The Relevance of Grundtvig's Teaching" in *Church and Life* (July 15, 1993).

gladly attest that the challenge was met, even to the second and third generation. But the old needs and the old context no longer prevail. Again, the Word
which is always new seeks a new incarnation.

Those who honor the heritage about which we gather do know the shape,
power, and wonder of creation. We are in awe of creation's unfolding and
dynamic surge. We identify that ongoing and ever new reality as the Word,
which, as it is incarnate in Jesus Christ, affirms and restores us to life. We who
through the Word came into being and are twice born in the first and second
Adam now not only anticipate but also participate in the Kingdom. We can
only know and speak of this holistically. In so many ways we can also speak
the language of the seekers who are attracted to what we call the "New Age."
We are a part of a new age, the new age of a humanism which, through Christ,
is life-affirming and which seeks harmony and peace.

All this is implicit within our heritage. It was implicit for Grundtvig in his
broad history-aware, humanity-celebrating views. It was implicit for Irenaeus, who with the Evangelist John rejoiced in the gift of life abundant. With
them we do need to lift up the first article of the creedal covenant of our baptism; we do need to celebrate the blessing of life. But as Irenaeus, we are given
a story, a Word to counter the gnostics of our time – a Word that takes on flesh
and becomes incarnate in our midst.

The challenge for our own time lies with the rediscovery and the sharing
of the story. The Word has created a community and a fellowship, the church,
which continues to be a vehicle of His incarnation, our nurture. The Word
alive at font and table and on the lips of those defined by His creative power
gives content to both the past and the future. No one knows this better than
those who have sung the hymns of Grundtvig and with him have confessed
their baptismal covenant.

Grundtvig Within the Ecclesiological Revival of 19th-Century Europe

By R. William Franklin

Grundtvig was always glad to have new friends around him. At the great party for his 50th anniversary of ordination to the priesthood in 1861, there were visitors from as far away as Norway. Now on this 50th anniversary of the foundation of the Grundtvig Society there are visitors from as far away as the United States. In this paper I want to say something more about Grundtvig's concept of the church in the context of the general ecclesiological revival of 19th-century Europe. In my last paper to a Grundtvig symposium I related Grundtvig to Johann Adam Möhler and German Roman Catholicism.[1] In this paper I want to relate Grundtvig to E.B. Pusey and the Anglican Catholic revival of the 19th century.

I focus on the double theme of the church and Grundtvig and Anglicanism for two reasons. First, the theme of the church is taken up because in church matters Grundtvigianism appeared already in the course of the 1860s as a sort of church party and the first real Grundtvigian Society formed in the 1860s was popularly called "the Church Society." Second, I have come straight from the United States where the defeat of the proposed Lutheran/Episcopal Concordat leading to full communion between the Evangelical Lutheran Church in America and the Episcopal Church was defeated: a stunning and devastating blow.[2] The turning point of the debate was on the relationship between the historic episcopate and apostolic succession in the life of the church.

Therefore, in this paper I am engaging in a kind of public exploration in the ruins, as I ask these questions: What do common themes and differences in the Lutheran and Anglican participation in the 19th-century ecclesiological revival in Europe have to say not only about our past commonality but also about any future hope of bridges which will allow us to move to full communion still in the future? How does our 19th-century heritage provide a resource for this moment of pause in which our two churches, both as national churches and as

---

1. R. William Franklin, "Johann Adam Möhler and N.F.S. Grundtvig: The Bridge of Romanticism" in *Grundtvig Studier* (1996), pp. 128-45.
2. R. William Franklin, "Does the Proposed Lutheran-Episcopal Concordat Compromise our Anglicanism?" in *The Anglican*, 25 (1996), pp. 3-7.

world bodies, must seriously ask what future relationship can exist between us in the light of this vote and this experience of the Concordat that Lutherans and Episcopalians have gone through with negative results. In this paper, I want to compare Grundtvig with the Oxford Movement; I want to compare him above all with his Anglican contemporary Edward Bouverie Pusey.

E.B. Pusey (1800-1882) was, with John Keble and John Henry Newman, one of the leaders of the Oxford Movement (1833-1845), the beginning of a revival of Catholic Tradition within the Church of England. Pusey and his allies maintained that the established Church was not the Protestant Church of England but the Catholic Church in England, and they fashioned their *Tracts for the Times* into instruments for a second, and Catholic, Reformation in England. In its own day, the Oxford Movement was viewed by some as a suspect, Continental challenge to the Protestant hegemony in England, though it was launched by a group of Anglicans at the heart of the British academic establishment. Yet in reviving the universal Catholic Tradition within Anglicanism, Pusey, like Grundtvig, rejected the Continental, Roman concepts of his day, such as "perfect society" that identified the church with hierarchy. He came to see, with Grundtvig, that the times required communities of faith showing how to keep the festival as well as the fast.[3]

As with Grundtvig, the parish focus and the economic focus of Pusey is important for a complete understanding, for it was Pusey who turned the Oxford Movement away from the better-funded parishes controlled by some of the most reactionary elements in British society, and it was Pusey who urged that the Anglican Catholic revival should focus on the modern cities and the outcasts of urban society. By contrast, in the case of Grundtvig we have Vartov and a concern for the small farmer, rather than for the gentry and for areas of former population concentration where the comfortable parishes were located. The established church in England, not unlike the Church in Denmark, had based its power and its privileges upon an alliance with the country gentry. Pusey had grown up among the landed aristocracy, and he had been appointed Regius Professor of Hebrew at Oxford in 1828 by the Tory Duke of Wellington when the previous incumbent in the chair, Dr. Nicoll, had died prematurely, some said, from breathing too much dust in Oxford's Bodleian Library.

But to the new Regius Professor at Oxford the old Anglican establishment, with episcopal palace, country parsonage with fire and sherry, the bare worship, these were not to be the ideal for modern Anglicanism. It is for this reason that in September 1833 Pusey launched a campaign to build "Eucharistic" parish churches in the new industrial cities of Britain. Pusey linked the

3.   R. William Franklin, "Pusey and Worship in Industrial Society" in *Worship*, 57 (1983), pp. 386-412.

network of new parishes as liturgical, architectural, pastoral advisor and guest preacher until his death in 1882.[4]

A central theme in Pusey's preaching and in the practical machinery of these parishes was the patristic focus on the incarnation of Jesus and on Apostolic Tradition, handed down in both the institutions and liturgies of the Church, as a reflection of the incarnation and therefore central, not peripheral, to the life of the Christian community. Christ-baptism-Eucharist-church: for Pusey, as for the patristic writers and for Grundtvig, these four are essentially one mystery; the liberating power of God unleashed through the coming of Christ, through baptismal regeneration, through the Eucharist, and through the church to restore the dignity of man and woman amid dehumanizing circumstances through the Apostolic Tradition of the church, which also, in Pusey's case, unlike Grundtvig, was closely identified with episcopacy.[5]

The patristic writers thus provided the theological vocabulary for Pusey as he turned the Anglican Catholic revival into a movement that focused primarily on the restoration of the centrality of Eucharistic worship in the life of a parish. In the atmosphere of the mechanized world of Victorian Britain, Pusey found that in order to make worship the act of all present who are members of Christ's body, the people's work – the patristic word for Eucharist until the fifth century is *leitourgia* (the "people's work") – the Eucharist, rather than Morning Prayer, a non-Eucharistic service of the word, should be celebrated weekly as the chief form of Sunday worship. Pusey's revival of the patristic tradition that held that the Eucharist is the action of a communal body is expressed in two lines from a hymn of his ally, the prime minister of England, W.E. Gladstone:

> We who with one blest Food are fed
> Into one body may we grow.[6]

The church as a community under the figure of the body of Christ, worship as the act of a community that receives this body of Christ under the form of bread: these key themes of Puseyite Anglican Catholicism are all a part of a 19th-century revival of patristic tradition within the Church of England.

4. R. William Franklin, "Puseyism in the Parishes: Leeds and Wantage Contrasted" in *Anglican and Episcopal History*, 62 (1993), pp. 362-77.
5. Three key texts of E.B. Pusey are: *Tracts 67, 68, 69, Scriptural Views of Holy Baptism* (Oxford, 1835); *Tract 81: Testimony of Writers of the Later English Church to the Doctrine of the Eucharistic Sacrifice* (London, 1837); *A Letter to the Bishop of Oxford on the Tendency to Romanism Imputed to Doctrines Held* (Oxford, 1839).
6. *The English Hymnal*, no. 322 (1933).

Pusey himself defined "Puseyism" as "in a word, reference to the ancient Church, instead of the Reformers, as the ultimate expounder of our church."

From this perspective it is possible to view Puseyism as a distinctive stream within the Anglican Catholic revival of the 19th century, and within the ecclesiological revival of the 19th century, one that was patristic rather than Roman in its definition of Catholicism, one that was urban rather than rural in defining the new focus of Christian action in the era of modernization. In 1943, in his classic *The Shape of the Liturgy*, Dom Gregory Dix, the most influential figure in the enterprise of 20th-century Anglican liturgical revision, captured the significance of the urban, parochial expressions of Puseyism in one sentence: "The Oxford Movement turned to the parishes and taught the parish priests and the laity in great numbers to think of the Eucharistic action as the patristic authors had thought of it."[7] It is this pointing to a local community centered about the Eucharist that distinguished Pusey's ecclesiology from that of the 17th-century Anglicans Pearson and Bull or that of the 19th-century American High Church Episcopalian John Henry Hobart. In time Pusey's revival of a patristic ecclesiology that focused on the Eucharistic liturgy transformed the worship of the Church of England in such a way as to lead to the parish communion, to the replacement of Morning Prayer, or Ante-Communion, as the normal way of Anglican Sunday worship. As a result of this process initiated within Anglicanism by E.B. Pusey and from the perspective of the change to a vernacular Roman Catholic liturgy at Vatican II, at last the English liturgy derived from Thomas Cranmer and the Catholic liturgy derived from the Council of Trent were hardly to be distinguished.

Can we think of Grundtvig as a contemporary northern parallel to Pusey within another great church? If we shift the prism of history and see the Copenhagen preacher and the Oxford scholar as part of one common European cultural dynamic, we begin to see things that 19th-century Anglicans and Lutherans had in common, also with some Roman Catholics of the period who were undergoing a parallel revival: above all Johann Adam Möhler in Germany and Prosper Guéranger in France.[8]

In his earliest years in Udby and in Jutland, Grundtvig had been of the opinion that the church's whole foundation was *sola scriptura*, the Bible and the Bible alone. But just a few years before Pusey in England, he arrived at a view, similar to that of Pusey, that it was the church itself and its tradition, especially as expressed in the Apostolic confession at baptism, that was the ba-

7. Gregory Dix, *The Shape of the Liturgy* (London, 1945), p. 717.
8. For further analysis of these parallel revivals see R. William Franklin, *Nineteenth-Century Churches: The History of a New Catholicism in Würtemberg, England, and France* (New York and London, 1987).

sis of the Christian faith. Christ was not to be sought in a book of the past, but in a living community of "the people," engrafted by baptism, nourished by the Eucharist. It is in the congregation, at baptism and communion, that Christ speaks his living Word to the community, or as Grundtvig put it himself: "No book can confer life, not even the Bible. The Christian community is no mere reading club; it is a fellowship of faith begotten and preserved through the spoken word as this goes down from generation to generation."[9] The people, not the text, is the vessel of the Apostolic Tradition.

This view Grundtvig put before the public for the first time in a publication that appeared in 1825, one year after Pusey's first published work, a short Latin speech delivered in the Sheldonian Theatre in Oxford. *The Church's Retort*, the reply which Grundtvig made on the church's behalf, was addressed to a professor of theology in Copenhagen, H.N. Clausen, who had brought out a book on the doctrines of Catholicism and Protestantism. For Clausen, the Bible was the undoubted foundation of Christianity, and the truth was to be deduced from it alone with the aid of reason. This view ran completely counter to Grundtvig's account of the Christian faith. He had become convinced that the church needs some authority which lies beyond question as the basis of sound spiritual life. His answer had come in what Grundtvig thereafter spoke of as his "matchless discovery," which fell into this period of 1825. The discovery, or more properly the recovery, was this: that modern Christians in a skeptical age may appeal to the letter of scripture not to a dead but to a "Living Word," the Church's confession of faith – as that has been handed down through the centuries by the human community – renewed continuously in the waters of baptism.[10]

In his ecclesiology, Pusey was concerned with unity as well as community, and during the same period, Grundtvig maintained in *The Church's Retort* that the essence of Christianity does not lie in any fixed text but in a spiritual unity, a preservation of apostolic faith which has somehow been present in the variety of diverse human forms which Christianity has assumed in the course of the centuries, a unity that is so rich that it brings forth these forms, sometimes contradictory and in tension, out of its own fullness and still has more to be revealed. As with Pusey, the church itself for Grundtvig is at the mid-point of this evolving unity. Grundtvig shares with Pusey an identical sense of the Church of Jesus Christ as one monumental, historic, organic reality. He means by this that the Church – not the Danish state or the University of Copenhagen or the city corporations – is the place, where the whole of hu-

9. Grundtvig quoted in E.L. Allen, *Bishop Grundtvig: A Prophet of the North* (London, 1944), p. 66.
10. Toivo Harjunpaa, "Grundtvig and his Incomparable Discovery" in *The Lutheran Quarterly*, 25 (1973), pp. 54-70.

man life, the whole of human existence, finds its integrity and meaning. Grundtvig reminds us, as does Pusey, sometimes both of them in violent language, that the lives of the Danish people or the English people have been rooted in another and greater tradition than that of the state. It is the apostolic tradition of the universal Church of Christ.

Grundtvig sets so high a value on the church as bearer of salvation that he used language which clearly suggested a departure from the Protestant position, as when he translated the great battle hymn of the Reformation in a form which suggested that the Church rather than God is the stronghold in which faith takes refuge. Yet there is a departure in the direction of the people here also in Denmark: Grundtvig's is a "people's church," not a church of the clergy. The community as such and not the ordained alone are the custodians of Apostolic continuity. He expresses this point clearly in a stanza from the Church Hymn,[11] *The Church, It Is an Ancient House*:

> Never forgotten shall be in the North
> The Church of living stones,
> which on the strength of the Word of God
> Are united by faith and baptism.
> As a builder of a church, the Spirit is best,
> It needs a king no more than a priest
> The Word only hallows the House![12]

He speaks in other verses of this hymn about the Apostolicum – the bearer of Apostolic succession – only in terms of confession, baptism, and communion, not in terms of ordained ministry. Obviously, Grundtvig also does not see the Apostolicum as a dogmatic confession of faith, but as an Apostolic confession of faith which bears a sacramental character. The Apostolic confession is a Word from the mouth of Christ himself as we living creatures open our mouths to speak and embrace it with our hearts as we unite with the community of the Living Word in the midst of a liturgical celebration. Apostolic continuity in Grundtvig is guaranteed and expressed not by way of succession from individual to individual, but in and through the convocation of the church in one place, that is, through its Eucharistic and baptismal structure,

11. In a variety of ways Grundtvigianism in the Danish Church was a development paralleling the Oxford Movement in the Church of England. On Pusey and Grundtvig see P.G. Lindhardt, "Grundtvig and England" in *The Journal of Ecclesiastical History*,1 (1950) , pp. 207-24; F. Aubrey Rush, "Letters from England: Grundtvig Writes Home" in *The Norseman*, 11 (1956), pp. 263-70.

12. GSV I, p. 81, quoted in Theodor Jørgensen, "Grundtvig's *The Church's Retort*" in A.M. Allchin et al., *Heritage and Prophecy. Grundtvig and the English-Speaking World* (Aarhus, 1993), p. 190.

not its ministerial structure. It is a continuity of communities and churches that constitutes and expresses Apostolic Succession in Grundtvig's approach.[13]

Pusey by contrast adopts an earlier linear model of Apostolic Succession, a historical model in which God sends Christ and Christ sends the apostles, and Pusey believed the apostles sent bishops as the basis of Apostolic Succession. This sending for Pusey is a linear and historical succession, for Grundtvig it is a continuity of communities and churches. The proposed Concordat between Lutherans and Episcopalians in the United States proposed a synthesis between what I am here calling a Grundtvigian communal model of Apostolic Succession and a Puseyite linear/historical model of Apostolic Succession. The ecclesiology of the future would have created a synthesis of a succession of bishops and a succession of Eucharistic communities. Yet I believe that in the 19th century there were already four points of convergence between this Grundtvigian Lutheran ecclesiology and the Puseyite Anglican ecclesiology which keep us sure that such a synthesis might still be possible in the future:

1) Both were concerned to make a firsthand "traditional" religion possible for the common man and woman amid the revolutionary circumstances of the 19th century.

2) Both wished to stress the universal elements of Christianity as opposed to the denominational elements of it.

3) Both wished through liturgical worship to reinforce a sense of universal solidarity not only among the living but also with the dead.

4) Both Grundtvig and Pusey ultimately believed that this apostolic solidarity is sacramental: it is in the celebration of the sacraments and within the congregation at worship that we hear God's Word to us, creative Word, which brings into being the church, the new people of God.

The coincidence of the appearance and of the survival of these common themes demands a proper explanation today if we are to evaluate the possibility that Anglicans and Lutherans might achieve full communion in the century ahead, if not in the past.

Pusey and the Oxford Movement, Grundtvig and the Grundtvigians each need to be understood as movements launched to restore a corporate concep-

---

13. Henning Høirup, "Grundtvigs Gedanken über Christentum und Volk" in *Grundtvig Studier* (1952), pp. 72-81.

tion of Christianity, a corporate ecclesiology for the first generation of Europeans forced to confront a democratic, industrial, and predominantly secular
civilization. For the first time since the Reformation era, there was a rediscovery by an Anglican and a Lutheran of liturgical prayer as a social act with humanistic implications. The similarities suggest that one historical root which
supports the possibility of a merging of Anglican and Lutheran ecclesiologics
in the future is the ecclesiological convergence of the 19th century, the parallel attempts in England and Denmark 170 years ago to address Christianity to
the newly-emerging forces of modernization, and political and industrial
revolution: to address Christianity to forces of dehumanization which
flowed from those revolutions.[14]

To see the similarity, Pusey and Grundtvig must be placed within a common secular historical setting. The rise of a new corporate Anglicanism in
England, the rise of a new corporate Lutheranism in Denmark can be understood as part of a single phenomenon if both are seen to be part of a much
larger search for community in the 19th century that took many forms and
has many sources and lines of descent. Grundtvig was sharply opposed to
and wanted to begin a reaction against the dominant individualism of his
time. In the 1832 introduction to his book, *Nordisk Mytologi*, he defined the fellowship needed in modern society to be an aspect of "folk-life." In addition,
Grundtvig reminded his contemporaries of the historic tradition of Eucharistic fellowship that the Lutheran churches had largely abandoned.

Similarly, in the first three centuries of Christianity, Pusey found a new
definition of Catholicism for the 19th century: faith establishes a living, organic relationship with other human beings as well as with God, and the Eucharist establishes this bond of faith fellowship.

To find some explanations of the parallels in Pusey and Grundtvig, it is
important to begin by stressing that this attempt to recover the corporate dimension of existence can be found in many areas of 19th-century thought,
and I believe that German Romanticism is a mutual source of common
themes in Grundtvig and Pusey. In a previous paper and article, I have made
my somewhat controversial assertions about Grundtvig's debts to German
Romanticism, and above all to Schelling. Here I will only summarize those
points. I believe that it is significant that in 1802 Grundtvig fell under the influence of the prolonged stay in Copenhagen of the Danish-Norwegian-Ger-
man philosopher and man of letters Henrik Steffens. In a lecture room in Copenhagen, Steffens presented ideas of the German Romantic philosopher
Schelling that would prove to be attractive to Grundtvig. The southern German Romantic philosopher Friedrich Schelling became interested in the

14. The relation to historical movements is analyzed in R. William Franklin and Joseph
    M. Shaw, *The Case for Christian Humanism* (Grand Rapids, 1991), pp. 140-76.

church because the church appeared to be a historic unity, touching the mass of humanity, always expressing itself in new forms, yet forever maintaining its essential core unchanged. The influence of the Romantic world showed Schelling a deeper understanding of what a body is. The idea of community came to him in opposition to the Enlightenment concentration on the single individual. I believe that the German Romantic Schelling ultimately was a door that led Grundtvig to an expanded understanding of the doctrine of the Incarnation as the center around which everything else in Christianity should revolve in a century in which faith was faced with a fundamental crisis provoked by the historical criticism of scripture and the development of a scientific worldview in the public at large, both of which seemed to undercut foundations of theistic belief: the Incarnation not simply as a doctrine about the nature of Jesus Christ but much more importantly as a way of understanding the relationship of the historic community of the church through the ages to the word of God. Schelling beckoned Grundtvig back to older, pre-Enlightenment views, ultimately by 1823 to Irenaeus and to a patristic way of thinking about the Incarnation: that human history and the created order as a whole can be the locus of divine presence, that God is present to humans not by negation but through a long process of perfecting and completing what humanity is. This patristic way of understanding the Incarnation, which Grundtvig found in Irenaeus, with its emphasis upon the authority of the worshiping community as in some sense an extension of the Incarnation, allowed Grundtvig to hold a particular balance, a particular tension, in which the authority of scripture could be recognized, but always as interpreted within the historical evolution and sacramental practice of the universal church. These were all elements in the background of Grundtvig's "matchless discovery" of 1825.[15]

In a parallel manner, also in 1825, knowing of Pusey's own troubles with the authority of scripture, Dr. Lloyd, the Bishop of Oxford and Pusey's patron, suggested to him that a young English theologian might best acquire the tools of biblical scholarship at the German universities. Pusey left London for Göttingen and Berlin in 1825, and he returned again in 1826. While Pusey was in Berlin, Augustus Neander was lecturing from the notes for the first volume of his *Allgemeine Geschichte der Christlichen Religion und Kirche*, which covered the first seven centuries of the Church. In these lectures Neander presented this patristic material in the context of a contemporary dilemma: All Europeans were now living "in a time of great crisis" and God was working in this generation of revolution to set right the imbalances of Christianity.

15. Sven Bergentz, *N.F.S. Grundtvigs religiösa Idealism* (Lund, 1923); C.I. Scharling, *Grundtvig og Romantikken* (Copenhagen, 1947); William Michelsen, "Om Grundtvig, J.A. Möhler og romantikken" in *Grundtvig Studier* (1996), pp. 146-49.

For the Enlightenment had turned faith into a rational exercise divorced from liturgy, and the evangelical movement of the German Pietists had dangerously weakened the institutional expressions of Christianity. By contrast, Neander maintained that Jesus Christ had left to his church institutional means and liturgical means, which form the Apostolic Tradition of the church, for the purposes of stability and growth. Neander the German Protestant thus set before Pusey the forgotten world of the patristic church: the intense consciousness of human solidarity in the institutions of the Church expressed in the writings of the Fathers and the Mothers; the fellowship, sharing, and corporate celebration the Church experienced in its liturgical worship; the essential vision of the patristic church as an institution propagating itself in opposition to the dominant pagan power.[16]

As a testimony of the influence of these German views on Pusey, A.P. Stanley, later the famous Dean of Westminster Abbey, provided this description of Pusey's Oxford classroom in 1838:

The whole atmosphere of the Professor breathed the spirit of Germany to a degree which I am convinced could have been found in no other lecture room in Oxford ... The table was piled with German commentaries ... to these lectures I certainly look back as to the most instructive which I attended in Oxford ... And it is certainly not from agreement with the peculiar views which the Professor extracted from the Fathers ...[17]

These lectures on "the peculiar views which the Professor extracted from the fathers" provided a national platform for Pusey's revival of patristic tradition within 19th-century Anglicanism.

Therefore, to be understood in their fullness, Pusey and Grundtvig must not be seen in their national context alone, but also within an international context of movements which transcended national borders, Romanticism, and also a common return to the patristic church as an inspiration for modern Christianity. Pusey and Grundtvig must be seen as part of an international development in which Christianity, confronted by modernization, turned back to themes of people and church and community which marked the pre-Constantinian era, a dynamic that owed much to the realization that, with the spread of mechanical power and the displacement of absolute monarchy, the social order that had been in existence for over 1,000 years in Western civilization had come to an end.

16. R. William Franklin, "The Impact of Germany on the Anglican Catholic Revival in Nineteenth-Century Britain" in *Anglican and Episcopal History*, 60 (1992), pp. 433-48.
17. E.G.W. Bill, *University Reform in Nineteenth-Century Oxford 1811-1885* (Oxford, 1973), pp. 252-53.

It is as a part of this international response to modernization that I as a foreigner to Denmark and as a traveler across the Atlantic to this celebration wish you on this 50th anniversary to think about the legacy which Grundtvig has left to his country, not just as a national figure but also as a prophet who could summon his people to such a love of their country as would make them leaders in international cooperation. He showed in the 19th century that the new world of democracy and industry and national solidarity is not opposed to Christian internationalism, but that these new forces can be enlisted and mastered in the cause of a beneficent humanization of the planet.

I also want to say that, for Christians, international cooperation cannot be isolated from the cause of a realized Christian unity in a concrete state of full communion. And particularly in the wake of this defeat of the ecumenical cause of reconciliation between Anglicans and Lutherans in the United States, I believe that there is a lesson to heed in this 19th-century material. It is this: This point of contact between Lutherans and Anglicans 170 years ago is an important phenomenon because it demonstrates the existence of a much more venerable dynamic toward reconciliation between Lutherans and Anglicans than many may have imagined, far transcending the fortunes, or lack thereof, of late 20th-century ecumenism, a dynamic which I am convinced will carry us forward in positive ways beyond the results of the moment. The forces of history, the chance encounter, the accidental friendship all play a role in this dynamic, alongside the vote counts which mark the progress or lack thereof of the ecumenical movement. But amid all of this, the constant factor has been the Christian individual willing to take a stand, the individual who has seized the opportunity and marshalled the potential of each moment that has marked the stages of this advance. Though theologians of the first half of the 19th century served only remotely as a preparation for the turning point at which we have now arrived, they do mark the starting point that beckons the churches even now forward toward a Christian consummation which is part of God's plan for the fulfillment of humanity. Pusey and Grundtvig beckon us forward from our current state toward that intended consummation with confidence.[18]

18. What is the proper understanding of the theme of ecumenism in Grundtvig? Though Grundtvig was certainly non-Roman, there are points where Grundtvig's teaching converges with catholicism, broadly understood. There is the catholicity of his teaching on the church, Scripture, and the human. On Grundtvig and the concepts of catholicity and apostolicity see P. Schindler, *Vejen til Rom* (Copenhagen, 1949); and P. Augustinus, "Grundtvig som Vejviser til Rom" in *Menighedsbladet*, XXXII (1950), pp. 132ff.

"The Noble Tribe of Truth"
Etchings on Myth, Language, and Truth Speaking

By Vítor Westhelle

Man first and then Christian,
This is a main article,
Christianity is given free,
It is purely our good fortune,
But a good fortune that only comes to him
Who already is a friend of God
By being of the noble tribe of truth
                    N.F.S. Grundtvig[1]

I. Introduction

Etchings, the hobby of my teenage years and the metaphor for these reflections, consist in covering a metal plate with a wax-based ink, leaving exposed the parts of the metal to be etched by an acid solution. A negative labor of corroding what one leaves exposed, and relieving what one covers, that which one protects from the acid touch by veiling it. A negative labor that relieves by concealing. I present the reader with two texts I will be submitting to my etching. Texts which, after read, will be covered for the etching work to perform its corrosive tasks at their margins so that at the end they might appear again in relief. My concern is neither to study them nor to appropriate them for my own construction, but to examine their edges, the rough contours of some critical issues they touch. What follows should be regarded as a supplement written on the margins, at the edges of a text by Luther and of another one by Grundtvig. Led by these etchings my notations will, firstly, lead me to an examination of the role of myth and language in biblical literature. Secondly, the question of truth speaking and its conditions will be explored. With these discussions I will, thirdly, move from the north to the south, and

---

1. N.F.S. Grundtvig, *Selected Writings*, ed. Johannes Knudsen (Philadelphia, 1976), p. 141.

take the metaphor for what it does: It carries me over to the place that holds my own genealogy and shows the implications of my etchings for the understanding of Latin American theology and literature. These are the texts by Luther and Grundtvig that after their presentation here will be covered for the etching work to begin:

We must not, like these asses, ask the Latin letters how we are to speak German; but we must ask the mother in the home, the children in the street, the common man in the market place about this, and look them in the mouth to see how to speak ...[2]

If the people really are to see, hear, and find what the spirit of the Lord, as a foreign guest, has to give, and what the essentials are, they must have a living participation, through their natural imagery, for this is where the living proclamation of Christianity of necessity must begin. As it is with the mother tongue, so it is with the life of peoples. Just as human language has a living presence only in the mother tongue, so can the human race exist only in a folk-life ... The question before us has nothing to do with merit, nor with what we find in Christ or Christianity. It has to do with what is really in the world and how the world can become Christian in spirit and in truth ... I have to believe that the incarnation of God's Son required that he was conceived and born of a woman. He could find his mother only in a prophetic people chosen by God and led to this.[3]

II. Edges

Two topics will signal the edges of the relief as they form the parameters of the texts above. One concerns the relationship between folk-life (the English translation of the Grundtvigian *folkelighed*[4]) and language. The other concerns the relationship between Christianity and truth speaking.

The juxtaposition of Christianity and truth, as well as of language and folk-life, needs not go without saying. The conditions for the possibility of Christianity entailing truth will not be my pursuit in what follows. My ques-

2.   WA 30/II:637; LW 35:189
3.   Grundtvig, *Selected Writings*, pp. 47-48.
4.   I am using this translation following Johannes Knudsen (Grundtvig, *Selected Writings*, p. 37, note 11). According to Knudsen the term is closely connected with the entire population of a country, a nation or a tribe in its cultural expression, not being therefore set in a simple opposition between what is "folkish" and what is elitist or sophisticated, as the English "folk" suggests. Instead, it demarcates itself from systems and institutions being thus close to the Heideggerian and Habermasian concept of life-world with the advantage of being restricted in its use to a concrete cultural context and national or tribal identity.

tion here is for the conditions by which truth speaking can constitute itself or by which it fails to do so, assuming that Christianity entails a claim to truth. What are the conditions for truth speaking? Is it an epiphany that takes place regardless of circumstances? And how to explain its failure when truth is deceptive or silence reigns? Are there conditions or contexts in which an utterance can be said to be true and another in which the same utterance will be cynical?[5] These are some of the questions I am interested in pursuing.

A similar pragmatic approach will also address the relationship between folk-life and language, suggesting that it is in and through an empirical language, through the vernacular, that a people binds itself into a visible and demarcated unit, a space of belonging. In other words, I am suggesting that an understanding of language needs to take on from the beginning the question of addressivity. To whom is the message addressed and under which circumstances does communication occur? What does happen in this process of addressing someone? And these are issues that conventional views of language fail to take into account.[6] From a pragmatic standpoint, language emerges as a communicative web that constitutes itself precisely in the movement of this cultural weaving within concrete and dynamic matrices of forces.[7]

In this dialogical dynamic of forces language implies communication and cohesion, a social bond, but it is always inscribed in a context of violence or severance. Language, as pragmatists have often insisted, is always a source of

5. One of the most remarkable commentaries on this problem is offered in a fragment by Dietrich Bonhoeffer in which, arguing against Kant's view of truth as unrestricted disclosure, Bonhoeffer argues that an "individual utterance is always part of a total reality which seeks expression in this utterance. ... it must in each case be different according to whom I am addressing, who is questioning me, and what I am speaking about. The truthful word is not in itself constant; it is as much alive as life itself." *Ethics*, ed. Eberhard Bethge (New York, 1955), p. 365.

6. I am avoiding here two traditional views of language. One can be labeled the Romantic subjectivist (Humboldt, Vossler) view of language (within which Grundtvig's view of language has been often framed) as the creative expression of a subject, as the inner impulse (*energeia*) of an idea that sediments itself in an external, inert linguistic crust (*ergon*). The other is a structuralist formal (Lévi-Strauss, Saussure) view of language as an abstract a-historical system (*langue*) over which idiosyncratic utterances (*parole*) produce creative deviations. I see two reasons why these theories of language ought to be avoided. Both imply an understanding of language that is monological and therefore can at most take social circumstances as external variables in linguistic performance, but not as integral to the formation of language itself. Because of this monological character they are also unable to account for what is going to be shown to be basic in the formation of language in a communicative process, namely, the power relations in which a language emerges and configures itself. See Richard M. Morse, *New World Soundings: Culture and Ideology in the Americas* (Baltimore, 1989), pp. 11-22.

7. Such a view of language has been forcefully rejected by Mikhail M. Bakhtin, *The Dialogical Imagination* (Texas, 1982), p. 428.

error that debases the very communication it entices.[8] In his book *On Aggression*, Konrad Lorenz describes this paradoxical relation between communication and violence:

It is a curious paradox that the greatest gifts of man, the unique faculties of conceptual thought and verbal speech … , are not altogether blessings … All the great dangers threatening humanity with extinction are direct consequences of conceptual thought and verbal speech.[9]

This tension between cohesion and severance, between communication and violence provides for an ever renewed possibility of recouping or renegotiating the social bond into a new communicative matrix. Communication and violence are intertwined. In this polarity folk-life constitutes itself, re-imagining itself. The possibility of social survival and therefore of the constitution of a folk-life is always bound to the equation between these intertwined poles.

III. Myth: a yonder story

In delusion, the echoing-word
Was cut off from its root,
Uttered only what can be revealed
Through flesh and blood,
Became a plaything for every wind,
Except where in poverty,
With a woman's sigh,
It fastened itself
On vague memory
Of God's voice in paradise[10]

This equation, the possibility of keeping a negotiation, a commerce, so to say, between communication and violence I will call, for brevity's sake, *myth*, the particular semantic construction upon which any folk-life gains its sustenance. But how does this work? How does the myth as a particular linguistic

8.   See the profound, if fragmentary, reflections on this theme offered by Antonio Gramsci, *Selections from the Prison Notebooks*, trans. and eds. Quintin Hoare and Geoffrey N. Smith (New York, 1971), pp. 348-51, 449-52.
9.   Konrad Lorenz, *On Aggression*, trans. Marjorie Kerr Wilson (New York, 1963), p. 230.
10. Grundtvig, *Sang-Vaerk*, V, quoted and translated by A.M. Alchin, *N.F.S. Grundtvig. An Introduction to his Life and Work* (Aarhus, 1997), p. 227.

genre handle this commerce? Let me illustrate it with what I regard to be the classical narrative about communication and violence. I am thinking of the biblical story of Cain and Abel. A tragic account that has as much to do with violence as it has to do with communication. But more than that, and this is what brings me to the examination of this story: it is a mythical narrative that works as a myth of mythology; it is in itself an attempt at accounting for why a myth is necessary and foundational. A myth explains the function of myths. This doubling, this curious reflexivity within a myth that explains the inner working of a myth must be examined further.

In the canonical narrative of the Hebrew Bible, redaction criticism apart, there is no mentioning of any verbal communication among human beings until Cain and Abel come into the scene.[11] Up to that point, any communication was between God and Adam or Eve, or between Eve and the serpent. Among themselves they only shared the fruit and fructified; at least this is what a narrative reading of the canonical text allows us to conclude. With the two brothers this is no longer going to be the case. Each one is a distinct human being, but no longer original or placed in a unique relationship to God. Unlike their parents they had to know who they were by being acknowledged. They were no longer those who shared from the single fruit of the tree of knowledge but the ones who would produce the fruits that would not be offered to each other but to the Lord in search of recognition. The search for recognition by the "other" is placed within a triangulation among Cain, Abel, and God in which each represents the desire of the other. The question posed regards the mastering of this desire. The conditions for an asymmetry that will be at the root of the violence that ensued is created: Cain's offering was not received with regard and Abel's was. In the asymmetric reception of his offering, Cain felt his own individuality denied. The fruit of his own labor, the production of his own self, was not recognized. He lost his face, his "countenance fell" (Gen 4.5) and he could not mirror himself in the desire of

---

11. I thank Max Konstham for calling my attention to this intriguing narrative reading of the Genesis account that was originally made by the Maharal, as the legendary Tehudah Löw Ben Betsal'el, Rabbi of Prague in the 16th century, was called. For a commentary on his work see André Neher, *Les puits de l'exil: la théologie dialectique du Maharal de Prague (1512-1609)* (Paris, 1969). This explanation for the emergence of violence offered by the Maharal is older and distinguishes itself from two other compelling and widely discussed theories. One is Hegel's dialectics of the master and slave relationship. The other is René Girard's scapegoat theory. But unlike the "happy" Hegelian solution and the "tragic" version offered by Girard, the one here presented raises the conflict itself as grounding the semantic material of the myth so that both narrative of conflict and the eirenic possibilities ensue from the same source: the myth. It is the myth about violence itself that creates what political theologians have called "anamnestic solidarity."

the other. The desire for recognition on the part of Cain did not find corre-
spondence in the Lord's desire toward him. The economy of offering was in-
terrupted by an expenditure on the part of Cain that had no return. The desire
for the other, to be recognized, to be oneself was taken away from him but
granted to Abel whose offering was accepted with regard.

This sets the plot in motion for the account of the first direct human communication. "Cain said to his brother Abel, ['Let's go out to the field.']¹² And
when they were in the field, Cain rose up against his brother, and killed him."
(Gen 4.8 (New Revised Standard Version)). Rivalry instates communication
and its very end. It is not even a matter of attributing the tragedy that occurred to a flawed character in Cain and to a pristine innocence in Abel. The
story goes deeper. It tells about the beginning and the end of human communication. Once communication begins, the pendulum that will identify the
assassin will end on the side of the one who initiates the communication. It so
happens that Cain killed Abel, for he was the one to direct the first word to his
brother, the word born of the desire to be recognized. Abel, who did not need
the word to be recognized, whose offering was enough to establish an economy of reciprocity with the other, became himself an offering in the cycle of
violence that communication set in motion. What establishes communication
is also what renders it impossible. In the words of Hannah Arendt:

Cain slew Abel, and Romulus slew Remus; violence was the beginning and, by the
same token, no beginning could be made without such violence, without violating.
The first recorded deeds in our biblical and our secular tradition … have travelled
through the centuries with the force which human thought achieves in the rare in-
stances when it produces cogent metaphors or universally applicable tales. The tale
spoke clearly: whatever brotherhood human beings may be capable of has grown out
of fratricide, whatever political organization men may have achieved has its origin in
crime.¹³

The story does not end, however. The tale goes on performing its doubling,
reflecting its own inner working. The myth raises *itself* as the possibility of the
impossible communication it has just described. Such is the paradox of communication: by describing its tragic impossibility it creates a semantic field

12. The Masoretic text announces this invitation but omits the actual words that other ver-
    sions (LXX, Syriac, and the Samaritan Hebrew Scriptures) fill in. Were these words too
    laden and grave for them to be registered or so innocent that a presumed copyist could
    not understand their terminal fatefulness? Or is the content of the address irrelevant
    when compared to the act of addressing itself – indeed, so irrelevant that to register the
    actual words would divert attention from the real issue: direct communication itself?
13. Hannah Arendt, *On Revolution* (New York, 1963), pp. 10-11.

that makes it possible. Through this myth itself, the human community identifies its own nemesis. In and through it, the community is able to sustain itself in the recognition of its virtual impossibility of coexistence. The myth itself is the shield that diverts the dart of direct communication which it describes, establishing this language by which we can coexist in and by the very awareness of its risk and danger. Cain and Abel might cohabit because the story of the impossibility of this cohabitation is being told, because we are reminded that Cain addressed Abel and thus killed him.

Hermann Gunkel called attention to the fact that this myth, unlike other myths, fails to have ethnographic identification; it is an "obscured" narrative.[14] The tradition does not identify who Cain is and who his descendants are. However, is it not in this obscurity, in this refusal to establish identities that the myth becomes a universal narrative in which we all are simultaneously Cain and Abel? Or are we all not, at least Cain, wandering on the earth beyond the limit of our tribe and thus able to survive only because, like Cain, we carry the mark of our own condemnation, the sign that communicates that we are communicators and, in that, engenderers of violence? What protects us from each other is the story of our own condemnation. Cain and Abel can coexist because between them comes the story that Cain killed Abel in the desire to be recognized by the other.

Here we must pause for a moment. If the universal character of this myth is its distinguishing feature, how can we have the story if all that we have is a sign in our front that we cannot even read but presumably it says that we are killers who should not be killed? How is this obscure story linked to a genealogy? How can it be owned, shared, and passed on if, like Cain, we carry it but cannot know it? How can we go on living without a habitat, as wanderers on earth carrying the mark of a violence that only protects us from being killed but does not allow us to belong? Are we condemned to inhabit the wandering itself, as the Hebrew ironically identifies the "place" where Cain "settled," the place which is no place, the "land of Nod (Wandering)" (Gen 4.16, an ironic *utopia*)? Where is the third party that carries the story further? How is it that we can decode the "mark" on Cain's forehead?

The narrative goes still further and offers a response. It ends with a reappearance, a *parousia*. A reappearance of a character that introduces for the first time a *narrator* within the biblical canonical account. From the "vertical" communication between God and the creatures, to the "horizontal" communication between humans that install violence, we now have the intervention of a third genre, the one that spawns the story itself between the words of Cain and the silence of Abel. And could it be anyone else but the "mother of the living" herself, Eve, that enunciates the story to be passed on? These are

14. Hermann Gunkel, *Genesis* (Göttingen, 1969), p. 232.

then the words of Eve, no longer to God, no longer to the serpent, but as a register for posterity itself, to an unnamed addressee, to an indirect audience: "God has appointed for me another child instead of Abel, because Cain killed him." (Gen 4.25) She not only names the violence which communication has instated but reinstates the broken genealogy itself. Her son, Seth, the "appointed" one, will be the carrier of the story that neither Abel, the dead victim, nor Cain, the wandering perpetrator, are able to pass on. The direct communication that between God and humans was the source of blessing and punishment and the direct communication between humans, which engendered violence, are now suspended in a narrative without a direct addressee, an oblique communication with an absentee interlocutor, a story that will create a living space for Cain and Abel to survive, a story being told for another place, for another time. Myth: a yonder story. This is the story of the mother, the mother *tongue*.

Storytelling, Christa Wolf reminds us, "is humane and achieves human effects, memory, sympathy, understanding – even when the story is in part a lament for the destruction of one's father's home, for the loss of memory, the breakdown of sympathy, the lack of understanding."[15] To keep the paradoxical relation between communication and violence in balance is this not the function of the myth? And is it also not the corrosion of mythology – of the mytho-poetic nucleus of language, as Paul Ricoeur called it – the reinstatement of violence in the murderous economy of direct communication?[16]

IV. Parrhesia

If every civilization is built upon a myth or a poem, as Octavio Paz has so often insisted,[17] it is so because it weaves the web of a story that tells us where we have come from, what went wrong, and thus also how we ought to live, a story that proceeds from the mother and is encoded in the mother tongue. *It is its encoding itself.* If we take this understanding of language and the function of myth within it, what does it mean then to tell the truth? What is the relation between Christianity and folk-life in its cultural, linguistic, and mythological constitution? What is the relationship between the Word and language? What are the conditions by which the truth can be uttered? Am I suggesting a continuing and unproblematic relationship between the Christian message

15. Christa Wolf, *Cassandra: A novel and four essays* (New York, Farrar, Straus, Giroux, 1984), p. 173.
16. See my article "Invisibility and Dissimulation" in *Prejudice: Issues in Third World Theologies*, ed. Andreas Nehring (Madras, 1996), pp. 141-60.
17. Octavio Paz, *Los hijos del limo* (Barcelona, 1974), pp. 91-114.

and culture? Am I reducing the Kierkegaardian abyss between heaven and earth to a cozy *Anknüpfungspunkt* celebrated, as if it were, at the table in mother's kitchen? Is the Christian story thus reduced to an Ebionite reading of Jesus, the son of Mary, period? Is the carrying on of the story, or the immaculate conception of the Word itself, a spiritless event?

In two of his final lectures at the Collège de France, the late French philosopher and social critic, Michel Foucault, engages in an analysis of truth-speaking going back to the ancient Greek concept of *parrhesia*, to speak the truth boldly or plainly saying it all, without reserve.[18] His whole argument in these lectures cannot be rehearsed here. However, what draws me to this text is his analysis of the necessary connection between truth speaking and freedom which is established by one's being part of a *demos*, of a people in and through which one knows one's own belonging. The example Foucault brings forth to conclude his study is illustrative. He comments on Euripides' play *Ion*. The main character in the play named after him is looking in Athens for the mother he does not know, hoping that she would be an Athenian, otherwise he would not have the right to speak freely, boldly, and would have to be confined to the rules and laws of the city of men. In Ion's words: "Even if the law itself would make a citizen of a stranger who enters a city, the possibility of speaking remains limited to the one of a slave; he would not have the right to say all freely."[19] Foucault is here probably relying on the psychoanalytical distinction between the law of the father and the language, the tongue of the mother. It is this theme of Lacanian analysis that links us to the discussion about myth that we had earlier. What is of import here is not so much the constitution of the myth itself, its inner structure, or its theme, but the search for the mother, from whom the myth spawns, that "constitutes one's personality that gives the right to speak and binds one to the membership of a *demos*." This is what grants one a genealogy and therefore a language that can be authentically uttered without reserve. "It is this right to speak, this *parrhesia*," continues Foucault, "which the individual possesses belonging to a community of citizens, that is transmitted through the mother."[20]

The relationship between the myth that generates the context in which *parrhesia* can be spoken, and the law (in Romantic jargon: between the living word and the dead letter) is worth considering further, particularly because it calls upon the theological relationship between law and gospel which has

---

18. Michel Foucault, *Das Wahrsprechen des Anderen: Zwei Vorlesungen von 1983/84*, introd. and ed. by Ulrike Reuter, Lothar Wolfstetter, Hermann Kocyba, and Bernd Heiter, trans. by Ulrike Reuter with Lothar Wolfstetter (Frankfurt, 1988), pp. 15-42.
19. Ibid., p. 41.
20. Foucault, *Das Wahrsprechen*, p. 42.

been the framework within which the relationship between Christ and culture, Christianity and folk-life, has often been cast. However, the distinction between myth and the law offers an important nuance for the understanding of the gospel which the simple relationship between law and gospel fails to account for. Myth opens a new territory between law and gospel which interfaces with both. A context in which the law can be owned and a conduit through which the gospel can be heard is thus provided by the myth. It introduces a difference in the realm of language and therefore also in folk-life. It is the difference between two functions of language in response to the paradox of communication as described above: the paradoxical relationship between communication and violence in direct verbal exchange. One averts the paradox by prescribing rules and regulations which presuppose the very breach it tries to address. Carrying on his forehead the order that proscribes killing and prescribes the protection of life, Cain is himself the symbolic embodying of the primordial legal code. The other, as we have already seen, averts the violence neither by proscription nor by prescription, but only by the telling of the story. In other words, what the myth accomplishes is not announced as its own intention or by the results it produces.[21] The latter is not yet *parrhesia* – in fact we know that a myth often prevents a truth from being told – but it shapes the idiom through which the truth can be uttered; it is the raft over which the survivors float.

Foucault, accordingly, distinguishes *Parrhesia* from other regulated discoursive strategies (demonstration, rhetoric, pedagogy, and heuristics), all of which have their own laws in which they are legitimized. This is what allows them to be analyzed from the perspective of the internal structure of the discourse, from its finality, the effect it produces, and the intention of the enunciator. Like the law in the legal and theological sense, all these strategies are inscribed in an economy of investiture, in the expectation of a return, a pay-off. But with *parrhesia* it is different; it does not invest in anything but itself. It does not imply a strategic calculation; it is simply saying a thing for what it is. What one buys is not some other result but *parrhesia* itself. In it there is a total expenditure that implies a critical risk.

Only from the perspective of risk and danger, Foucault tells us, can *parrhesia* be read. "The parrhesiasts are those who undertake the truth speaking and for that they will have to pay a price that has not been determined in advance, but can imply even their death."[22] *Parrhesia* is not something "natural" in the sense of being spiritless or lacking serendipity. Not only the telling of a story is here implied but also the circumstances in which it happens, the pow-

21. This distinction parallels the one between direct and oblique communication. See Tzvetan Todorov, *The Poetics of Prose* (Oxford, 1977), p. 25.
22. Foucault, *Das Wahrsprechen*, p. 31.

ers it conjures, the forces it releases. Truth speaking demands a sacrifice and is framed in a context of risk, a risk for the sake of the truth. However, this spirit-filled circumstance is not only an existential decision, a moment of madness defined against, or made independent from, the cultural milieu in which it emerges. On the contrary, it is its fulfillment, not its suppression.

Foucault's concern and criticism of the West probably prevented him from taking a story out of the Semitic tradition to make his point equally well or even better. The Exodus narrative in the Hebrew Bible tells us about a boy who like Ion was left by his mother to have his life saved. Moses was placed in a basket by the river in order to conceal his origin and protect him from being killed. As we know, he was rescued by the Pharaoh's daughter. Although raised by his mother hired as a servant, he was only the adopted son of the daughter of the Pharaoh. When commissioned by God to tell the Pharaoh the truth about the condition of his people and demand freedom to hold a feast to God, he could not do it. Many times Moses claims lack of legitimacy, "suppose they do not believe me" is his plea (Exodus 4.1). Moses, the one to become the giver of the law, could not articulate the story of his own belonging: "I am slow of speech and slow of tongue" (Exodus 4.10). What he wanted was a strategy for legitimacy by which a risk could be calculated. But that was not the nature of the message he was given to proclaim. A strategy was not to be put in place. The question was not to establish an alternative jurisprudence, of finding another source of legitimacy, of reckoning the expenditure of power. Truth speaking, under these conditions, rescinds all calculations allowing no longer for a give and take: its investiture is total. It can be described as a tactical move in the sense that Michel de Certeau defined it: "a tactic is determined by the *absence of power* just as strategy is organized by the postulation of power."[23]

Only through his brother Aaron, the one who presumably knew his mother and had his mother tongue, Moses did gain a voice to speak the truth. Moses became the parrhesiast through the one who knew where he came from, who knew his story, his genealogy, and so gained a voice and could enter with competence the risk field in which truth speaking could be practiced with efficacy. *Parrhesia* does not require legitimacy, but authenticity, and its strength, paradoxically, grows out of a vulnerability. The one who has the story alone can risk entering the agonic context in which the truth can be uttered.

---

23. Michel de Certeau, *The Practice of Everyday Life*, trans. Steven Rendall (Berkeley, 1988), p. 38.

V. The Palimpsest

This, I submit, is the relationship that establishes a connection between folk-life and Christianity, between being human and being Christian, between culture and the condition for the possibility of speaking the truth.

Here the interest invested in these marginal notations comes to the surface. The edges of this surface upon which texts from Luther and Grundtvig were inscribed begin to reveal their sharp contours. The etching I am engaged in carries me to another place, the place of my own wanderings, the Americas that have to a large extent, except for surviving and isolated indigenous populations and ethnic enclaves of various origins, buried their mother tongue, encrypted it under the lid of the legal idioms brought by the colonizers. They were given the "law of the father," the Iberian father, under which the mytho-poetic nucleus survives at most in dissimulation.

The association of the law of the conqueror with the imposition of language is an intentional project of colonization. The colonization of the tongue suppresses the soul. We can take as an example the words in the Prologue of the influential work of Antonio Nebrija, *La Gramática Castellana*, published in the same eventful year of 1492, which not only marked the *official* arrival of Europeans in the New World (the Vikings' landfall notwithstanding) but was also the year of the expulsion of the Muslims from Granada, the last stronghold in a territory which the Moors had conquered and fought for for 800 years, and of the exile imposed on those Jews who resisted conversion. The Prologue was Nebrija's presentation of his work, the first modern grammar in the Western world, to Queen Isabel:

Language has always accompanied domination and follows it to such a measure that both have begun together, together they have grown and, finally, their fall was joint. When in Salamanca I presented this work to Your Majesty, you asked me what would it be worth. The Right Reverend Bishop of Avila anticipated my own response, and speaking on my behalf he said that, once Your Majesty has imposed your yoke to numerous barbarian peoples and nations of different languages, as a consequence of their defeat they would be obliged to receive the laws that the winner applies to those who have been defeated. Then they would be able to acquire its knowledge through my grammar.[24]

The implications of this can still be confirmed 500 years later in the studies done by Brazilian sociologist José de Souza Martins. Documenting research carried on among marginalized peasants, Martins describes a cultural formation in which people living in marginal conditions, in order to survive,

24. Apud Ruggiero Romano, *Mecanismos da Conquista Colonial* (São Paulo, 1973), p. 79.

were forced to speak the language of the conqueror and to hide in it the language of the conquered, a language demarcated by a code of prohibitions and allowances, a code of subjection, a language of jest ... Metaphor, occultation, dissimulation, silence remain as the language that documents the persistence of the same violence that gave birth to it.[25]

What is the connection between this observation and the intentions of the colonial project? Are the texts of Nebrija and the condition of marginalized peasants in Brazil united only by coincidence? Or else, is there a necessary continuity between the two? Let me explore this with another text.

In *The Tempest*, a late play of Shakespeare (1611), a very perceptive description of the role of language in the conquest is presented that I will take the liberty to quote at length. In it a dialogue between Prospero, the conqueror of the American island, and Miranda, his daughter (the representation of higher beauty, chastity, and innocence); the subject is Caliban,[26] (the representation of the natural being, the native inhabitant of the island):

Prospero	We'll visit Caliban my slave, who never yields us kind answer.
Miranda	'Tis a villain, sir, I do not love to look on.
Prospero	But, as 'tis, we cannot miss him: he does make our fire, fetch in our wood, and serves in offices that profit us. What, ho! slave! Caliban! Thou earth, thou! speak!
Caliban	There's wood enough within.
Prospero	Come forth, I say! there's other business for thee: Come, thou tortoise! when?
...	
Caliban	This island's mine, by Sycorax my mother, which thou tak'st from me. When thou cam'st first, thou strok'st me and madest much of me; wouldst give me water with berries in't; and teach me how to name the bigger light, and how the less, that burn by day and night:

---

25. José de Souza Martins, *Caminhada no Chão da Noite* (São Paulo, 1989), p. 116. Rubem Alves offers a similar observation: "Their language was not an expression of a historical self-consciousness ... They spoke a language that did not belong to themselves: they repeated, like an echo, the slogans of those who dominated them. Determined by ... mutism, the oppressed consciousness was reduced to paralysis." *A Theology of Human Hope* (St. Meinard, 1969), p. 10. De Certeau (*The Practice*, pp. 15-18) makes a similar remark about "popular" language in the context of domination as "a dark rock that resists all assimilation ... ceaselessly recreating opacities and ambiguities."

26. For the Caliban character, Shakespeare was inspired by Montaigne's essay on the cannibals of the New World, of which Caliban is an anagram. The word comes from the self-description, *Carib*, of the first natives the Spaniards encountered. See Roberto Fernández Retamar, *Calibán y otros ensayos* (Havana, 1979).

and then I lov'd thee and show'd thee all the qualities o'th'isle, the fresh springs, brine-pits, barren place and fertile: Curs'd be I that did so! All the charms of Sycorax, toads, beetles, bats, light on you! For I am all the subjects that you have, which first was mine own king: and here you sty me in this hard rock, whiles you do keep from me the rest o'th'island.

...

Miranda   Abhorred slave, which any print of goodness wilt not take, being capable of all ill! I pitied thee, took pains to make thee speak, taught thee each hour one thing or other. When thou didst not, savage, know thine own meaning, but wouldst grabble like a thing most brutish, I endow'd thy purposes with words that made them known. But thy vile race, though thou didst learn, had that in't which good natures could not abide to be with; therefore wast thou deservedly confin'd into this rock, who hadst deserv'd more than prison.

Caliban   You taught me language; and my profit on't is, I know how to curse. The red plague rid you for learning me your language!
(Act I, Scene 2)

After this, with curse as the *ultima ratio* of the one who does not have a weapon any longer, Caliban, stepping outside of the main scene, concealing his speech (for the one he had received as a gift was at the same time his prison), admits that there is no other way out of slavery: "I must obey. His art is of such pow'r it would control my dam's god, Setebos, and make a vassal of him."

The island of the mother Sycorax is lost; kept, however, are her curses as an ultimate underground possibility of resistance. What would be the possibility of truth speaking under these conditions? The scenario practically inverts the one we have considered above. It is not the stranger's genealogy that is called into question. It is rather the impossibility of the mother tongue to raise itself above the crust of an extraneous legality. Octavio Paz offers this comment:

The speech of our people reflects the extent to which we protect ourselves from the outside world ... The dissembler never surrenders or forgets himself ... the person who dissimulates is not counterfeiting but attempting to become invisible, to pass unnoticed without renouncing his individuality.[27]

Is truth speaking an impossibility under these conditions? What is the relationship between *parrhesia* and dissimulation? Where is the authentic reser-

27. Octavio Paz, *The Labyrinth of Solitude*, trans. Lysander Kemp, Yara Milos, and Rachel P. Belash (New York, 1985), pp. 29, 42.

voir of language hidden when the story of the mother is covered by the "law of the father" and only curses are left of her? Is the fate of the Americas inscribed in the code of violent communication in which Cain cannot but carry out his crime? Is the history of the Americas not a testimony to this? Octavio Paz' suggestion that dissimulation is not counterfeiting but an attempt at gaining invisibility insinuates an answer. Unlike counterfeiting, dissimulation is not a way of entering an economy pretending a false value to pass for a true one. It is a refusal to accept the economy. Like *parrhesia* it sets an end to the strategy of exchange. But while truth-speaking does it by risking all, dissimulation does it by hiding the value, which will only surface in a curse uttered in the language of the other. But does it ever succeed in conveying the truth? For this to be elucidated I need to go back briefly to the biblical story of Moses and its rich symbolism.

Again the mother. She is the one who in order to save her son's life puts him in a basket made of papyrus to be found and kept by someone else. Moses, the infant, becomes himself the inscription on a papyrus, a palimpsest onto which the child of promise was himself inscribed, once again a story for others left floating in the water of dissimulation in which his origin was hidden and protected so that he could become the one to part the waters through which his people would march to freedom. I have insisted earlier on Moses' incapability of speaking an authentic word without Aaron, his mouthpiece. My point now goes further. Moses, even if he was unable to articulate the story, was the one who had it from the moment of his being laid in a papyrus basket to the epiphany he received by the burning bush. He was the inscription itself laid in a palimpsest. Even when hidden, encrypted, or dissimulated, folk-life is not lost. It is there in stories of survival. It might have to wait for an Aaron to come along and articulate it and speak through it the truth of the tribe making it into the "noble tribe of truth."

Allow me to use a last illustration of this point, a contemporary example from Latin American literature. Isabel Allende in her book *The House of the Spirits* tells the story of three generations of women culminating with the story of Alba, the storyteller who, after being tortured and raped by the military police, finds the diaries of her grandmother, who used to call them "notebooks to write life." In the notebooks she recovers the story around those women who wove her life together in order to have *parrhesia*, to tell with boldness what has happened to her. She writes while she waits for the uncertain return of her lover Miguel. She writes while she waits for better times; she writes to indict the present regime. And she writes while she carries in her womb a child, a daughter, she says, "of so many rapes, or maybe the daughter of Miguel, but above all my daughter."[28] She is the one who will

---

28. Isabel Allende, *La casa de los espíritus* (Barcelona, Plaza & Janes, 1982), p. 380.

inherit the story and the right to tell it further with boldness and freedom. A story of survival.

The key to the reading of recent Latin American theology and also our literature is in the relief encrypted by the wax-based ink in the plate of a southern mythology stirred in the silent depths over which the acid performs its labor of negation. From north to south, from the awareness of the importance of northern mythology to the requirement of relieving the concealed mythologies of the south, the metaphor has carried me. At the edges of Luther and Grundtvig's texts, a lesson has been learned; it has less to do with construction than with the corrosion of narratives that has robbed the mother tongue and threatened the existence of folk-life. This is why Luther and Grundtvig have been catalysts for etchings done far beyond the latitude of their own mythological cradle.

Old Europe and its Aftermath: Poetry, Doctrine, and Western Culture

By Jakob Balling

I have chosen a rather wide-ranging theme, if not a downright preposterous one. Of course, it is a little more modest than the theme allegedly chosen by an ambitious Frenchman for his dissertation, namely "God and His Time", or for that matter by Sartre when he conceived of "Being and Nothingness"; but all the same, it is comprehensive enough for one afternoon! No wonder that I have had, and still have, my misgivings about it. If after all I have, to some extent, overcome those scruples, the reason lies in my conviction that some general and preliminary observations on the relation between poetry and doctrine and a bird's eye view of the connected problem of the periodization of European history constitute one of the useful ways of approaching Grundtvig.

This has to do with two simple circumstances. First, Grundtvig was a poet, but he was also a theologian, a formulator and communicator of doctrine. Consequently, one of the questions that have to be asked when seeking to understand him is: How do the two aspects relate to one another? And second, Grundtvig grew up and flourished in a period of time which is reasonably regarded as a period of major transition between an old European order and a new one. Consequently, one has to ask: what significance does this have for the understanding of the man, the poet and the theologian?

In the following, I shall elaborate on these two points and their mutual relationship. I shall begin with some remarks on the relationship between doctrine and poetry in the European tradition; then I shall go on to remind you of the case for placing the watershed between the Old and the New Europe in or near Grundtvig's time and also of the need to consider the question of how the two sets of reflections relate to one another. I hope to show the bearing of these matters on the understanding of Grundtvig and shall therefore conclude with some remarks pertinent to that. It goes without saying, however, that the main purpose of my contribution is to sketch out things that have to be taken into consideration *before* one embarks on a closer reading of Grundtvig.

First, then, the relationship between doctrine and poetry in the European tradition. When asking that question, the first thing that comes to mind is the fact that from very early times, through the Middle Ages and beyond, Christian doctrine itself has encompassed a strain of poetic modes of thought. I am thinking of a dominant pattern in ancient and medieval interpretation of Scripture, a pattern consisting in the events of sacred history seen as interconnected and mutually illuminating in a way closely resembling the interpenetration of poetic images. To be more explicit and concrete: As Augustine implies in a passage in ch. 20 of his *De catechizandis rudibus*, the door-posts of the Israelites in Egypt, smeared with the blood of the first Paschal lamb, the cross of Jesus on Golgotha and the sign of the cross on the forehead of the candidate for baptism belong together in such a way that their respective meanings are revealed when all three are taken into account simultaneously, notwithstanding the fact, or indeed because of the fact, that the cross of Christ is what determines everything else. That, I would maintain, is a poetic way of thinking, closely related to the interweaving of poetic images and metaphors, and it has put its stamp on the formulation of Christian doctrine through many centuries, not least because of the concomitant notion that each and every key event of sacred history is present in what happens now. That is what is apparent when the history of salvation is summed up for the new Christian when his forehead is anointed with the sign of the cross "as on a door-post", as Augustine puts it. And it is equally apparent in medieval liturgical writers' approach to the mass and in their attempt, so to speak, to compress the crucial events of past history into the eucharistic acts and gestures.

This is, of course, a wide field of which I can only scratch the surface, but I believe that I have said enough to make plausible the claim that the early tradition of Christian doctrine has a meaningful relation to poetry while of course at the same time being a set of non-poetical propositions open to the kind of discussion that takes little account of the interplay of images. Incidentally, I would ask you to note the qualifying adjective: *early* Christian tradition, which implies a contradistinction to modern doctrinal tradition, something to which I shall briefly return in the course of my remarks on periodization.

Let us now look at our question from the other side, the side of poetry.

John Milton can guide us into the subject in more ways than one. In one of his prose reflections[1] on the "office" (as he calls it) of a poet he describes the poetic inspiration in terms of the prophetic calling of Isaiah. The great and worthy poem can only come into existence, he says, "by devout prayer to that eternal Spirit who can enrich with all utterance and knowledge, and sends out his seraphim with the hallow'd fire of his Altar to touch and purify the lips of whom he pleases". Of the poetic abilities he says that they "are the inspired guift of God rarely bestow'd ... and are of power beside the office of a

---

1.   See the extracts from "The Reason of Church-Government" in J. Max Patrick (ed.), *The Prose of John Milton* (1967), pp. 107-11.

pulpit, to inbreed and cherish in a great people the seeds of vertu, and publick civility, to allay the perturbations of the mind, and set the affections in right tune, to celebrate in glorious and lofty Hymns the throne and equipage of God's Almightinesse, and what he works, and what he suffers to be wrought with high providence in his Church ... ". No wonder that poetry is something that consists, as he says, in "teaching over the whole book of sanctity and vertu", in short something "doctrinal and exemplary to a Nation".

Passages like these present in a nutshell one important aspect of our theme. The poet is a teacher of civic virtues, a promoter of calm and harmony of mind, an instrument of praise; but most importantly: he is entrusted with the task and the authority of a prophet and a preacher, and in that capacity he is a co-labourer in the restitution of fallen mankind.

This could easily be taken to be a purely didactic "activity" – in other words, a pouring forth of versified dogmatics and ethics. That, however, would be to miss the point. Versified dogmatics is not poetry. What the "doctrinal" poets of Old Europe, the poets that want to be of service to doctrine, are up to and aiming at is an attempt not only to formulate a rationally coherent view of the Christian message in all its implications but also to do it in the poetic mode, as poets, using the specific tools of the craft: the metaphorical interplay of meanings, the epic narrative and the dramatic confrontation, and by these means, to do something to doctrine that cannot be done by means of ordinary doctrinal exposition.

In order to elucidate this statement a little further I would like briefly to quote myself and repeat a summary which I have given elsewhere of the common characteristics of the classical theological poems of Dante and Milton.[2]

In the first place: in *Paradise Lost* as well as in the *Divina Commedia* the speaker's voice is a prophetic voice. Its utterances are divinely authorised, the bearer of the voice is sent to pronounce judgment, to promise salvation, to teach the way of the world, and of God.

Secondly: This task entails an obligation to make clear what – in Goethe's words – "holds the world together". To put it another way, the obligation to make clear the shape of history and of the cosmos. In both the great poems the whole of history is presented in a series of narratives, long or episodic, as well as in a series of dramatically shaped confrontations and conflicts. In both poems the course of history is interpreted by means of a guiding principle which – to put it briefly – could be described as the Augustinian concept of love and of order. This same principle holds good for the cosmic order set forth – in widely different ways – by the two prophetic voices.

---

2. "Grundtvig, Dante, Milton, and the Problem of European Continuity" in *Heritage and Prophecy. Grundtvig and the English-Speaking World* (Aarhus, 1993), pp. 75-76. See also J.L. Balling, *Poeterne som kirkelærere* (Copenhagen, 1983).

Thirdly: In accordance with the prophetic dignity of the poet's voice and with the task of universal interpreter entrusted to him, both poems assume the shape of what I venture to call a modernized Scripture. By this concept, which, incidentally, can be seen hinted at in Dante's *Epistle xiii* to Can Grande della Scala, I try to express not only the combination just mentioned (the combination of prophetic inspiration and universal exposition and interpretation) but also the calculated effort which is common to both poets of supplementing the "old" Scripture by putting in what it omits, by straightening out and rationalizing its lines of thought, by commenting on it, and by prolonging its course of narrative down to the poet's own time.

Fourthly: One of the things which constitute the calculated novelty of the "modernized Scripture" is the way in which the historical and the cosmic strands in the exposition are mutually interwoven. The combination, the "poetic universe", is worked out as a vast network of narrative, of metaphorical associations, and of dramatic confrontations, whereby one realm of experience (history) is seen to "comment upon" and deepen the understanding of the other (the cosmic order) and *vice versa*. Most importantly, however, the ultimate point of these interrelated structures is to be found in the fact that the meaning and the "drift" of both realms are concentrated in one person's experience. Both "orders" as well as their combination, their mutual commentary, are mirrored and internalized in Dante's pilgrim and Milton's Adam respectively.

Finally: From the "modernized Scripture", organized as a "poetic universe", springs an inherent appeal. The appeal is not an outwardly-added "moral" but that which by means of metaphor, narrative action, and dramatic confrontation is, as it were, spoken by the order of things to persons in lack of order, the protagonists, the poet, and the reader.

Taken as a whole, these fundamental common characteristics can be said to coincide in one common intention, that of giving expression to the Christian postulates concerning order – the creation, the breakdown, and the restoration of order.

I mentioned above that this mode of discourse was meant to "do something to" Christian doctrine, something that cannot be done by means of ordinary theological exposition. Something of what I mean by that has already been made tentatively clear; now I shall try to push the investigation a little further.

The two epics are theological statements insofar as they express a rationally coherent view of the Christian message which can be shown to be meaningful when translated into theological prose. That is worth remembering! There is, to that extent, common ground between the poets and their prosaic colleagues. But above and beyond this, the poetic mode of discourse does something to the doctrinal matter. What is it?

One aspect of an answer can be gained by closer consideration of what I called the "poetic universe". The "poetic universe", thus defined, is the outcome of the poets having exploited the possibilities uniquely available to them for a clearer, richer and more concrete exposition of some of the most

fundamental tenets of Old European Christian thinking, namely the following assertions: 1) the assertion of coherence and mutual illumination between
a cosmic, an anthropological and an historical order; 2) the double assertion
that God is involved in the world as its Creator and Saviour, knowable as
such by way of the world, which He has created and redeemed, and at the
same time as the Totally Other, dwelling in an existence unknowable by "natural" means; and 3) the assertion that everything that has happened in sacred
history is relevant for the self-understanding of the now-living individual by
being, so to speak, summed up and actualized in him or her.

These, then, are common tenets of Old European theological thinking;
but the freedom enjoyed by the poets to build an imaginative universe of
meaning by means of interrelated images, open-ended narrative and dramatic confrontation – the freedom, in other words, to establish a mutual
"mirroring" of macrocosm, microcosm and history – enables them to make a
statement about the coinherence of creation and redemption, about God's
nearness and otherness, and about the summing up in every human being of
God's entire purpose and action that cannot be made by traditional methods
of doctrinal exposition.

A couple of brief illustrations of this point could appropriately be taken
from Dante's *Comedy*. Throughout the poem a calculated effort is made to let
the cosmic edifice, with its narrowing and widening spaces, illustrate the
moral and religious assertions about the human condition. This is strikingly
exemplified in two passages. One of them is the traveller's experience on top
of the outermost sphere. Here his vision of the entire cosmic edifice is sud-
denly turned inside out to reveal an arrangement of things totally different
from the one previously perceived. That is to say, the Triune God is revealed
as the centre and the transcendent goal of everything that is. The other passage is the one in which Vergil tells the traveller of the fall of Lucifer. We are
given to understand that when the rebellious angel hit our earth in the middle of the southern hemisphere and bored his way down to the centre, there
to lead his frozen and helplessly wing-flapping existence, the earth-masses
that he pressed up in the process were used by the Creator in the infinite in-
ventiveness of His love to form the mountain of Paradise for the first human
couple, and later on, when man had fallen and the great redemptive events
had taken place, they were used again by Him for the purification of sinful
souls. In interactive poetic constructs like these (a great many more are discussed in my book), theological statements are made concerning God and the
world, statements that are capable of translation into theological prose, but
not without the loss of something that only poetic diction can provide.

Something similar can be said concerning another salient point in Dante's
(and also in Milton's) way of doing theology: his attempt to let all humanly
possible spatial and temporal experiences – as well as their interaction – be

summed up and concentrated in what is lived through by one human agent. In the course of his journey the travelling poet (the "I" of the poem) encounters the whole of human history and its reflections in the cosmic edifice and absorbs it all into himself through a process of learning about love, order and sacrifice as well as about selfishness, hatred, disorder and destruction – a dynamic process, in short, during which he himself gradually becomes an organized whole, turned upward towards the source of being, love, sacrifice and order. Here again, a presupposition common to all forms of Christian thinking: the notion that – rightly understood – "all history is contemporary history" is given an expression whose clarity and concreteness cannot be rivalled by any form of prosaic exposition.

Until now, my remarks on what the poets "do to" doctrine have been focussed on the possibilities inherent in the concept and reality of a "poetic universe". I would like, for the same purpose, briefly to touch on two other aspects of the poetic way of doing theology.

First, I refer to what is implied in what I called the appeal, inherent in the theological poems. Again, this is something which in principle is inseparable from prosaic modes of Old European theology (where it was always self-evident that, as Nathan the prophet said to king David, "Thou art the man", or, as the Latin speakers said: "Tua res agitur"); but in the poems it is given an expression of unique pungency because of the specific means available to the poets, enabling them to make of the appeal something other than an outwardly-added "moral", something (as I put it) spoken by the order of things to persons in lack of order: the protagonists, the poet and the reader.

This is what becomes abundantly clear when we consider the experiences undergone by the travelling poet in Dante as well as by Milton's Adam. The process through which the poet comes to himself – that is, learns who he is and what he is destined to become in relation to his fellow-beings and surrounding nature – is shaped by a long series of appeals in the form of demands and promises; demands to strive for insight into the order of things and to find his place in it, in accordance with its driving principle: the love that moves the stars; promises that he is going to succeed if he engages himself in the task, in spite of his fear and confusion. Demands as well as promises come to him in the course of the journey from the prophetic messengers and mediators who are, so to speak, "out to get him", as well as from the utterances of resentful or sorrowful dead souls and from terrifyingly silent demonic creatures. But the promises and demands also spring from the order of things itself, the narrowing and widening spaces, the bottomless depths and the arduous slopes, the icy blasts and the fructifying breezes, the all-swallowing darkness of perdition and the blinding light of heavenly joy. To what is thus "said" to him in hell and purgatory by men and things, by cosmos and history, the traveller reacts by embarking on the experience in the only way possible to a fallen human being – that is to say, with hesitation and fear, with frequently repeated misunderstanding, but staggering on all the same. The brutal realism of the description of himself given by the "I" of the *Commedia*, his self-exposure to scorn and ridicule, is there in order to serve a realistic understanding of what it means to be a fragile creature, an average man – and that includes in a calculated and purposeful manner the reader! – a fragile creature under claim and promise, whimpering under the weight of his freedom. Last but not least, it is meant to serve the understanding of the traveller's self-assurance once he has arrived in the spheres, and the naturalness and joyfulness of his responses there. The central lesson taught by the *Paradiso* consists in the assertion that Truth – the truth about the world and the self – has by slow degrees made that creature free, worthy and assured who ventured to engage in it with fear and trembling and unworthiness when it came to him and reached for him down there in the depths. Accordingly, the poem as a whole teaches that God's order of love gradually embraces the traveller in such a way that at last he embraces the order as his own. This, the poet tells us by the means in his power exclusively, this is how freedom and dependence meet each other and merge as a consequence of responses to appeals.

My final comment on what poetic diction "does to" the doctrinal matter concerns the posture taken and the claim made by the poet. The poetic voice is, as I said, a prophetic voice, endowed with authority to proclaim, to interpret, to organise and supplement, to actualize and to appeal. And, as I also said, it is a voice whose utterances pretend to what can appropriately be called a "modernized Scripture". What does that teach us as far as our present question is concerned?

One thing it definitely does not teach us is that such is the poet's attitude outside his poem. The Old European theological poet is a sane human being, no raving maniac. The pretension is internal to the poem, it serves a theological purpose there and only there. What purpose?

This is, of course, a question that cannot be answered conclusively and indisputably. But in the light of what the poems can otherwise be shown to teach us I think it justifiable to suggest that the prophetic and "scriptural" pretension is there because this is the clearest and most convincing way the poets can find to express a view of what is meant by Christian freedom. By formulating the pretension they bid to make good the import of what the Church confesses about man's free service being the goal of God's entire action towards His fallen creature. If this – we can hear the poets saying – if this is true, then the follower of Christ is someone of whom He makes a king, a prophet and a priest in His own image. A liberated creature is someone who, notwithstanding his knowledge of what separates God's word from human words and the creature from its Creator, dares to take God on His word and to utter that word himself in the conviction that the message of the one and only Holy Scripture can only be heard as it demands to be heard when the hearer's reflection and decision meet it in freedom, a freedom acted out in the post-biblical situation. This is what is made clear by the poet when he does not confine himself to a mere retelling of the message of creation and redemption, but reorganises it, supplements it and interprets it on the basis of the radical assertion that what is spoken here is spoken with prophetic and "scriptural" authority. The poet is as aware as the next man that this way of formulating the idea of Christian liberty is impossible in a normal, communicative context, but it is his proud and humble claim that it can be risked in the serious play in the sight of God played by His poets. The poet's way of realising the freedom of the Christian man is not the way followed by the "ordinary" theologian, and the poet remembers that prosaic theology is able to say things the poetic one cannot, but he makes the claim that something similar can be asserted the other way round. As John Milton puts it, the poet's muse is Wisdom's sister, coeval with her and her coequal playmate: "Before the Hills appear'd or Fountain flow'd, / Thou with Eternal wisdom didst converse, / Wisdom thy Sister, and with her didst play / In presence of th'Almighty Father, pleas'd / With thy Celestial Song".[3]

Now, saying, as I have done, that the theological poets of Old Europe "did something to" traditional doctrine is equivalent to saying that the study of those poets is relevant for understanding the history of doctrine and of the Church, for defining the great watersheds in the course of Western culture and for setting the theologian and the poet that Grundtvig was into his proper historical context. What follows are some, necessarily perfunctory, remarks on those themes.

If it is true that the poets "did something to" doctrine, then it is evident that the student of doctrinal and church history and of the course of European civilisation at large must take their poems into account and do it along several different lines, out of which I shall mention a few in the form of short postulates, on which available space forbids any extensive comment.

One: The study of the theology of two poets, from the 14th and 17th century respectively, makes clear that here we have a form of doctrinal communication that is closer to ancient and medieval Biblical and monastic theology than are the forms prevalent from the 13th century onwards, that is, from the breakthrough of the scholastic method. By their way of letting theological reasoning emerge from scriptural narrative, by their amalgamation of exposition and appeal, and by their way of realising Christian freedom by means of a prophetic pretension, they share a vitally important set of differences

---

3. *Paradise Lost* VII, 8-12, in Christopher Ricks (ed.), *Paradise Lost and Paradise Regained* (1968).

from mainstream theology, Protestant as well as Catholic. Acknowledging those differences must necessarily entail consequences for the mapping out of the course of doctrinal history.

Two: Furthermore, acknowledging the common ground shared by the two poets, the wide-reaching analogies of thought and structure I have tried to sketch out must inevitably lead in the direction of a reconsideration of traditional ways of defining the essential watersheds in European history. As is well-known, this reconsideration is a task which has been undertaken recently from a whole lot of different angles in different countries. On the basis of an increasing understanding of the great staple continuities (economic, political, social, cultural) in European life from the 11th to the 18th centuries, an attempt has been made to construct an alternative model of periodization, called, by one of the pioneers, "Alteuropa" or "Old Europe".[4] The builders of this model emphatically do not propose that little has changed during those centuries; they are, in short, not aiming at replacing one simplistic orthodoxy with another but they want, on the one hand, to stress the connections between Renaissance/Reformation and what went before, and on the other, to place the essential epochal divide in the period of the industrial and political revolutions. The dynamics of Old Europe, they maintain, is thus something that must be viewed as organically embedded in abiding structures that were not irrevocably broken until the turn of the 19th century. There is no need to expatiate on these matters generally; my concern is solely to point out that the similarities and analogies between two poetical theologies, separated as they are by three and a half centuries and a breach of church unity, lend a powerful support to this model.

Three: The support lent to the model is, furthermore, and importantly, a support lent to its "dynamic" aspects as well as to the "static" ones. That becomes clear by appreciating not only the great common patterns of thought and structure, but also the significant differences between the ways in which the two poets use the common patterns. Two differences stand out above all. Firstly: the difference between the Dantesque and the Miltonic interplay of cosmos and history. Milton's asymmetric conglomerate of worlds corresponds to his clash of personal wills, forcefully acting in conflict; and this complex is tellingly different from Dante's interplay of cosmic symmetry with an historical action conceived in monistic terms. This difference can, by the way, be said to be partially epitomised in the difference between Dante's Lucifer and Milton's Satan. Secondly: the contrast between Dante's emphasis on large and small social communities: the Church, the Empire, the city and the family; and Milton's comparatively jaundiced view of society, his stress on the lonely individual and his "paradise within". Something must indeed

---

4. Dietrich Gerhard, *Old Europe: A Study of Continuity, 1000-1800* (1981).

have happened between the 14th and the 17th centuries, one is apt to conclude, even if not as much as tradition has it.

Four: My last point in this section concerns the position of the poets, viewed in the context of ecclesiastical history. It seems to me to be of some interest for the church historian that something which must by all accounts be called real and substantial theological thinking is presented by men outside the guild of professionals. It is not quite clear to me exactly what conclusions may be drawn from this; but I dare say it is worthy of further investigation.

By what I have said until now, I hope to have made a case for considering the theology of the poets as legitimate objects of interest for the theologian as commonly understood. And I also hope to have made plausible the proposition that the study of poetic theology reinforces the sense of "Old European" continuity as well as that of the dynamic inherent in Old European civilisation – that, in other words, the study of poetic theology can contribute usefully to the permanently necessary discussion about the periodization of European history.

This last point could be usefully elaborated and illuminated by an extended consideration of the insights gained by the American literary scholar M.H. Abrams in his study of the Romantic poets.[5] Abrams offers abundant and detailed proof of the tendency of the Romantics to utilise traditional biblical and theological concepts and lines of thought, reflecting a "supernaturalistic" view of things, for their own purpose: that of interpreting human life within a resolutely "naturalistic" conceptual framework. That means, for example, that the traditional notions of primal innocence, fall from innocence and restoration of harmony are applied, and in practice exclusively, to man's experience of his progress from childhood to adulthood. That tendency can, I am sure, be interpreted as evidence of continuity insofar as each and every form of secularization bears an indelible mark of what has been secularised; but I certainly would be much more inclined to view it as a symptom of fundamental change, a much deeper one than the one from Dante to Milton, a phenomenon, in other words, that supports the "Old European" model from, so to speak, the "modern" side of things.

But it is high time for at long last throwing in some remarks on Grundtvig, considered in the light of what I have been looking at until now.

The remarks must, once again, take the form of short postulates or theses, without the ideally requisite extensive comment.

Grundtvig was a poet whose poetry served a theological purpose by poetical means; and he was a theologian whose theology had strong affinities with those ancient and medieval theological forms that made use of poetical or quasi-poetical means of expression. In this respect, he was a man of the

---

5.   *Natural Supernaturalism: Tradition and Revolution in Romantic Literature* (1971).

Old Europe, with deep roots in the patristic tradition. Something of that can be ascertained by considering the following four points (always remembering, of course, that they represent a selection).

One: Only a brief glance at his output of hymns is necessary to establish how natural he finds the early Christian way of viewing God's history with mankind as a whole, consisting of interconnected and mutually illuminating images. A good example is provided by the Paschal hymn: *Tag det sorte Kors fra Graven* (Take the black cross away from the grave). There, by means of the dominating image of a garden he interweaves a series of crucial events: the one in Eden, the one in the garden where Mary Magdalen met the risen Christ and the future one in the garden of graves that surrounds the singing congregation's parish church, and everything is subsumed in the notion of an awakening that happens now. This is, as I suggested, a genuinely patristic and Old European approach to the Christian message, put to use in fresh and totally un-antiquarian Danish 19th-century speech and thus, by the way, implying an acute challenge to conventional modes of distinguishing between ancient and modern. – How intimate Grundtvig's ties were to that tradition is, perhaps, even more strikingly demonstrated by his version of the *Te Deum*. Even a cursory comparison between his version and the Latin original (as well as the intermediate versions) makes clear not only that Grundtvig, as we already know, felt comfortably at home in these surroundings but, more significantly, that he felt sufficiently at home to make the *Te Deum* more copiously and densely patristic than it had been in patristic times.

Two: As I have elsewhere tried to show in somewhat greater detail,[6] Grundtvig, in *Nyaars-Morgen* (New Year's Morning), his long poem from 1824, makes use, be it consciously or otherwise, of some of the self-same procedures as the ones used by both Dante and Milton: the prophetic voice, the prolonging of sacred history, the summing up of history in one person's experience; and he, moreover, reproduces, in his own way, and by no means as an imitator, some of the Dantesque settings for the encounter with past history. In other words, he conducts himself in the manner of an Old European theological poet. At the same time, and this is a crucially significant point, his way of formulating his poetical-theological message is in other respects strikingly different from the Dantesque and Miltonic strategies. *Nyaars-Morgen* is almost totally devoid of any sense of cosmic coherence and cosmic-historical interplay; its sense of what constitutes significant past history is exclusively national insofar as it is not biblical; last but not least, the isolation of the perceiving and reflecting self is much more marked than in Milton, not to speak of what is the case in Dante's *Comedy*. The study of "New Year's Morning" thus provides material for reflecting on the meeting and merging in one

6. See "Grundtvig, Dante ..." (note 2, above).

19th-century man of a vitally present Old European or classically Christian manner of thinking and another one, distinctly characterised by a modern sensibility.

Three: Largely similar conclusions can, I believe, be drawn from Grundtvig's use of himself and his own life-story as some sort of crowning point of previous history. As I have tried to point out, this is something that genuinely and quite unaffectedly belongs to traditional Christian thinking. As this thinking tells us in multiple ways, every Christian is meant by God to be an epitome of all history; when I receive the cross on my forehead all sacred history and God's whole purpose are summed up in me. Provided that this is understood in the way it was meant, it has nothing whatsoever to do with delusions of grandeur or with the idea of an exceptionally interesting personality. On the contrary, it makes a point that is inseparable from the Christian understanding of what the words humility and common humanity mean. At the same time, when hearing Grundtvig make use of the device, one has trouble avoiding the impression that something new is afoot alongside what stems from the tradition – something, in other words, that has to do with a typically modern way of conceiving the human person; how much is a moot point, open to discussion, one that would have to include a comparison with similar traits in Dante and in Milton.

Four: One of the things that have struck me during my attempts at providing myself with an idea of what Grundtvig is up to in his prose histories is the all-pervading struggle to establish patterns in the flow of profane as well as sacred history and the reader's consequent impression that here an essentially and intrinsically poetic mind is at work. It would indeed be strange if that were not so; at all events, such is the impression gained from seeing Grundtvig organising the course of history along lines drawn from the realm of interconnected metaphors and images: the ages of man, the seven churches of the Apocalypse, and so on. I am aware that over-extravagant conclusions could be drawn from this. Grundtvig had, after all, a thoroughly matter-of-fact side to him when working as an historian. But I consider it legitimate to point out this trait as the final of the signs of his being, in the last resort, a poet. Not in the sense in which it was once meant by one of our literary Grundtvig experts. Grundtvig, he said, was of course a priest, a theologian, an educator, agreed, but above all, he was a poet. I do not mean it in that sense, but in the sense that this theologian had a distinct way of doing theology; and his distinctive way is one that brings to mind that long line of poetic theology which I have tried to sketch out above.

Grundtvig's View of the Bible

By Christian Thodberg

Grundtvig was a poet, an historian and a prophet. This must be clearly understood in dealing with his view of the Holy Scripture. It is commonly claimed that Grundtvig's "matchless discovery"of the Apostolic Creed in 1825 so to speak abolished the Holy Scripture inasmuch as the Apostles' Creed came to replace the Bible. In its brevity such a statement fails to cover what actually happened. Grundtvig's view of the Bible can only be described through an account of how it actually came about.

I. The Romantic heritage

After his experiences at Egeløkke, Grundtvig became deeply absorbed in Romanticism, working as a poet and an historian for a national awakening after the disasters in 1801 and 1807. His main subject was Norse mythology and history, which he wrote about in both poetry and prose with a view to encourage national self-reflection among the Danes. History, in Grundtvig's view, is not dead; it is the spiritual property and identity of a people, and history may repeat itself. What is at stake is a spiritual and moral awakening which ultimately stems from the Romantic idea of the two worlds: the physical, visible and the spiritual, invisible one. Spiritual/physical and good/evil are contrasts which, through spiritual and moral improvement, cancel out each other in the course of history because the physical and the evil are merely an absence, something not present. Art – and to Grundtvig the art of poetry – is the means to permit man to sense the height from which he has fallen.

Grundtvig never relinquished the Romantic idea of the two worlds and history as a meaningful sequence. After he had experienced his Christian awakening in 1810-11, and eagerly reassumed the Christianity of his childhood, he worked the idea of the course of history and the two worlds into his Christian universe. There were others who attempted to christianize the idea but no one as radically as Grundtvig. For that reason, in spite of any Romantic inspiration, he never became a true Romanticist. In his view, good and evil, God and Devil, could never be harmonized. The Biblical dualism, as expressed for example in the Gospel according to St. John, remained un-challenged. Salvation and damnation are real possibilities. The Romantic view of history inspired Grundtvig to understand the course of history from an interpretation of the Biblical history of salvation.

The change in Grundtvig's view of the Holy Scripture can hardly be explained better than through his first hymn, *Dejlig er den himmel blå* (Lovely is the Night Blue Sky). The hymn has nearly always been regarded as a children's song, but an intense preoccupation with the prophet Daniel lies behind it. What is depicted is the exile of Israel in Babylon which becomes an image of the position of Christianity at that time. Christianity is a faint star glimpsed by the mighty rulers in Babylon through the guidance of Daniel. On the surface, of course, the hymn tells about the wise men from the East, but the three wise men are described as a king, a king's son and an astrologer. This takes us back to the Book of Daniel, for the wise men of the hymn are pictures of King Nebuchadnezzar, his son Belshazzar and their astrologers. They again are images of the scholars and the poets of Grundtvig's own time. They should heed Christianity and return to it, follow the star to the goal, that is, let their lives and the course of history be determined by God's word, and they will discover that the star at the goal is in the mild eye of the child; the mild eye of the child refers not only to the eye of Jesus but to the child's eye in general for the deepest secret in the poem is its dependence on the words of Jesus: "Except ye be converted, and become as little children, ye shall not enter into the kingdom of heaven" (Matthew 18.3). Thus, what has been expressed here is an understanding that does not attain its full scope until much later.

So, the course of history is determined by the relationship of the people with God's word, and this aspect of salvation history recurs in Grundtvig throughout his life. It applies to Daniel's talk about an age of gold, an age of silver, an age of brass and an age of iron, and to the peculiar interpretation of the seven churches in The Revelation of St. John, the first one being the Hebrew church, the second the Greek, the third the Roman, the fourth the English, the fifth the German, the sixth the Nordic, the seventh being either the congregation that Grundtvig will restore himself, or alternatively, possibly the Indian church.

Grundtvig knew the Bible by heart and his supreme use of Biblical images is already recognizable in *Dejlig er den himmel blå*. His view of the Holy Scripture is interwoven with his practical use of the Bible: half or more than half of many of his sermons consist of literal or hidden Bible quotations.

II. Grundtvig as preacher in Udby

It is with this view that Grundtvig begins work as a curate to his father in Udby, 1811-13. He had already announced his Biblical-theological programme in his famous probationary sermon in 1810: only the holy teaching of Jesus, sprung from a higher root, can mitigate the despair which human reason in all its powerlessness has resulted in – and can do so only through an unconditional faith in the word of Jesus and a humility that subjects itself to God's guidance. Grundtvig saw himself as a prophet, as the Luther of his time, and as such he set himself up as a Christian judge of his own age in the famous or infamous World Chronicle of 1812. The same attitude was held towards the plain peasants of Southern Zealand. It was a regular ministry of conversion which, with abundant references to God's guidance of his people in the Old Testament and the New Testament, calls for conversion before the imminent judgment.

The sermons are above all Biblical because they make use of Biblical images as a lever for the ministry of conversion. The idea of the two worlds is given a Christian interpretation, for example on the basis of Col. 3.1-4, and so is the Biblical imagery and its reflection of contemporary affairs on the basis of 1 Cor. 13.12. Life is temporary and preparatory compared to life in Heaven.

By virtue of the Biblical content, the sermons are full of power and rich in imagery but as always in a ministry of conversion they alternate between admonitions and threats. Though this is generally the case, there are exceptions, for example in the Christmas sermons in which there is a change of tone: here he repeats the saying, "It is good to be child at Christmas", and for once Christianity is given a positive interpretation based on Luke 2.14, which was to acquire significance at a later time as was the idea behind *Dejlig er den himmel blå*.

III. Contemporaneity

The question of the historical truth of the Bible is not one of immediate urgency. The moral pathos is too pervasive for that to be the case. Yet, it is repeatedly pointed out that those listening must put themselves in the place of those listening to Jesus and enter, so to speak, into the Biblical account. Relevant references may be Hebrews 13.8: "Jesus Christ the same yesterday, and today, and for ever" or Matthew 28.20: "Lo, I am with you always, even unto the end of the world".

But gradually the question of the truth of the Bible emerges. The frontline facing Grundtvig was the vapid Rationalist creed of self-improvement: God, virtue, immortality. Inasmuch as Grundtvig constantly refers to the unconditional words and demands of God, the christological events assume decisive importance, and precisely those were denied by the Biblical criticism of the age.

This impelled Grundtvig to reflect deeply about the truth of Christianity. It was not just a theoretical question to him – it was vital to him personally: how might the christological events and thus salvation itself become contemporaneous with him? How could he come to hear and know that the words of

Jesus applied to him? It is not too much to say that this was the main problem in his life and the driving force in all of his theological thinking.

How a solution of this problem develops is what we shall follow in the time after Udby; the fact that the problem was not solved immediately may be the reason why, on December 26, Grundtvig solemnly relinquished his post as clergyman. The problem was a product of the idea of the two worlds, and to Grundtvig it was deeply personal: his vitality, his fear of death, his need for salvation were so intense that he strongly needed to feel God's nearness. It is his perseverance at this point that makes his theology so interesting and inspiring for posterity, and we must necessarily understand Grundtvig's problem on his own premises. For the sake of his own salvation and his life he needed to be contemporaneous with Jesus and the history of Jesus.

IV. Grundtvig's psychological elaborations on the word

In various treatises in the 1810s and particularly in the periodical *Danne-Virke* 1816-19, Grundtvig reflects on the importance of the word. The power of speech is man's wonderful gift, and Grundtvig relates it to pre-historic times. Then the word was above all the bearer of love between people and has remained so. By means of the word one may express everything to somebody else and thus hearing becomes as wonderful as speech. In pre-historic times, the word was forceful and vigorous and was evidence that man had been created by God, prophesying about what man may become. Grundtvig mainly confines himself to the boundaries of human experience but at a later time he includes this understanding in his theology.

V. The imagery

Beside the word, imagery is a reminder of man having been created by God. In the beginning the original written signs, that is, the letters, were images, and man communicated with others in images, that is, poetry, and this ability has not been lost entirely by man. In particular man is still able to receive images. The imagination has remained intact; it is not an active capacity in man but a quality that enables man to receive images. God in particular can create images in man by means of the supreme imagery that has remained with us, the Biblical imagery. The Hebrew written signs are the last evidence of the origin of the Biblical imagery.[1]

1.   Christian Thodberg, "Om Grundtvigs poetik med særligt henblik på den bibelske inspiration" (On Grundtvig's poetics with special reference to the Biblical inspiration) *Grundtvig Studier* (1982), pp. 30-32.

The imagery is not only found in the Bible for the God who created the earth left traces of his goodness and love behind him in nature, corresponding to Jesus referring to the lilies of the field and the birds in the sky. The lilies and the birds are constant reminders to man's sight and hearing about how man should live in the world – in perfect security under God's will. That capacity is found, even after the Fall, in the people of Israel, for example among the shepherds, but the capacity did not disappear with the shepherds. It is still to be found in the child. The child has a memory of a life in perfect security together with birds and flowers. It is "the child's sweet dream of the heart" for, above all, that memory is carried in the human heart, and in the woman or the feminine element which, in Grundtvig, merges with the heart as the place where man's divine origin or likeness to God's image is to be found more than anywhere else.[2]

So, on the basis of purely human experience, Grundtvig is able to establish the particular force of the word, the special capacity of the word to communicate the connection between heaven and earth and finally the heart, the childish or feminine, as the special place in man for that communication. This will leave its mark on his sermons and does so already at the time of Udby.

VI. The Bible reflects past, present and future

To Grundtvig the Bible exhibits the whole history of salvation, that is, people's past, their present and their future, brought home to the actual experience of the congregation present; this happens in a form of sermon which consciously manifests itself as the word of God, that is, in an imagery which is immediately derived from the linguistic forms of the psalms of the Old Testament, and of Isaiah and the rest of the prophets. In other words, the sermons imitate the Biblical poetry and therefore the text should be written out in stanzas of short lines, reminiscent of the Psalter.

This can be made clear from the sermon on the fifth Sunday after Trinity 1822, which deals with that one theme: hearing God's word.[3] The sermon falls into five sections; the first one retells the history of Israel where God's word was the force at the beginning of time but the people turned away; there was a hunger for God's word (Amos 8.11-12), but in vain; there was no

---

2. Erik Krebs Jensen, "Hjertets gudbilledlighed" (The likeness to God's image) in *For sammenhængens skyld* (For the sake of context) (Århus, 1977), pp. 65-96.
3. It is presented and analyzed in detail in my treatise: "Grundtvigs skovoplevelse 1811 og prædikerne over Peters fiskedræt i tiden, der fulgte" (Grundtvig's forest experience 1811 and the sermons on the miraculous draught of fishes in the following time) in *Grundtvig Studier* (1986), p. 20-26.

prophet left, and the people fell into the legal bondage of the scribes and pharisees. The second section tells about the testimony of John the Baptist, and the third, in a high-flown style, about the coming of Christ when the people found what they were searching for. In the fourth section, the present congregation reflects on this crucial sight and pronounces the Christian confession: We beheld his glory (St. John 1.14), while the fifth and last section prophesies about the future from the viewpoint of the present, which looks like the time in Israel before the coming of Christ; history repeats itself: Christianity must be renewed when the congregation returns home from "Babylon" to "Jerusalem", that is, when, in the near future, Grundtvig will come from Præstø to Copenhagen where the hunger for God's word is felt!

To put it in different terms: the imagery has made the congregation and Grundtvig contemporaneous with the salvation history; indeed, they are part of it themselves. Thus it has been established more clearly than many words can do what Grundtvig's view of the Bible was at that time: referring to the decisive historical events he maintains the reflection of the present as part of an historical process in which the congregation is involved but it is an involvement, of course, which is preached.

Preaching, however, can only happen by a word of God, and what precisely is the way Grundtvig understands God's word? Here his understanding of the power of the word, formulated on the basis of human experience, comes into play. Towards the end of the 1810s and in the beginning of the 1820s, there is a decisive change in Grundtvig's use of the Bible. The imagery is not abandoned but from now on the images that are applied become the framework of a certain word of God. They are usually short words and brief phrases with a special ring to them:

1) Christ has risen from the dead
2) Let there be light
3) Those are dead who seek the child's life
4) God has visited His people
5) He has managed everything well
6) Unto you is born this day a Saviour
7) God is Love
8) John 3.16 (frequently)
9) Fear not
10) Weep not
11) Rise up
12) Happy Christmas
13) Happy festival
14) etc.

that is, they are on the one hand summaries of Biblical preaching, functioning already, in the New Testament, for example, as conscious refrains to the accounts of Jesus healing the sick, and on the other hand imperatives. Once again it is the question of contemporaneity that is Grundtvig's problem. He needs the strongest possible words from the Bible and thus from the living God. The imperatives are high on the list because as imperatives they are unconditional commitments. The imperatives in particular are said to "ring through time and eternity", that is, they attempt to establish the contemporaneity that is necessary.

About the summaries of the Biblical preaching, statements like "The Lord has risen from the dead", and John 3.16 it is said again and again before and after 1820 that they are valid because they have passed from mouth to mouth in a long chain from the Apostles down to us. Thus they are valid by virtue of an unbroken tradition in the congregation, which is seen, already in the late 1810s, as a unity of the generations from the time of the Apostles to the present generation. When, on the first Sunday in Advent 1822, Grundtvig preaches on the theme of "The Lord is at hand" in Philippians 3.4, he is aware that people well-versed in the Scriptures will point to expectations at the time of the Epistle of an imminent return of Christ. He also refers to 1 Thessalonians 4.17 about those who are alive at the Second Coming being moved to heaven together with the dead: "They would not understand that which is evident that when the Apostles wrote the word of the Lord to teach the congregation, they wrote to the whole large congregation in Jesus Christ which was to be gathered until the end of time ... "(GP 1, p. 78).

The inherent power of the word, ringing through time and eternity, the chain of tradition from generation to generation and the congregation in the all-embracing sense contribute to secure contemporaneity: that God's word applies to us.

With the emphasis on the importance of the congregation it also follows that the preaching of the Bible comes to be heard in a special place: in the church service. In the church service the address by God should release an echoing word, a reply in the form of songs of praise and confession. Already in the early 1820s, Grundtvig can write enthusiastically about how certain he is that there will soon be a revival of singing songs of praise to the Lord, even though he did not, of course, renew the hymn singing in the Danish Church until the time of the *Sang-Værk* (Hymnary) in 1836-37. In other words, the prophecy came true – a memento to the exegetes that want to explain the prophecies in the Old Testament and the New Testament as subsequent rationalizations!

VII. The change of Grundtvig's view of the Bible in 1824

During 1824 in particular, changes occur in Grundtvig's view of the Bible. He now distinguishes with greater clarity between the various books of the Bible. The Old Testament is mainly a promise and a reflection of what the New Testament recounts, and in the New Testament those books are valued highest that were written down by eyewitnesses. The Gospel according to St. Luke is down-rated, but despite this view the Epistle of James has no value at all, however, because it is used in support of the teaching of God, virtue and immortality that Grundtvig fights against. The Pauline Epistles are given a prominent position, but it is the Gospel according to St. John that ranks supreme, and from St. John 3.16 is singled out so strongly that this word alone might almost be sufficient foundation for the Christian church. This is bound up with the significance that is attached to the concept of love in 1824. Already love at the human level is acknowledged as the force that gives coherence to life, and for that reason John 3.16 becomes a divine confirmation of God's word's high degree of validity to man. Together with the heart, the childish and feminine element, love becomes the experience and emotion that makes God's word credible.

This development reaches its peak around Whitsun 1824 in the poem *De Levendes land* (The Land of the Living) which we know as beginning with *O, Kristelighed* (literally, O, Christ-likeness). In the original poem this is the culminating final stanza which intends to establish what Christianity really is, namely likeness to Christ. Grundtvig puts this into words in his sermon on Whitsunday in his familiar Biblical imagery in a daring paraphrase of the hymn in Philippians 2.6-11 (GP 2, pp. 17-18). There is a direct line from *Dejlig er den himmel blå* to the Christ-likeness in the baptized child. It is that Christ-likeness that the adult must recapture, and even though the final Christ-likeness is not attained until the end of the world and the Second Coming and even though the idea of the two worlds has been preserved, Christianity has become a reality in the world in that enclave that man constitutes as a God-created and reborn being. "It lives still within us, we feel in our heart" and "My Land, says the Lord, is both Heaven and Earth, where Love reigns supreme". The present life has its own value by virtue of the love from God and the love among people. True life is no longer referred, in the manner of the Evangelists, to a life after death, as it was in the 1810s.

VIII. The "matchless discovery" in 1825

Grundtvig was fighting a battle on a different front from that of the pulpit, namely in his study, in an attempt to substantiate and prove the truth of Christianity on a philosophical and dogmatic basis.[4]

In spite of the enthusiasm about the Bible that pervades the sermons in 1824, he is troubled by the modern Bible criticism which undermines his enthusiasm from within.

Grundtvig himself was attacked for his new orthodoxy which to his own age seemed a provocation. His emphasis on the great christological events was seen as a romantic enthusiasm for great deeds which he used poetically only, and at the same time his opponents felt that he broke down moral standards by referring to the power and sole validity of the word.

Purely intellectually he had to fathom the problem of the truth of Christianity. Since 1813 he had made use of an 18th-century philosophical principle, namely the axiom of opposites which he formulated himself as follows: "That must be true which one cannot deny without contradicting something that is absolutely certain."[5] He transferred this principle to Christianity as it came to appear historically in the purely historical existence of the church: Christianity cannot be false when, in spite of so much opposition and contradiction before and now, it has continued to exist. This is logically impossible. To this should be added that Grundtvig's theological contemporaries, especially the exegetes, presented an interpretation of the Bible that was sometimes diametrically opposed to Grundtvig's. Just as the Pope used to hide the Bible to the people, the popery of the exegetes now prevailed, since they maintained that the scientific interpretation was the only one credible. Thus Grundtvig was caught in a serious dilemma, partly because he asserted his own interpretation of the Bible on an unscientific basis, partly because he was troubled by doubts himself as a consequence of the results of the modern Bible criticism.

In his sermons from the 1820s Grundtvig had repeatedly epitomized Christianity in confessions, couched in poetic prose, and as early as 1823 he had cited the second Article of the Apostles' Creed in such a statement. Already in 1819 he had claimed that the message of the Resurrection had passed in one oral tradition from the Apostles down to us. The ground was prepared, when in the week ending July 31, 1825, he came to realize that renunciation and the Apostolic Creed were a firmer and more genuine foundation of

---

4.　See "Om den sande Christendom og om Christendommens Sandhed" (On true Christianity and the truth of Christianity) in *N.F.S. Grundtvig's udvalgte Skrifter*, IV, ed. H. Begtrup (Copenhagen, 1906) pp. 443-733.

5.　Henning Høirup, *Grundtvigs Syn paa Tro og Erkendelse* (Grundtvig's view of faith and cognition) (Copenhagen, 1949).

Christianity than the Bible inasmuch as baptism had been a reality from the very first Whitsunday and thus also the conditions of baptism, since the opposite must be unthinkable.[6] In fact, it was not primarily an historical theory, for the realization corresponds closely to the confessional statements, repeated several times in his sermons up to 1825.[7]

In other words, there is a direct line from these confessional statements to the emphasis on the Apostles' Creed. Thus the discovery did not signify the kind of confessional fundamentalism that may be true of the older Grundtvig – and at least of those who shared his thinking – as a word imposed on the Apostles and taught them by the Lord himself in the 40 days between Resurrection and Ascension.

The discovery is peculiar in two respects: Firstly, in his sermon on the eighth Sunday after Trinity (July 24) on the text about the false prophets, Grundtvig recommends studious readings of the Bible, but on the following Sunday (July 31) he proclaims his discovery of the Apostles' Creed, that is, as a factual realization, not as a subject in preaching.[8] Secondly, the discovery does not result in a changed sermon in the following time, neither in content nor in style. Something entirely different happens: Baptism and Holy Communion are emphasized with increasing strength as the foundation of Christianity. Grundtvig had discovered the church in earnest, and that finds a vehement expression when shortly after he attacks H.N. Clausen's book with its speculative church view, founded on modern exegesis.[9] But then, in turn, the subsequent libel action knocks him out completely so that he gives up his clerical post on the sixth Sunday after Easter, 1826, just before the Whitsunday for which he had written *Den signede dag* (The blessed day) and *Tusind år stod Kristi Kirke* (For a thousand years stood the Church of Christ).

In the following period Grundtvig revised his sermons from the beginning of the 1820s in the comprehensive three-volume collection of sermons: *Søndags-Bogen* (The Sunday Book). Especially volume three, in which the sermons are mostly like a kind of treatises, is used to cement the discovery of the Apostolic Creed, but it is difficult for him to apply it to his preaching. The main thing is that his church view is clarified: the church is the faithful, gath-

---

6. Kai Baagø, "Grundtvig's mageløse opdagelse. Et bidrag til dens tilblivelseshistorie" (Grundtvig's matchless discovery. A contribution to its genesis) in *Grundtvig Studier* (1957), pp. 36-50.
7. Christian Thodberg, "Grundtvig som prædikant" (Grundtvig as a preacher) in *Grundtvig og grundtvigianismen i nyt lys* (Grundtvig and Grundtvigianism in a new light), pp. 117-62.
8. Cf. GP 3, pp. 199-211, and Kaj Thaning, "Den 'mageløse opdagelses' tilblivelse" (The genesis of the "matchless discovery") in *Grundtvig Studier* (1981), pp. 7-29.
9. In *Catholicismens og Protestantismens Kirkeforfatning, Lære og Ritus* (The church constitution, doctrine and ritual of Catholicism and Protestantism) (Copenhagen, 1825).

ered round Baptism and Communion. Moreover he read and in part translated Irenaeus's tract against the heretics,[10] and the inspiration from that
work strengthened a conviction, already alive in him, that Christianity takes
its point of departure in natural man. The created man has so much of the
likeness to God's image in him that the natural man is not eradicated from the
Gospel but on the contrary is taken back to his created originality. This led to
a new view of man in Grundtvig, and this again becomes important for his
freer view of human life and Christianity in the 1830s, but in particular for his
preaching and view of the Bible; the consequence is that the human precondi-
tions for the reception of the Gospel are emphasized. Every true man must
become a Christian, and a true man is the one who understands the conditions of life, a life in fear and helplessness and hope, that is, with a self-recog-
nition that opens up to salvation.

IX. Preaching in the 1830s

All this leads to an entirely new view of the Bible when Grundtvig resumes
work as a preacher in 1832. As an example we may select the sermon on the
fifth Sunday after Trinity, 1832, once again on the miraculous draught of fish,
the historicity of which was questioned then as it is now. But historical authenticity cannot be any proof of our faith but vice versa: our real faith must
prove this and other miracles by Jesus (GP 5, pp. 272f.). In itself, the miraculous drought of fish cannot be the foundation of faith, but we know firstly
that God must perform miracles in accordance with his nature and secondly
that a miracle was needed for an uneducated fisherman to be called to establish the church that still exists.

    Thus Grundtvig develops a type of sermon, characterized by a certain
hermeneutical principle. When, in 1833, he delivers a sermon on Jesus curing
one who was born deaf, he makes clear that it is evidence from the God who
is still master in his congregation through his living word and not through
the Biblical account, dead to us now, about what happened then:

For when we remember these things and lay them to heart, then we shall know good
counsel, and see Him laying His fingers on the ears of the babies and baptize them
with the Holy Spirit that they may be heedful where His Gospel is preached, and feel
that He touches our tongue, when we kneel at His table and hear Him speak the great
Effata: Be opened, to our hearts ... (GP 6, p. 267)

10. *Om Kjødets Opstandelse og det evige Liv af Biskop Irenæus* (On the resurrection of the flesh
and eternal life by Bishop Irenaeus) (Copenhagen, 1855).

... Indeed, dear friends in Christ! The house of the Lord, the house of our Lord Jesus Christ, it is no bone-house and no corpse-house, no book-shop or writing-room, but it is a divine establishment for the spiritually deaf-and-dumb as we all are in mother's womb ... " where the Lord repeats what he then did: " ... it was not botched-up work, it was creation, and thus baptism is a true rebirth and renewal, and Holy Communion a true union with the Lord to lead to salvation Amen, in the name of Jesus Amen! (GP 6, p. 299)

In his great sermon on the reviving of the widow's son at Nain, Grundtvig says that the "Weep not!" that was spoken to the widow is found

... wherever there is baptism, wherever bread is eaten and wine is drunk on His behalf and with His words, and it is He Himself that speaks to those who are willing to hear His voice, He Himself who asks: "Do you believe!" It is He Himself who says to the believer: "I baptize you in the name of the Father and of the Son and of the Holy Spirit." It is He Himself who invites the believers and the baptized to His table and says to them: take this and eat, this is my body which is given to you. Drink, all of you, this is the cup of the new covenant in my blood which is poured out to you for the forgiveness of sins. (GP 9, p. 310)

X. The liturgical exegesis

Thus the problem of contemporaneity had been solved for Grundtvig. The words, personally addressed at baptism and communion, are unequivocally and indisputably the words of Jesus spoken to us. The same is true of His actions; this applies to the sign of the cross being made at baptism and the words connected with it: "Receive the sign of the holy cross", cf. the hymn:

God's gentle fingers
Made the cross on your forehead,
The voice of God's only begotten
Made the cross on your breast,
So no devil shall harm you.

That was what happened at baptism, but the one baptized can repeat and renew it:

Now in your baptism
With the hope of salvation
Both your soul and your heart can be bathed.
(DDS 488.2)

Something similar applies to the ritual of laying on hands. It is not only found in the New Testament. When the believer asks where Jesus is now, he understands:

> O, Covenant with joyous heart
> Now it is clear to me as light,
> Jesus! You Yourself were there,
> Now I know both when and where,
> You laid Your hand upon my head,
> I know now clearly what You said,
> When I was baptized with Your word,
> Where to Your table You bade me come.

This also applies to the Lord's Prayer – strangely enough, because the Lord's Prayer is, of course, regarded as a prayer we say to God, but rightly the prayer only attains its power because Jesus Himself says it for us when we pray in his name. God is not mistaken:

> The Son of God with fatherly embrace
> Gives us the name of children,
> God speaks to us about our prayer:
> It comes from my Son.
> (DDS 376.7)

It shows itself when we are most deeply troubled, and our prayer dies on cold lips. Grundtvig prays to the Holy Spirit to

> Have mercy on our mortal clay!
> Show us that You can remedy all!
> And whisper to us the Lord's Prayer,
> So our tongues will be on fire.
> (DDS 250.7)

In this connection, the confession of faith, too, finds its place – not just as a mere summary of the content of faith, a yardstick of faith, but precisely in its inquiring form as a promise and a gift:

… the confession of faith, it is true, does not sound like God's words to us, but like our words to God", namely in its general denunciatory form, but the confession of faith must be regarded as a pledge: "For as long as we look upon our baptismal covenant, or the renunciation, and the confession of faith as human commandments, they will lie heavily on our shoulders: demand much and give nothing at all; but when we look upon them as testimony from *Jesus Christ* our Lord about what we must believe and confess in order to live with Him, as he lives with the Father, as a legacy from Him who would rather give than take, whose commandments are all great offers, whose command, like his Father's, is eternal life; when we look upon it like this, we shall see at once that it demands little and gives infinitely much. It only demands honesty and confidence, but gives all that it speaks about: that is the Father and the Son and the Holy Spirit: the Creator as father and the Judge as brother and Providence, the almighty ruler as advocate, comforter and companion! (Whit Monday 1835, GP 8, p. 42)

– altogether a powerful contribution to the ongoing debate about the rite of questions!

The character of a personal pledge which is implied in the baptismal words has already been discussed. A special role is played by the greeting of peace: "Peace be with you!" which to Grundtvig is the true blessing as against the Aaronic blessing which he distinctly depreciates. For one thing, "Peace be with you" is said by Jesus Himself as the first word to the disciples after the Resurrection, for another, it occurs in the baptismal ritual – at Grundtvig's time just after the prayer during the ritual of the laying-on of hands ("The almighty God ... "). That word is spoken to the troubled heart as the supreme comfort – for example in a little used hymn:·

> Do we not have, the few of us,
> The fairest hope of all?
> What did not Jesus, our Lord,
> Say to us in baptism?
> Was it not the word which only suits
> To those who go to Heaven:
> Peace be with you all, peace be with each of you!
> (DDS 38.2)

The blessing of peace, especially, is where absolution is given because the word occurs immediately after the sentence "and has forgiven all your sins":

> In baptism He forgives me
> The guilt of all my sins:
> In "God's peace" he washes me
> And heals the boil of death.
> (DDS 445.8)

It is also, by the way, Grundtvig's emphasis on the blessing of peace which, in the 19th century, results in the blessing of peace being said after the completion of Holy Communion.

As far as Holy Communion is concerned, Grundtvig stresses the imperative parts of the words of institution. This must necessarily be the case since it is meant to be the words of Jesus to us. For the same reason the imperative words at Holy Communion constitute "corporeality" rather than the elements of Communion, for the oral pledge is the corporeality of Jesus, the corporeality of the Word. The bread and the wine are indispensable, but serve above all to clarify the meaning and significance of the words. The bread and the wine are visible signs which only at the end of time will merge with what they signify. The salutation "The Lord be with you" is a word directly pledged like the blessing of peace.

The Biblical enunciations and their worldly parallels as well as the Biblical imperatives do not disappear from the sermons, but from now on it is the task of the sermon to give a precise, modern clarification in the ritual words that are spoken now, and the ritual words are not only spoken in connection with baptism and communion but are also taken up and repeated in the sermon.

The words of the Bible are like parables, but in the actual ritual words Jesus speaks straightforwardly in accordance with Jesus' words: "These things have I spoken unto you in proverbs; but the time cometh when I shall no more speak unto you in proverbs, but I shall shew you plainly of the Father" (John 16.25). In the context of the Bible passage in question, that is the task of the Holy Spirit, and with unparalleled strength Grundtvig interprets the valedictory speeches in St. John, emphasizing the Holy Spirit as the one who, after Ascension, is the Lord's vicar on earth. It is precisely that Holy Spirit that speaks out freely in the ritual words, "For it is not ye that speak, but the Spirit of your Father which speaketh in you" (Matthew 10.20):

> You are not the ones who speak,
> Says He who can command,
> But the Spirit of my Father.
> Therefore though you died so early,
> Will your speech forever glow,
> Melting all the soul's chains.
> (DDS 242.5)

As a book of images, the Bible is still indispensable, and the believers now see in the church the Lord wandering about before their eyes and repeating all His miraculous deeds,

… so the deeds of the Lord, by His visible presence, will be for His believers what the visible world with its sky and earth and ocean, mountains and valleys, field and forest, animals and plants, sun, moon and stars, sky, earth and ocean are, naturally, for man, a mirror of the invisible God's power and majesty, where that is of corporal and visible shape which in the world of the Spirit has eternal power and reality. (21st Sunday after Trinity 1839, GP 12, p. 354)

Thus the Bible becomes a book of images, one in which it is not the book that creates faith, but the repetition of the Lord's deeds which are now heard and felt in His congregation. Now the Bible has come alive; the old orthodox preachers produced a sermon consisting of a "collection of Bible words, learnt by heart and read from the page", but the living preachers – and Grundtvig himself certainly – bear testimony "with few or many Biblical expressions as they would occur to us and as they come naturally into our speech" (Sexagesima Sunday 1839, GP 12, p. 137).

With the Holy Spirit as the interpreter of the Lord's living voice in the congregation, a good many of the pseudo-problems raised by Bible criticism cease to exist. The temptation of Jesus in the desert (Matthew 4.1-11) has been questioned as an historical event, but its historical authenticity is testified by the necessity of the renunciation at baptism. Grundtvig openly admits that he finds it difficult to understand the account of the Ascension in Acts 1.1-11, but the Ascension is testified much better by the confession of faith and by the reality of the congregation when the Holy Spirit reigns as the representative of Jesus who ascended. Grundtvig often defends the authenticity of the addition to 1 John 5.7, the so-called Comma Johanneum: "For there are three that bear witness in heaven, the Father, the Word, and the Holy Ghost; and these three are one" – a passage that was left out in the 1819 translation. The authenticity is testified by baptism in the name of the Trinity.

The same view is applied when the authenticity of the baptismal covenant in Matthew 28.19-20 is questioned by contemporary Bible criticism.

The credibility of the Bible is testified by the Lord who is present in his congregation: one may remember the golden days of Christianity with enthusiasm but Grundtvig has found, it is true, a reality slightly less glorious:

... this reality have we found when we found that word of the Lord which will not perish with heaven and earth, when we heard His voice not from afar, but at our side, in our midst, where verily he is baptizing with the Holy Spirit, feeding with the bread that fell from heaven, and pouring wine from the cup of salvation, and now it is our delight to read the Book of the Lord, for now all the graves of the Word burst open, and the holy people, who have been asleep, rise with the Lord and reveal themselves to us, indeed, now all the good words He used to speak come alive to us and are heard anew in the closet and in the congregation to our hope and comfort, to our delight and joy. (Second Sunday after Easter 1838, GP 11, p. 193)

Grundtvig also claims with great force that the Holy Scripture itself points to oral preaching, for example when Paul refers in 1 Corinthians 11 to the account of the communion which he has received orally, and which must for that reason be passed on orally. The account of the walk to Emmaus is evidence of the limitation of Scripture; a spoken address was needed before it was believed, and referring to his scholarly opponents in his own age, Grundtvig says:

… what can the Lord do about our turning everything upside down, calling his own spoken word at baptism a mere word of man that we dare not trust, and, contrariwise, calling the spoken words of the scholars about what the Scriptures say, calling that which is merely man's word, the Lord's and God's word. (Easter Monday 1838, GP 11, p. 185)

It is obvious that Grundtvig had to come into conflict with Luther's theology and view of the Scriptures. That applies to Grundtvig's understanding of the status of the elements of communion, as stated above. But it also applies to Luther's emphasis on "sola scriptura". With this principle Luther shook off the bondage of the Roman Church, and that, according to Grundtvig, was understandable in the heat of the struggle in the Age of the Reformation. All the same he feels in agreement with Luther when, in the Shorter Catechism, the latter explains the sole working of the Holy Spirit:

… well, then there is not, in fact, the slightest disagreement about church matters between Luther and us, so the difference may only be that perhaps we may be better able than he was to develop and clarify the inner nature of things, for which, however, we are also indebted, next God, to him who, through the power of our Lord, broke the yoke of popery on our shoulders and opened up a free school where, under the guidance of the Holy Spirit, we may grow ever wiser about the Kingdom of God (All Saints Day 1837, GP 10, pp. 69f.).

Grundtvig does not see a difference from Luther in the view of the Scriptures but rather a logical continuity.

In Grundtvig's case it might be a cause for concern that, with his focus on the Lord's presence in the congregation and on the Holy Spirit as the exclusive interpreter of the Scriptures, he might relinquish the connection with the historicity of the Scriptures so that the spiritual repetition of the life of the Lord, demonstrated to the believers, would become an enclave, mysteriously understood. This is not so. Grundtvig was the first one in Denmark to take up David Friedrich Strauss and his book *Das Leben Jesu*.[11]

Unlike the old Rationalists who openly rejected everything heavenly and divine, Strauss appears on the scene at a time when neo-orthodoxy in Germany is breaking through. In Strauss, Grundtvig sees a new opponent who

11. David Friedrich Strauss, *Das Leben Jesu* (Tübingen, 1835-36).

wants to explain Jesus' miracles as mythical events or as images of the redemption that man himself might bring about. They do not deny the miracles,

… No, the adversaries of our faith will ridicule suchlike as childishness from the boy-
hood years of human reason, and raise to the skies the story of Jesus Christ, God and
man, His miracles, resurrection and ascension as affirmation of their own dreams, as
the unshakeable proof of the fundamental unity of divine and human nature, and as
the brilliant example of the glorious victory of the human spirit over death and its eternal self-idolization. (Trinity Sunday 1837, GP 9, pp. 37f.)

Grundtvig must reject even a demythologized understanding of a more
Christian complexion; he refers to the many who want to

… understand both the resurrection, ascension and return of the Lord only spiritually,
and yet derive complete comfort and blessing from that, but those same people will
then say that they expect no other resurrection and ascension than that which may fall
to their lot in this life when the soul rises from the dead and lets Christ light the way
before it, and ascends in thought and hope to God's presence which is the true Heaven
…

No, to Grundtvig, resurrection, ascension and return to earth must be understood as literally as the birth, crucifixion and death of Jesus for the transformation of life that is defined by the confession of faith at baptism must be real
for the sake of life itself and salvation. It is certain

… that the spirit which proudly rises above flesh and bones, the visible and the tangi-
ble as something merely of the senses and of the earthly world, which the Lord dis-
carded in the tomb, and which we, likewise, must abandon, that is not the spirit of
truth but of delusion, precisely as John the Apostle writes: that it is the spirit of delusion which will not profess Jesus Christ coming in the flesh. (Ascension Day 1839, GP
12, p. 221)

A powerful influence on Grundtvig from Irenaeus is traceable here but apart
from that the line of thinking is consistent: Grundtvig had abandoned neither
his distinction between the two worlds nor the course of salvation history
with the actual creation as the beginning, the actual redemption as the centre
and the actual consummation as the ultimate goal and purpose.

XI. Summary

Grundtvig's view of the Bible is only brought home to us in earnest if we pay heed to his background in the Romantic conception of history and the idea of the two worlds connected with it. It is on the basis of this background that he approaches the Bible as an historian, a poet and a prophet – first as a national-Christian revivalist preacher, but later urged on by the problem of how God's Word becomes contemporaneous with man – or modern, to put it differently. It is his perseverance in tackling this question that makes Grundtvig's view of the Bible interesting or inspiring, regardless of whether one accepts his solution of the problem or not. As an historian he must necessarily leave place for Christianity in reality as the decisive driving force in the passage of time. At the same time he acknowledges the human condition with the fear, the helplessness and the hope that only the spoken and personally meaningful word is capable of meeting. As a poet he knew the magical power of imagery.

It is also on the basis of this background that he used the Bible which he probably knew better than any other Dane. With unerring certainty he selects those cardinal points in preaching that later have been recognized by New Testament scholarship as the "Sitz im Leben" of the gospels in the life of the first congregation. Effortlessly, he advances the claim that the truth of this preaching depends on an unbroken tradition from the Apostles, from generation to generation, until today. The Holy Catholic Church embracing all generations since the Apostles confirms this truth. The "matchless discovery" of the confession of faith is the theological codification of this very early understanding.

The real "matchless discovery" is the elevation of the ritual words at baptism and communion or in the church service as a whole to an interpretive key for these central words of preaching. Even today, this liturgical exegesis together with the particular form and use of the imagery in his hymns is the strongest basis of the Danish church service and Danish Christianity, and for the same reason Grundtvig's view of the Bible is not just a 19th-century phenomenon.

Grundtvig's view of the Bible is important for exegesis in general because he pinpoints the peculiarities of the single pericopes with a rare accuracy, for example their points and their characteristic refrains. Grundtvig is so familiar with the Biblical language that even in his prose he elaborates on the Biblical hymns from the Book of Psalms, the Prophets, the Gospel of St. John, the hymn in Philippians, and the Revelation of St. John. His exegesis of the writings of St. John are of permanent value; this is true especially of the valedictory speeches and the view of the Holy Spirit as a person that is connected with them. The same is true of his understanding of the life in Christ and its growth in Paul as well as in the Pastoral Letters. In brief: Grundtvig's exegesis is a treasure which has not yet been raised by New Testament scholarship.

The Holy Spirit in the Teaching of N.F.S. Grundtvig

By A.M. Allchin

The aim of this article is exploratory rather than definitive. It is based on a lecture given in the Faculty of Theology in the University of Copenhagen in April 1998, in connection with the 50th anniversary of the Danish branch of the Fellowship of St. Alban and St. Sergius. While it reflects something of the Fellowship's concern to encourage interaction and exchange between Western and Eastern Christendom, its principal focus is on Grundtvig's understanding of the relation of the Holy Spirit to bodiliness, a subject which is explored from a number of different points of view.

I

The subject of the Holy Spirit in the teaching of N.F.S. Grundtvig is of course a very large one. I want to start from what may seem a strange place, from Hans Lassen Martensen's report of his conversations with Grundtvig to be found in his memoirs. I have been struck by this passage, firstly because it shows the two men at a moment when they were still on friendly terms with one another and secondly because it shows a point on which Martensen felt complete and wholehearted agreement with Grundtvig. I think we often understand people better when we agree with them than when we disagree with them; and Martensen was after all one of the finest theological minds of his time in Denmark.

The matter on which Martensen found himself in full agreement with Grundtvig was that of bodiliness.

Although the spirit was for him the first, indeed the only truly real, yet he could not think of the spirit without bodiliness, and the spirit from which nature and the bodily was excluded, was for him an abstract spirit, the spirit of the rationalists with which he would have nothing to do. Thus he had in his viewpoint a higher, spiritual realism, which is also found in Lutheranism, particularly in the teaching about the sacraments. Here I was in complete agreement and thereby also in the great importance he gave to image language, which for him had a greater truth and reality than abstract concepts and whose highest form he found partly in holy scripture in the utterances of the prophets and the sayings of Christ, partly in the myths and symbolic language of the North. There was to be no playing with image language, and he often said that true poets were serious in their use of such language and that through it they expressed the *truth* in their view of life.[1]

There are four points in this passage on which I would like to remark. First, there is the question of bodiliness and its inherent link with the spirit. Second, there is the question of the relationship between the human spirit and the divine Spirit, which is not explicitly mentioned but is certainly presupposed in the conversation. Third, there is the way in which this relationship between spirit and body illuminates the theology of the sacraments. Fourth, there is the way in which it also illuminates the use of image language in the Old and New Testament, in the worship of the Church, and more generally in the language of poets and prophets of all nations, and especially those of the North.

II

From this starting point I want to explore Grundtvig's discussion of these matters from different periods in his life. First I want to go to 1841 and to his work *Kirkelige Oplysninger især for Lutherske Christne*. The passage with which I am concerned begins with the thought of the Church and the place of the Holy Spirit in the Church, it then moves to a more general consideration of the role of the Holy Spirit in human society as a whole. Grundtvig declares that the proclamation of the Gospel presupposes "a living relationship between Christ and his faithful disciples ... and such a living relationship can only come into being when his Spirit, as a divine, self-authenticating power of life, dwells in and works through the Church". It was Grundtvig's belief that lack of this understanding of the Holy Spirit "as a divine person, Christ's representative on earth, his Church's power of life, its pastor, teacher and guide", was one of the principal causes of the 19th century's "abstract conception of Spirit and spiritual reality and its material conception of freedom and personality, which, where they are dominant, make any living relationship between heaven and earth, God and man, and between Christ and us, evidently impossible".[2]

In this particular work, which is written in dialogue with the Tractarians and in particular with Newman, Grundtvig is concerned about the way in

1.   A.M. Allchin, *N.F.S. Grundtvig. An Introduction to his Life and Work* (Aarhus, 1997), p. 63.
2.   G. Christensen, Hal Koch (eds.), *N.F.S. Grundtvig, Værker i Udvalg* (Copenhagen, 1942), III, p. 430.

which the work of the Spirit creates the unity of the Church across space and still more across time. He maintains that the Lord and the Spirit are not bound by space and time.

They can and will work just as powerfully, livingly, and joyfully in all believing gener-ations, and under all the quarters of heaven, so that in this connection there can be no more separation between the first and the nineteenth century, than there was between Jews and Greeks, Scythians and Barbarians; all difference falls away in exactly the same degree as the Spirit of the Lord works with power bringing all together into com-munion with the Lord who is the same yesterday and today and forever.[3]

In this passage we see how the Spirit is central and vital to the life of the Church in Grundtvig's understanding of things, and how it is the power of the Spirit which makes us contemporary with Christ. This, he maintains however, is a truth not generally recognised; and from this lack of recogni-tion there are disastrous consequences not only for the life of the Church but also for the life of society in general. Grundtvig suggests that this deficiency in theology has had consequences far beyond the strictly theological realm; he also suggests that a consequent deficiency in philosophy and anthropol-ogy in general has had disastrous consequences for the life of the Church. There has been, as so often in his thought, an interaction between sacred and secular, between ecclesiastical and national. The work of the Spirit is vital not only for the life of the Church, for redeemed humanity, but for the life of soci-ety, for the life of humanity as a whole: without it we are left with an abstract concept of spirit and spiritual reality and a material concept of freedom and personality.

III

We turn back to a very different period of Grundtvig's life, when his circum-stances were very different, and look at two of the essays in *Danne-Virke* dat-ing from 1817.

At this time Grundtvig had no public office in the Church. He lived as a freelance writer and scholar, studying, writing and translating. He was partic-ularly involved in early medieval texts from Danish and Scandinavian history, immersing himself in the distant past of the people to whom he belonged. He was also involved in the translation of *Beowulf*. He was thus in touch with the great early Anglo-Saxon epic poem, which he saw – but at that time almost no one else did – to be profoundly if often implicitly Christian in its basic struc-

3. Ibid., p. 431.

tures and intentions. In this very year he published a poem *Ragna-Roke* in which he celebrated the Anglo-Saxon seer and poet Cædmon as a true successor to King David, a model for future Christian bards in the North.

He is therefore, in this essay, discussing our question of the relation of spirit and body in a very different context; in relation to the nature of human knowledge. He is seeing the question in the context of philosophical idealism on one side and philosophical materialism on the other. He is also seeing the question in the context of a romantic view of poetry which sees the inspired poet as himself the creator of his material, and a classical view of poetry which sees the poet as the careful craftsman who shapes and adorns material which he has inherited from the tradition to which he belongs. In both cases Grundtvig rejects the oppositions described and takes a middle way. The poet is both *apprehending* and *active*, to use the terms of Anders Pontoppidan Thyssen,[4] the poet both receives and innovates. We may remark that this is precisely what he is doing in his creative appropriation of the Anglo-Saxon heritage. And, as we shall see, this is not for him something true of poets alone. In a different way it is true of all those who take an active part in the life of the society to which they belong and the Church of which they are a part. And this, as we shall discover, is because the human situation is at once necessarily bodily and spiritual.

As bodily creatures located in space human beings are destined to play their part in the natural world and as bodily creatures located in time they are destined to play their part in the historical community to which they belong. But in both cases the element of spirit which is inherent in the human condition links them to a higher and eternal reality, which enables them to share in some measure in the creative power of the eternal realm.

So in his discussion of the nature of human knowledge Grundtvig affirms that all knowledge rests on sensory experience. "Bodily and spiritual are in no way in opposition to one another, in the way in which falsehood and truth are. They in no way abolish or deny one another, but are linked in a friendly interaction, which presupposes a common reality and a common origin."[5]

The human condition "consists of something bodily and something spiritual which together make up a unity, fused together in a self-consciousness which constitutes neither bodily nor spiritual existence alone, but *human* existence, the reasonable personhood which is a conjunction of both". This inward conjunction of spirit and body creates "an unshakeable wall against all idealism; against all denial of the rational reality of our bodily nature".[6]

---

4. "Grundtvig's Ideas on the Church and the People 1848-72" in Christian Thodberg, Anders Pontoppidan Thyssen (eds.), *N.F.S. Grundtvig: Traditional and Renewal* (Copenhagen, 1983), p. 112.
5. *Danne-Virke*, II (1817), p. 39.

In other words Grundtvig is asserting that spirit is never disembodied; that human flesh is never without reason or spirit. Humankind is always a conjunction of body and spirit and in this conjunction human beings become living souls. Furthermore, we know through the conjunction of body and spirit, and this necessarily means that we know and express ourselves in and through bodily images. Bodily images rather than abstract concepts are the primary way in which human beings express their understanding of life.

In theological terms, Grundtvig sees these matters in the light of the verse in Genesis, "God breathed the breath of life into man's nostrils, and man became a living soul".[7] In his understanding the breath of life is the gift of the Holy Spirit and it brings spirit and body together into one. Thus human spirit is understood as given by, and energised by, God's Spirit. So man lives in the closest dependence on and in the closest relation to God.

Human self-awareness develops as man's awareness of his relationship with God the Holy Spirit develops. Humankind comes to see everything truly in the light of the Spirit, the light of eternal truth. "Man sees himself as created in God's image, and he sees the universe, as God's handiwork."[8] In other words man sees and knows himself as a unity of body and spirit, and sees in and through bodily images. It is the nature of poetry to reveal the universe in this light. "Image language has greater truth and reality than abstract concepts", as Martensen remarks in the passage quoted above.[9]

Man grows in his consciousness "of this double relationship, this relationship to the world which his body expresses, this relationship to the divine to which his spirit bears witness".[10] It is interesting to see how carefully Grundtvig differentiates the relationship between the body and the world around which is a simple relationship of solidarity which the body can fully express, and the relationship between the human spirit and the divine to which the human spirit bears witness, thereby recognising the distance which exists between the Creator and the creature. Grundtvig goes on: "the one relationship is kingly, the other relationship is that of a servant, so that both together united constitute a representative or ambassadorial relationship. To work out this union, to embrace this double relationship with thanksgiving and afterwards to hold it fast in love, this is the human calling".[11]

6. *Danne-Virke*, II (1817), pp. 39-40. I am deeply grateful to Dr. Kim Arne Pedersen for his guidance in this part of Grundtvig's work.
7. Ibid., p. 159.
8. *Danne-Virke*, III, pp. 260f.
9. Quoted in *Grundtvigs Erindringer og Erindringer om Grundtvig*, eds. H. Høirup and S. Johansen (Copenhagen, 1948), pp. 181ff.
10. Ibid., p. 164.
11. Ibid., p. 174.

In this way the human person is seen both as a microcosm and as a mediator – linked with the world around by his bodily nature, linked by his created spirit with the Creator Spirit who breathes his life into him. We are very close here, not so much in language as in ideas, to some of the basic themes of much patristic theology. So we are not altogether surprised to discover Grundtvig himself using Greek terms to express this situation. Humanity he tells us is to be understood *cosmologically* in relation to creation and *theologically* in relation to God.[12]

IV

We have been looking at Grundtvig as the essay writer. Now we come to see him as the preacher and to discover his understanding of how the Bible uses these terms flesh and Spirit, both in the Old Testament and in the New Testament and in particular in St. Paul.

The sermon from which I am quoting dates from October 1825 (Trinity 15). It was preached in the very week in which Clausen was initiating the court case against Grundtvig. Grundtvig is now very much in the midst of affairs. His mature point of view on the Church, his "kirkelige Anskuelse" has developed rapidly and become much more articulate. But his view on the relation of body and spirit as expressed in this sermon is, in its basic outline, the same as it had been some ten years earlier. Now, however, it is explained in biblical terminology.

We soon learn that the Scripture uses the word flesh for everything that is earthly and spirit for everything that is heavenly in us, and now it follows of itself that flesh very often means something evil, because our flesh has become sinful, but yet it can also mean simply our earthly nature in its necessary created limitation and weakness. So when it says "the Word was made flesh and dwelt among us", there flesh evidently means only our earthly nature, for the Son was made like us in all things except in sin, and as the Lord says "the spirit is willing but the flesh is weak", and when the apostle speaks of the weakness of the flesh, he refers only to what in the course of time is inseparable from our earthly condition. We can all understand that sin was not a necessary consequence of this weakness, for God saw all that he had made and behold it was very good, and the Spirit witnesses to this when he says that the Son came in the likeness of sinful flesh and condemned sin in the flesh, and thus showed that there could also be flesh which was without sin, and that it was thus that flesh was created, for just as Jesus became man without an earthly father, only of an earthly mother, through the power of the Holy

12. Ibid., p. 200.

Spirit, so also Adam became man, for the earth was his mother, and his father was God, who breathed the Spirit of life into his nostrils, so that he became a living being.

We see again the vital importance of this verse.

Thus the flesh in humankind is originally God's creation, weak in itself, but in conjunction with the Spirit of God capable of obeying God and doing his will, and by degrees of becoming spiritual, being changed and transfigured into his image, in whom it was created. ... Flesh and spirit are therefore in the beginning in no way set in opposition to one another, so that they should come into conflict, for in Jesus they were not in conflict.[13]

We see in this passage Grundtvig's insistence on the creation of Adam through the breathing in of the Spirit and on the conjunction of flesh and Spirit in the incarnate life of the Son. Grundtvig goes on with a quotation from the prophet Ezekiel:

"[I] ... will give you one heart, and give you a new spirit, and I will take away the stony heart out of your flesh; I will give you a heart of flesh so that you will walk in my way and keep my law and be my people, and I will be your God." When the Lord talks in this way and foretells the wonders he will do in the Church of Our Lord Jesus Christ, then at once we see that flesh here does not mean what is sinful, but what is soft and flexible, as opposed to what is hard and unfeeling, and so it means flesh as it was in the beginning, conjoined with spirit, and as it was in Christ Jesus ... And now we can well understand Jesus when he says and he will give his flesh for the life of the world, and that we shall eat his flesh and drink his blood, so as to live by him, as he lives by the Father, so as to be raised by him at the last day. Truly he speaks here of his true, real flesh and blood, but when he says that he gives his flesh for the life of the world, that is his pure unspotted body which was always the tool and temple of the Holy Spirit, and when he speaks of his flesh and blood which we shall eat and drink, that is his spiritual, transfigured body, with which he ascends on high, as he himself says: "the words that I speak to you are Spirit and life; for this body was born of the Spirit and all that is born of the Spirit is Spirit".

Therefore no-one shall tell us that we are fleshly and rely on the flesh, when we believe the Lord's words about the means of grace in his Church, and trust in their power; for what is given us there is both spiritual and bodily, like himself, in whom all the fullness of the Godhead dwells bodily. Our heart is by nature flesh, with faith and love it could become spiritual, but with sin it is ruined; but through baptism and communion, Jesus gives us his heart, so that a new man is born and grows, created according to God, in true righteousness and holiness. All our body is by nature flesh, and

13. Christian Thodberg (ed.), *N.F.S. Grundtvigs Prædikener 1825*, (Copenhagen, 1983), p. 233.

through sin it is made subject to death and corruption, but through baptism and communion it is renewed inwardly so as to be raised up again at the last day.[14]

In this sermon we see very clearly the consequences of this understanding of the interaction of flesh and spirit for Grundtvig's theology of the sacraments.

V

Let us now go on another ten years and see a little more in detail, what this conjunction of flesh and spirit will imply for the life of the Christian community, particularly for the life of the Christian community at prayer in the Eucharist. Here Grundtvig is preaching at Septuagesima 1834 and his text is taken from *Psalm* 104 ("Wine which maketh glad the heart of man so that his countenance becomes joyful").

"Wine maketh glad the heart of man, so that his countenance becomes joyful." So says the Psalm, and although drinking songs say the same thing that does not mean that psalms must become drinking songs nor that drinking songs become psalms. It only shows that the Spirit who inspired the psalmist and all the prophets and apostles of the Lord, understands how to speak gracefully and how to choose images for himself and his divine activity where they are rightly to be found and where they are foreordained for this purpose from the beginning of the world ...

Although therefore we ought as Christians always to remember the apostle's warning not to be drunk with wine wherein is excess, but to be full of the Spirit, so it is also true that at the Lord's table both bodily and spiritual realities are at work. It is true both in a bodily and a spiritual way, as the psalmist sings, that wine rejoices man's heart and bread strengthens it, because there the bread and wine are not just images of the Lord's body and blood, in which we share spiritually; rather they are incorporated and taken up into them, by his word which says Take this and eat it, drink ye all of this. Therefore one of the early fathers rightly said that the Lord in the eucharist took to himself the first creation and put the seal to his word that he had come not to destroy but to fulfil, just as he sent out his servants not to break down but to build up.

The world, I suppose, can certainly not bear to hear this, for its conceptions of Spirit are so fine and empty that for even the least evident reality to be linked with the Spirit seems to the wise of the world something coarse or crass, as they say, something which not only weighs down and dishonours the Spirit but scares it off and drives it away. This however, only follows from the fact that the world, as the Lord says, in no way knows the Spirit of truth and cannot receive it, but is deceived and blinded by its own spirit, which is the spirit of the air, i.e. the spirit of delusion and deep emptiness.

14. Ibid., pp. 234-35.

We Christians, however, who are baptised in the name of the Holy Spirit, that is to say plunged into and rooted in his divine personhood, as well as in that of the Father and the Son, should naturally only smile at the world's superstitious faith in a ghost under the name of Spirit.[15]

Yes, my friends, what the Christians had for a time almost entirely forgotten, that they may now again see through the Spirit of the Father, who brings to our mind all that the Son has said, who so livingly reminds us of it, to God's glory and our own great gain, that we never forget it again, who so livingly reminds us that he who said, "what God has joined together, let no man put asunder", he the perfect man, will never use his divine power so ill, as himself to do what he forbids. No, just as surely as the Creator has brought soul and body together within our human nature, so will the Saviour free both soul and body from the bonds of corruption ... and just as human-kind is created of the dust of the earth to be its king and to eat of its fruit and to live eternally, so the Saviour will in no way abolish or derange this nature's order, but only loose the bonds in which nature has been placed on account of the sins of its king, that is to say of humankind. So, when by the world we understand the world which God created in six days by his Word, which he saw and found to be very good, then we shall also see that what the Lord says is joyfully and literally fulfilled, that God sent out his Son into the world, not to condemn the world but that the world through him might be saved.[16]

We have here an insistence that human flesh, which is made alive together with human spirit, through the creative and redemptive work of God the Holy Spirit is in total solidarity with the world, which is itself God's creation, and thus that the salvation, the transfiguration of the flesh of the believers, involves the salvation and transfiguration of the whole world. The water of baptism, the bread and wine on the Lord's Table, are fully part of the world of nature, but they become part of God's work in the redemption and transfiguration of the world. Similarly the images which the Spirit takes and uses in order to speak of the things of heaven are taken from among the things of earth because from the beginning the things of earth were intended to convey a heavenly meaning, and to be open towards realities greater than themselves.

We also see here another instance of the importance which Grundtvig gives to John 3.16 and the way in which he sees this verse in the context of the gift of the Spirit to humankind and to all creation. "God so loved the world that he gave his only begotten Son." It is in the Holy Spirit that the love of God is poured out into the world through the coming of his Son. It is in the Holy Spirit that the world is caught up into the eternal joy of God's kingdom which this love brings. Thus, this verse speaks of the transfiguring power of

15. Ibid., p. 104.
16. Ibid., pp. 105-6.

God which descends into humanity and through humanity into the whole creation and draws all creation up into the communion of the divine life.

So, in the great Pentecost sermon of 1838, preached on this very text, Grundtvig concludes:

God so loved the world that he gave his only begotten Son; so that we shall not imagine that it would help if we had faith such as to move mountains, but had not love, the divine mother not only of all true virtues and all good deeds, but of all true joy and of eternal life, so that we shall never imagine that the all-powerful and divine love is something which can arise naturally of itself or can be created and brought into our hearts by some effort or skill of our own, but that it is God's gift of grace in Christ Jesus, a drop of dew from the Father's eye with eternal life in it, a gift of grace which he will grant to all those who believe in his only begotten Son, grant to all who believe, through the Holy Spirit in baptism, and will develop throughout the whole course of Christian life into an almighty power within us, which reveals his glory, and overcomes the world and death, so that we, like the apostles, do not hold our lives dear, for love challenges the last and most dangerous foe to fight, and praises the Lord in the fire, and thanks the Father in the moment of death, he who did not spare his only Son but made him to be a way out from death and a way into life for all who believe.[17]

Grundtvig here speaks in terms of martyrdom, a theme more common in him than we might think. The gift of the Spirit is the gift of a life which is stronger than death. And this we see in the deaths of those who give their lives for their love of God. This we see "with the strength of the martyrs in a trembling reed".

But we also notice the baroque image of the drop of dew from the Father's eye which occurs in this passage, an image which might suggest H.A. Brorson rather than Grundtvig. The dew is a symbol of the morning, of the blessing of new creation, of light which triumphs over darkness, of love which triumphs over death. But here the drop of dew is also a tear. It is from the love of the Father, who in Grundtvig is always the centre of love in the Godhead, from the compassion of the Father which descends into the world creating from nothing in the beginning, redeeming in the victory of Christ in the midst of human history and at the end transfiguring all in the glory of the kingdom.

VI. Postscript

In this article we have looked at Grundtvig's attitude towards this question of the relation of spirit and body in the life of humanity, and the relation of the

17. Ibid., pp. 228-29.

Creator Spirit to the life of creation as a whole, at different periods in Grundtvig's life, from the 1810s to the 1840s and in different contexts, some discursive, some homiletic. Certain common themes have emerged and they have emerged in ways which suggest a deep affinity between Grundtvig's theology as a whole and that of the teachers of the early Christian centuries. As Niels Thomsen remarks in an admirable article in *Tradition and Renewal*, "What is astonishing is the naturalness with which Grundtvig constantly speaks out of a harmony with early Church faith and thought. Most powerful of all is perhaps where he sings and speaks out of a faith in the Trinity".[18]

One has a very similar impression re-reading some of the essays in *For Sammenhængens Skyld* and particularly that of Mortensen on the Holy Spirit. I find myself asking yet again how it can be that Grundtvig's approach to theology is so profoundly patristic and in some respects so profoundly Eastern as it seems to be? I am reminded again of the way in which in a recent discussion, Christian Thodberg has spoken of "the spontaneously patristic nature of Grundtvig's exegesis".[19]

How are we to account for this quality in Grundtvig's thought? This is a question which I pose but do not pretend to answer. It is important for our understanding of Grundtvig himself; it is also important in the context of the dialogue between Lutheranism and Eastern Orthodoxy. In a more general way it can help us to see how Grundtvig could be a teacher for all Christians. In his unself-conscious way he seems able to speak out of the common faith and experience of the earliest centuries, to which all Christian confessions look back.

The influence of Irenaeus on Grundtvig in the 1820s is of course evident and acknowledged, and the influence of Grundtvig's liturgical translations from Greek and Latin in the 1830s is also widely recognised. But already before that it seems to me that there were other influences at work. Perhaps Grundtvig's first attraction to the poetry of the Anglo-Saxons was not only literary and historical but also seriously theological. That is a line of thought which I believe deserves further exploration. But perhaps we need to look again at a Danish work which Grundtvig must have known as a student, and which, even if it did not excite him, may have influenced him in ways of which perhaps he was not fully aware. I refer to Frederik Münter's *Haandbog i den Ældste Christelige Kirkes Dogmehistorie* (1801 and 1804). Münter's work is not exactly exciting. He was too good a man of the 18th century with his instinctive revulsion from *enthusiasm*, *mysticism* and *fantasy*, to write an exciting

18. "Grundtvig in the Mirror of the Early Church" in Thodberg, Pontoppidan Thyssen (eds.), *N.F.S. Grundtvig*, p. 198.
19. Christian Thodberg, "Grundtvig's View of the Bible" in *Grundtvig in International Perspective. Studies in the Creativity of Interaction* (Aarhus, 2000), p.134.

study of the earliest Christian teachers. Perhaps also he was too much of a systematician to enter into their characteristic ways of seeing things. Having only recently come to recognise his possible influence on Grundtvig's understanding of Christian faith, I have not been able to look carefully enough at his work to feel confident in my judgement. But a first impression suggests that there are features in Grundtvig's theology, its pre-Nicene Trinitarianism, its emphasis on the doctrine of the divine image and likeness in humankind, its non-Augustinian attitude towards the fall, where memories of Münter's lectures may have been of real importance in forming Grundtvig's way of seeing things. Münter is certainly not in love with the writers of the second and third centuries, with Irenaeus, Clement and Origen; but he treats them with respect. They are at least, in his eyes, much preferable to their successors. In particular he seems pleased when he is able to show that their anthropology is certainly not that of the later Augustine. In his work he gives us a general picture of the Christian faith as taught in the first centuries, which may at least have had some influence on the way in which Grundtvig's mind grew and which therefore might help us to understand "that fundamental agreement that existed between Grundtvig and the early Church", to which Niels Thomsen points us.[20]

20. Thodberg, Pontoppidan Thyssen (eds.), *N.F.S. Grundtvig*, p. 207.

"A Truly Proud Ruin":
Grundtvig and the Anglo-Saxon Legacy

By S.A.J. Bradley

I am aware that I am inviting many in my readership to leap not just the one hurdle – that of yet another analysis of N.F.S. Grundtvig's idiosyncratic ideas – but two hurdles: Grundtvig's idiosyncratic mind *and* Anglo-Saxon literature. One might argue long over which of these two subjects is the more arcane and inaccessible! I hope I can do a little in this paper to clarify the arcane and make some inroads into the inaccessible.

The problem, of course, is the very one with which Grundtvig himself confronted his early 19th-century readership. When, between 1815 and 1820, he began eliciting affirmation of his problematical theories of universal history, of "Ordets Kamp til Seier" (The Word's struggle to victory) from the Anglo-Saxon epic poem *Beowulf*, there was hardly anyone in Scandinavia and hardly anyone in England – hardly anyone in the world, therefore! – who could adequately read Anglo-Saxon or who knew very much at first hand of the scope and content of surviving Anglo-Saxon literature.

Grundtvig was thus perforce a pioneer in Anglo-Saxon, one of the founding fathers, in fact, of Anglo-Saxon scholarship. Depending upon viewpoint, he was a catalyst or a gadfly or a menacing viking threatening to plunder England's literary heritage as his forefathers had plundered English silver and carried it off to Denmark in their ships (the metaphor is his, not mine).[1] In modern editions of *Beowulf*, Grundtvig's name will be found in acknowledgement of his contribution to the establishment of the text of the damaged sole manuscript. In modern studies of the history of Anglo-Saxon scholarship he receives (rather belated) recognition for what Professor Eric Stanley called the "astonishing brilliance" of his work upon *Beowulf* and for his role in advancing the cause of then grievously neglected literature of the Anglo-Saxons.[2]

---

1. See, for example, "Grundtvigs Levned indtil ca. 1843 kort fortalt af ham selv" in S. Johansen and H. Høirup (eds.), *Grundtvigs Erindringer og Erindringer om Grundtvig* (Copenhagen, 1948), pp. 74-75; *Mands Minde*, Lecture for November 16, 1838, in Johansen and Høirup, *Grundtvigs Erindringer*, p. 121; and "Fortale" in *Phenix-Fuglen*, p. 11 (see note 13 below).
2. E.G. Stanley, "'The scholarly recovery of the significance of Anglo-Saxon records in prose and verse: a new bibliography" in *Anglo-Saxon England*, 9 (1981), pp. 223-62.

But if it may be said that he *made his impact upon* Anglo-Saxon literature as a *scholar*, then it may also be said that he *felt* the impact of Anglo-Saxon literature upon him *as a poet*. He claimed as much for himself on more than one occasion: in *Mands Minde* (Within Living Memory) (1838), though he was actually referring to the imagery of Norse poetry, we may legitimately extend the situation to cover the Anglo-Saxon as well. In this lecture upon England and her relations with Denmark, his discourse had evidently run away with him and – in a manner of which he made a practice (indeed, a *principle* which was to become a hallmark among his followers particularly those teaching in the Danish folk high schools)[3] – he had seized upon a string of metaphors from Norse mythology to illustrate his argument. Then he pulled himself up and said, revealingly from our point of view: "Well, gentlemen, the old imagery of Scandinavia came to life in me before I knew it, and that is the bardic vein in me, but it is also the source of my view and study of world history, as well as of my knowledge of history."[4] And it is clear enough that the impact of Anglo-Saxon, as of Norse literature, was upon him not only as a poet and an historian but also as a theologian – as a theologian with a sense of history – as a philosopher, as a patriot, as a zealous believer in the paramount role of the mother tongue, and as one who put his trust in *folket*, the community of God's people, of God's Danish people, of God's northern peoples. It became his aim to incorporate the matter and the meaning of Anglo-Saxon literature, along with those of the more strictly Scandinavian Norse literature, into the cultural resources of his nation.

He never accomplished all that he had once dreamed of achieving to the honour and promotion of Anglo-Saxon literature. Certainly when he tried to get an international project going, he was outmanoeuvred by the English antiquaries. And perhaps he bit off more than he could chew anyway. Even so, the accomplishment is enough to impress. It spans some 50 years (at least) of his working life. If we want a couple of dates to bracket this span, we might take 1815 and 1861. In 1815, his fellow-countryman Grímur Jónsson Thorkelin published the first-ever edition of *Beowulf* – being primarily interested in it because, as its opening lines declare, it is about the ancient heroic deeds of the people's kings of Denmark. Grundtvig, astonished at what he read there, and

3. There are interesting and fittingly anecdotal illustrations of the bitterly fought-over role of myth and mythologising in Danish folk high school teaching, in which fidelity to Grundtvig's founding principles was perceived to be at stake, in Jens Peter Ægidius, *Bragesnak: Nordiske Myter og Mytefortælling i dansk Tradition (indtil 1910)* (Odense, 1985) and *Bragesnak 2: Den mytologiske Tradition i dansk Folkeoplysning i det tyvende Århundrede (1910-1985)* (Odense, 1992).
4. *Mands Minde* (1838), excerpt translated in Edward Broadbridge and Niels Lyhne Jensen (tr.), *A Grundtvig Anthology: Selections from the writings of N.F.S. Grundtvig (1783-1872)* (Cambridge and Viby, 1984), p. 118.

dismayed at the shortcomings of Thorkelin's handling of it, began to learn Anglo-Saxon ("as though I meant to become professor in it")[5] in order to produce a Danish translation and an interpretation of the poem. Indeed there was talk of producing, in collaboration with the prodigious linguist Rasmus Rask (following their meeting in 1816),[6] a new *edition* of the Anglo-Saxon text itself to replace Thorkelin's flawed version. Though this particular plan came to nothing, Grundtvig nevertheless finally published his own edition of *Beowulf* in 1861.[7]

The Anglo-Saxon poem *Beowulf*, then, conveniently – and significantly – provides the *alpha* and the *omega* of this schematization: but it also accounts for much of Grundtvig's activity in between the two dates. He published from 1815 onwards (in his own periodicals) specimen translated excerpts of *Beowulf*,[8] along with a considerable quantity of more or less popular and polemical critical discussion of text, content and interpretation.[9] And in 1820 he brought to press his Danish translation (or rather, paraphrase) of *Beowulf*, furnished with a copious introduction.[10] But then the decisive chance came. While the polemicist Grundtvig was languishing under censorship following his calamitous confrontation with Professor H.N. Clausen in 1826, in an audience with the King he mentioned he would be interested in going to England to find out more about these Anglo-Saxon manuscripts which languished largely unread in the great English libraries. The king awarded him a grant of money, and so Grundtvig visited England in the three successive summers of 1829, 1830 and 1831. He studied manuscripts in the British Library, in Exeter Cathedral Library, in Oxford and Cambridge; he met some of the leading British antiquaries, found a publishing house and, in 1830, published his ambitious *Prospectus* proposing systematic publication, by subscription "of the most valuable Anglo-Saxon manuscripts, illustrative of the early Poetry and Literature of our Language".[11] He returned in 1831 to find that he had been outflanked by the London antiquaries who had earlier seemed (but only *seemed*) to support his initiative: they had laid their own plans to avoid the

---

5. "Indledning" in *Bjowulfs Drape* (Copenhagen, 1820), p. xxxiii : "... som om jeg vilde være Professor i det."
6. "Indledning" in *Bjowulfs Drape* (Copenhagen, 1820), p. xxxiii.
7. *Beowulfes Beorh* (1861).
8. *Nyeste Skilderier af København* (1815).
9. Particularly of *Beowulf*; notably in his periodicals *Danne-Virke*, 1816-19, and *Brage og Idun*, 1841.
10. *Bjowulfs Drape* (Copenhagen, 1820).
11. *Prospectus, and Proposals of a Subscription, for the Publication of the most valuable Anglo-Saxon Manuscripts, illustrative of the early Poetry and Literature of our Language. Most of which have never yet been printed* (London, Black, Young and Young, Foreign Booksellers to the King, 1830).

disgrace of foreign intervention.[12] Grundtvig was unable to conceal a bitter-
ness, despite his jocularity: "People openly regarded and treated me as a
Danish Viking who, after the example of my dear forefathers, meant to enrich
myself and Denmark with England's treasures, and the publisher was close
to saying straight out that he did not dare to have anything more to do with
me, so as not to be branded a national traitor."[13]

But he continued work on his transcriptions of the Exeter Book. It is clear
from the relevant fascicle of his original papers in the Grundtvig Arkiv that
he yet hoped he might be the one to bring out the *editio princeps*.[14] As late as
1840 he was standing by. In that year he published *Phenix-Fuglen*, his edition
of *The Phoenix*, one of the poems in the Exeter Book. In its introduction, which
I just quoted, he speaks sharply of the English delay in publishing and of the
credentials of English scholarship. He was ready himself to step into the
breach, he declared. Only the call and a bit of financial assistance were
needed. Anyone who has worked through the surviving papers has, regret-
fully, to doubt the confidence of this offer, remarkable though the enterprise
is to which the papers testify – but anyway in the event his rival, the London
antiquarian Benjamin Thorpe, brought out the *editio princeps* in 1842.

Grundtvig carried on his intermittent work on the Anglo-Saxons. He was
interested in the contents of yet another Anglo-Saxon codex, Oxford Bodleian
Library MS Junius 11 (the so-called "Cædmon" manuscript): there are signs
in his papers in the Arkiv that he had ideas for the publication of at least parts
of this too. And he became interested in the contents of a recently discovered
and published fourth codex, the Vercelli Book. Extensive extracts from these
codices, going back to his days in Oxford, London and Cambridge or taken
from printed editions, survive in the Arkiv in Copenhagen. In 1860, he published his great poetic cycle the *Christenhedens Syvstjerne* (The seven stars (or
Pleiades) of Christendom) a section of which represents his assessment of the
place of the Anglo-Saxon congregation in world history. And in 1861, his edition of *Beowulf* came out.

Such intensive exploration of the poetry and culture of the Anglo-Saxons
yielded other fruits too, of a more specifically creative kind. To the body of
Danish hymnody Grundtvig contributed free renderings of passages of An-

12. Much of the story has been traced by Helge Toldberg in "Grundtvig og de engelske
    Antikvarer" in *Orbis Litterarum* (1947), Tom. 5, fasc. 3-4.
13. "Fortale" in *Phenix-Fuglen. Et Angelsachsisk Kvad, etc.* (Copenhagen, 1840), p. 11: " ...
    man aabenbart betragtede og behandlede mig som en *Dansk Viking* der, efter mine
    kiære Forældres Exempel, vilde berige mig selv og Danmark med Englands Skatte, og
    Boghandleren var nær ved reent ud at sige, han ikke turde befatte sig mere med mig,
    for ikke at stemples til en Landsforræder."
14. Royal Library Copenhagen, Grundtvig Arkiv, Fascicle 316, nrs. 1-8. See S.A.J. Bradley,
    N.F.S. Grundtvig's Transcriptions of the Exeter Book: An Analysis (Copenhagen, 1998).

glo-Saxon poetry in the form of hymns – most notably *I Kvæld blev der banket paa Helvedesport* (Yestereve came a knock on the portals of Hell) (1837) which was inspired by lines from the poem *Christ and Satan* in the early 11th-century Junius codex mentioned above, and *Kommer, Sjæle dyrekiøbte* (Come, you souls so dearly purchased) (1837) which is freely based upon lines in Cynewulf's poem, *Christ II (The Ascension)* in the Exeter Book. On top of all this, Grundtvig actually *composed* poetry in Anglo-Saxon. As early as 1817 he published (in his own periodical *Danne-Virke*, III) a pastiche poem (*Ragna-Rok*) based partly upon Anglo-Saxon poetry; and he furnished Anglo-Saxon verse prefaces to his editions of *The Phoenix* and *Beowulf*. I shall return to some of this shortly.

Grundtvig revealed himself as a poet with a craftsman's interest in the language of this ancient and Christian poetry, the poetry of the early Church in the North. He underlined words and phrases in the copies he made from manuscripts of Anglo-Saxon poems and he compiled word-lists drawn from these poems. And these words and phrases then seem to come out, sometimes perhaps unconsciously, in his own poetic compositions. Though the matter still awaits fuller exploration, there may well prove to be embedded in his writings a wealth of recall – from direct reference, through reminiscence to half-unconscious echo – of this poetry of the early Church in the North. For example, I have myself elsewhere tentatively suggested that the recall of Anglo-Saxon poetry he had himself transcribed from the Exeter Book may have been involved on the occasion of Grundtvig's breakdown on Palm Sunday 1867 and also in the poignant seafaring imagery and idiom of his last poem, *Gammel nok er jeg nu blevet* (Old enough have I become now) (1872).[15] Nor need this exploration be restricted to his formal poetry. It is a familiar truth in Grundtvig studies that his prose sermons use a rhetorical range extending far into the register we conventionally think of as belonging to poetry. It is true that his distinctive sermon-style was already in formulation before he immersed himself in the study of Anglo-Saxon poetry, and before he met the

---

15. See, for example, Niels Thomsen, "Grundtvig in the Mirror of the Early Church" in C. Thodberg and A.P. Thyssen (eds.), *N.F.S. Grundtvig Tradition and Renewal* (Copenhagen, 1983), p. 198: "All the time, images are flashing into Grundtvig's hymns that build bridges to the early Church and the Eastern Church." Also Bent Noack, *Helvedstorm og Himmelfart* (Copenhagen, 1983), p. 104: "Grundtvig's word-choice and mode of expression, especially in the eighteen-thirties, is flavoured by this (Anglo-Saxon) poetry and, not to be forgotten, its premises, and his, deriving from the early Church" (my translation). See also S.A.J. Bradley, "The First New-European Literature: N.F.S. Grundtvig's Reception of Anglo-Saxon Literature" in A.M. Allchin et al. (eds.) *Heritage and Prophecy. Grundtvig and the English-Speaking World* (Aarhus, 1993), pp. 45-72, especially pp. 64-70; and "Grundtvig's Palm Sunday 1867" in *Grundtvig Studier* (1993), pp. 198-213.

many surviving Anglo-Saxon prose homilies and the prose chronicles which display, in parts, a similar rhetorical breadth. And it is true that he was already furnished with the idiom and imagery of Old Norse poetry from which the kind of poetic idiom found in his sermons might derive. Nevertheless, it is likely to prove that in some measure in his prose sermons, as in his poetry, Grundtvig has profitably carried Anglo-Saxon grist to his mill.

This then is some account of the extensive and long-sustained engagement of Grundtvig with the literature of the Anglo-Saxons. It did not end in 1861: One of the very last conversations Grundtvig had was on Anglo-Saxon literature, at the very end of his long life, but I will save this to the end of my paper.

Now what is this Anglo-Saxon literature? And what was this zeal of his all about? Essentially, it is a Northern literature, an early medieval literature, a Christian literature. Grundtvig himself declared: "It is in the writings of the Anglo-Saxons that we have the most unequivocal remnants of the poetic language of the ancient North, within which we shall learn to know and to receive its spirit."[16] It was older than the highly-esteemed Norse (that is, Old Icelandic) poetry on which Grundtvig had hitherto fed his zeal for the ancient form and idiom of Northern poetry.[17] And crucially it was Christian: rooted in Northern antiquity *and* Christian – for Grundtvig, the best of both worlds. True, it was not rich in Northern *myth* as was the Norse poetry, which Grundtvig quarried for such myth as supplied metaphor in the statement of his arguments on practically any subject under the sun. But it had a legend component, notably in *Beowulf*, which he could and did use in the same way. And there was in it Christian, or christianised, myth. In *Mands Minde*, for example, he metaphorically applies to himself the myth of the Phoenix, and speaks of the remnants of this Eastern myth surviving in Western use – and here he must necessarily have in mind the Anglo-Saxon poem *The Phoenix*, which he was shortly to publish – as "above the best poem by Oehlenschlaeger", "for in these scraps I have found the human spirit's own ideal of its great destiny expressed with confidence, magnificence, and life".[18] In the preface to his edition of *The Phoenix*, he declares that the Anglo-Saxon poet has handled the Christian interpretation of the myth even better than did the Fathers of the Church.[19]

---

16. "Indledning" in *Bjowulfs Drape* (Copenhagen, 1820), p. lxviii: "Det er i Angel-Sachsernes Skrifter vi have de meest utvilsomme Levninger af det Gamle Nordens poetiske Sprog, hvori vi skal lære at kjende og fatte dets Aand."
17. Indeed, Grundtvig believed that the Icelandic Edda poetry showed many outward signs of having had its origin in Anglo-Saxon poetic tradition. "Indledning" in *Bjowulfs Drape* (Copenhagen, 1820), p. lv : "…Eddas Mythe-Kvad, som selv udvortes bære mangt et Spor af Angel-Sachsisk Oprindelse …" (… the mythic poesy of the Edda, which itself bears externally many a trace of an Anglo-Saxon origin …).
18. *Mands Minde* (1838) in Jensen and Broadbridge, *Anthology*, p. 98.

It was as much as anything this figure of the Northern, ancient, and Christian poet which seems to have captivated Grundtvig. According to the evidence of the papers preserved in the Grundtvig Arkiv, one of the earliest notices he records of Anglo-Saxon poetry concerns the Venerable Bede's story of Cædmon, the unlettered lay-brother in the monastery at Whitby, who miraculously received the gift of poesy at the dead of night, in a stable, and thus became (some time before the year 681) the first Christian poet in the English language. Bede tells the story within his *Ecclesiastical History of the English People*, completed in 731, in order to illustrate the informing thesis of his *History*, that from the age of conversion onwards the Holy Spirit was at work among the English nation, sanctifying what formerly had been profane. Tacitly, this is what Bede sees in the story of Cædmon, and it seems to have been a suggestion which appealed much to Grundtvig. The Holy Spirit approaches through the medium of poetry, poetry of traditional (Northern) form, in the vernacular (English) language. The form, the language of poetry are continuous from out of ancient (and originally heathen) tradition; but, sanctified by the Holy Spirit, they now enshrine the truth of Christ and are thus made an instrument of enlightenment, of conversion, of solace – as, explicitly, Bede says the poetry of Cædmon was.

Grundtvig, as a poet (I stress yet again), understood and took this testimony to heart. He was eventually to see and proclaim that the historical event itself had, literally, epoch-making consequences. With Cædmon was born, so he says in the preface to his edition of *The Phoenix* (1860),[20] nothing less than a new-European literature: the literature of new-Europe, of Christian Europe. Grundtvig, as a poet, was himself an heir to Cædmon; acknowledging in Cædmon the Christian and Anglo-Saxon equivalent of Brage, the legendary father of Scandinavian poesy.[21]

---

19. "Fortale" in *Phenix-Fuglen*, (Copenhagen, 1840), p. 18-19: "… *Kirke-Fædrene* … saae i Phenix-Mythen et deiligt Forbillede baade paa Herrens Opstandelse og paa vores … denne Forklaring findes endnu langt varmere og dristigere udfört hos den *Angel-Sachsiske* Skjald end hos Nogen af Kirke-Fædrene" (The Church Fathers saw in the Phoenix-myth a beautiful prefiguration both of the Lord's resurrection and of ours … This interpretation is found much more warmly and boldly worked out in the Anglo-Saxon poet than in any of the Church Fathers).

20. The text is in Johansen and Høirup, *Grundtvigs Erindringer*, p. 75.

21. I have subsequently discussed Grundtvig's characterisation of Cædmon more extensively in "Stridige Stykker snild jeg forbandt: Grundtvig's creative synthesis of Anglo-Saxon sources" in *Grundtvig Studier* (1996), pp. 97-127. The article includes a transcription of his unfinished poem in Anglo-Saxon on Creation and Redemption, which was pretty certainly intended as a verse preface to a putative edition of the poems in Oxford Bodleian Junius 11. For a recent English-language discussion of these ideas in broad context, distinguished by much insight, see A.M. Allchin, *N.F.S. Grundtvig: An Introduction to his Life and Work* (Aarhus and London, 1997), particularly Ch. 3.

That Cædmon was a monk, that Bede was a monk who wrote in Latin, that the whole *History* celebrates the indebtedness of England to Rome did not unduly trouble Grundtvig the Lutheran. He went on speaking disparagingly of monastic Latin with a roundness which makes any modern medievalist wince[22] and yet he seemed tacitly to set aside from such strictures the Venerable Bede and the monastic productions of Anglo-Saxon England – which pretty certainly include most if not all of the surviving codices of Anglo-Saxon poetry. Indeed, so significant was Bede's *History* held to be in Grundtvig's circle that in 1864, under Grundtvig's encouragement, Christian Kragballe published a Danish translation of the work, furnished with a preface commending it in categorically Grundtvigian terms of its universal-historical worth. There, he blames the German-Lutheran school for being "so ultra-Lutheran and so disregarding of the church" (saa ærke-luthersk og saa ukirkelig) that they have forgotten the Hebrew, Greek and Latin Fathers, but also – "and this above all" (og det allermeest) – they have forgotten the witness of the Anglo-Saxon Church. It was through the Anglo-Saxons, he reminds his readership, in Grundvigian concepts, that "the royal road of the Gospel" (evangeliets kongevej) reached into the North. Bede's *History*, he says, can offer the Danish people "enlightenment and consolidation" (oplysning og opbyggelse) as an antidote to what he saw as the ill-effects of the German brand of Lutheranism.[23]

The fact seems to be that the more Grundtvig strove to find out about surviving Anglo-Saxon literature, the more accommodated he became to the conformity of this literature with the orthodoxies of the early Western Catholic Church. As he transcribed the Exeter Book, and worked back home to prepare it for an edition, he read, for example, fine lyrics celebrating Mary as Virgin of virgins, splendour of the world, Lady of the heavenly host and of the earthly orders below the heavens and of the dwellers in hell; poetry celebrating the mystery of the Incarnation, the testimony of the saints; a lyrical poeticisation of the Lord's Prayer, homiletic injunctions to the giving of alms; and he found, in this oldest Northern vernacular poetic language, in this traditional Northern alliterative form of poetry, vividly imaged treatments of the Harrowing of Hell and the Day of Judgement. None of this elicited from him the outrage, the sneers, the denunciations of thralldom to monasticism and to Rome one might have expected, and could have heard, from men of

22. For example, in *Nordens Mythologi eller Sind-Billed Sprog* (1832), translated in Broadbridge and Jensen, *Anthology*, p. 37: "… this Italian, or neo-Roman, this monastic-Latin, papist spiritual culture, which from its very beginning was an artefact, like Dante's Divine Comedy, and at best a hothouse plant…".

23. Christian Kragballe, "Forord" in *Angler Folkets Kirkehistorie af Beda den Ærværdige* (Copenhagen, 1864), pp. 1-2.

less ecumenical instincts, of less wilful independence in matters of belief and knowledge, than Grundtvig.[24]

But Grundtvig was in fact already learning to distinguish crucially between the early (and, as he perceived it, pure) church of the age of the Anglo-Saxon conversion (end of the sixth century) and what the church (the Church of Rome, that is) had become in the age of Luther. The distinction becomes a thesis and forms part of that view of history and of humanity expressed in Grundtvig's writings on universal history[25] and, notably, in his *Christenhedens Syvstjerne* in 1860. And in doing so, he sets himself apart – for better and for worse – from other major 19th-century Anglo-Saxon antiquarians:[26] because of course he is far more than an antiquarian.

Grundtvig *the antiquarian* read Bede's story of Cædmon and tracked down some of the poetry of Cædmon (or what was then held to be his work). Grundtvig *the universal historian* perceived the essential continuities between the age of Cædmon, the age of Luther and the present age. Grundtvig *the theologian* harmonised the testimony of King David the Psalmist, of the poets of the early Church whom he saw illustrated in Cædmon, and of Martin Luther. Grundtvig *the poet* devised, in an early poem he called *Ragna-Rok*,[27] a vision-

---

24. Of course, this openness to the testimony of the early Church has to be understood in the light of Grundtvig's simultaneous exploration in other traditions too, notably in those of the Greek Church. For a convenient and sympathetic English-language account, see Allchin, *N.F.S. Grundtvig*, particularly pp. 56f. and pp. 242f.

25. Including *Lærebog i Verdenshistorien* (1808); *Kort Begreb af Verdens Krønike i Sammenhæng* (1814); *Udsigt over Verdens-Krøniken fornemmelig i det Lutherske Tidsrum* (1817); *Tidens Strøm eller universalhistorisk Omrids* (1829); *Haandbog i Verdens-Historien. Efter de bedste Kilder. Et Forsøg af N.F.S. Grundtvig*, I-III; and *Christenhedens Syvstjerne* (1860). Grundtvig also makes significant reference to such views in *Nordens Mythologi eller Sind-Billed Sprog* published in 1832, the year after his third and for the time being last visit to England. The work is important as a more direct and overtly polemical application of ancient literature to the present age; and because it was particularly influential since it «became the book of reference for all the lectures given at Grundtvigian folk-highschools in the 19th century» (William Michelsen, introduction to excerpt in Broadbridge and Jensen, *Anthology*, p. 33), and was a staple text in the protracted debate over the role of myths and mythologising in Danish folk high school teaching.

26. Grundtvig discusses his attitude towards legend-history, relative to shifting fashion among historians, in "Indledning" in *Bjowulfs Drape* (Copenhagen, 1820), pp. lii-liii, where he says that his own wish, as historian, is to "forbinde de ældre Dages Godtroenhed med den følgende Tids Forsigtighed, og det nys-undfangne poetiske Saga-Blik" (to combine the old days' *bona fide* credulity with the following age's meticulousness and the newly-embraced poetic saga-view) and asserts that "det er med Vidende og Villie jeg stræber at forbinde, hvad der sædvanlig findes skarp adskilt" (it is with awareness and intention that I strive to combine what is usually to be found sharply separated).

27. *Ragna-Rok. Et dansk Æmter*, published in *Danne-Virke*, III (Copenhagen, 1817).

ary exposition of this harmonisation which incorporated Cædmon's own poetic utterances in their original Anglo-Saxon poetic form and language.
Grundtvig – who "from childhood" (fra Barnsbeen) loved "the literary art,
antiquity and the land of our fathers" (boglig Konst, Fortid og Fædreneland)[28]
– mingled with Cædmon and Luther the figures of Holger Danske, the
mythic Norne-Giæsten and En Lys Alf (A Good Elf). Grundtvig *the polemicist*
published the whole confection in *Danne-Virke*.

In this long, somewhat bizarre poem, featuring both Cædmon and Luther, Grundtvig proclaims Cædmon as heir to the harp of King David. "I
dreamed, I dreamed, I saw David the king", intones the Spirit of Cædmon,
"into my hands he gave his harp so fair. Its golden strings I struck with might:
and still in the world my song is recalled".[29] And he begins to sing, in Anglo-Saxon, the opening lines of the Anglo-Saxon poem *Genesis* (which was
once widely thought to be Cædmon's work). Norne-Giæsten longs for the
power to cause the Vatican to sink into the yellow waves of the Tiber and
praises Luther as a hero brave and bold because, despite fire and streams of
venom, he has maimed the Pope, "the troll of Rome": "Yea, doomed he fled
from the din of battle, from his arm and shoulder, as Grendel did."[30] The reference to *Beowulf* here (Grendel, of course, is one of the monsters in *Beowulf*,
whose arm the hero rips off in a mighty struggle which purges the Danish
king's hall of the monster's ancient tyranny) and the conflation of the
dragon-fight with the Grendel fight and thus of Luther with Beowulf ("humankind's Northern hero who ... disarms the Power of Darkness and by his
strength saves the dying life of the people"),[31] all this is highly characteristic
of Grundtvig's exploitation of early Northern myth and legend for metaphorical purposes.

But once the church *had* been pure, and Cædmon's divine gift of poesy
witnessed that the Anglo-Saxons had taken over custodianship of truth, by
the divine will, and would soon, through their missionaries into North-west-
ern Europe in the seventh century, pave the "royal road of the Gospel" into
Scandinavia.

28. *Danne-Virke*, II (1817), p. 208.
29. *Ragna-Rok. Et dansk Æmter* in *Danne-Virke*, III (Copenhagen, 1817), p. 340: "Jeg
    drømde, jeg drømde, / Kong David jeg saae, / Han gav mig i Hænde / Sin Harpe saa
    prud, / Strængene gyldne / Slog jeg med Vælde, / End vel i Midgard / Mindes mit
    Kvad."
30. *Ragna-Rok* in *Danne-Virke*, III (Copenhagen, 1817), p. 327: "Du Helt, som kiæk og bold,
    / Trods Ild og Edder-Strømme, / Lemlæsted Romas Trold! / Ja, feig fra Kampens
    Bulder / Alt fra sin Arm og Skulder / Som Grendel flygted han."
31. "Indledning" in *Bjowulfs Drape* (Copenhagen, 1820), p. I: "Menneske-Slægtens Nor-
    diske Helt, der ... afvæbner Mørkets Magt og redder med Kraft det døende Folke-
    Liv."

All this typifies Grundtvig's approach to the literature he had "discovered" for himself – not least to *Beowulf*. The story line there is of humanoid monsters and dragons and feuds and wars, and of human heroism in the struggle to preserve community against them. But Grundtvig perceived here, in much the same way as he did in the Anglo-Saxon telling of the Phoenix-story, a far greater, profounder, more universal statement in the poem. For him, it narrates poetically a symbolically typical episode in the struggle, as old as the world, as long as time, between Truth and the Lie, between the Word and the worldly enemies of the Word, of the Word's struggle to victory within the world, within time.[32] These were truths and issues burningly alive for Grundtvig in his own day and, through him, amongst his own community and congregation; and in *Beowulf* he found another way to talk about them, to prove their ancient relevance to the past and the present progress of human society.

The Anglo-Saxons then, as an historical community and culture, formed an essential link in Grundtvig's symbolic and schematic account of universal history: They were among the guarantors of the stance of the Lutheran congregation; their participation in the ancient culture of the North posited a certain fundamental unity of the North of the modern age, which categorically transcended ephemeral international politics. They put Grundtvig in touch, on one of several fronts, with the early church and encouraged in him a liberal, non-sectarian understanding of the catholic dimension of the Church and helped move him towards a new and surer understanding of the "catholicity", that is, the universal oneness, of Christ's Church. Their poetry authorises the service of the Truth, the Word, and allows Grundtvig endorsement of a certain image of himself as prophetic bard, latest in the same continuous line as Cædmon: it was the same living word as lay upon Cædmon's lips that lay now upon his own.

A similar authorisation was entailed in Grundtvig's habit of appending an original composition in Anglo-Saxon to accompany his Anglo-Saxon publications. I will take, as my very last topic, just one small but significant example, to stand for the many that are to be found, from his Anglo-Saxon composition prefacing *Bjowulfs Drape* (1820).

The opening section of the poem *Beowulf* is taken up with a definition of exemplary kingship. This definition of an ideal king is thereafter a yardstick throughout the rest of the long poem. When we meet other kings, and particularly Beowulf himself as king, we feel compelled to respond to the poet's

---

32. I have discussed this interpretation of *Beowulf* at some length in "Grundtvig, Anglo-Saxon Literature and 'Ordets Kamp til Seier'" in *Grundtvig Studier* (1989-90), pp. 216-45 where bibliographical information may be found upon other studies of the subject.

signals and ask is *this* a good king, is this a *good* king – by comparison with the exemplary model proposed in the opening of the poem? *Is* this a king manifestly favoured and succoured by God – because he rules for the well-being of his people and gives them security, prosperity and peace? The exemplary king chosen by the poet is of course the ancient legendary Danish king, Scyld, founder of the Scylding dynasty: *Þæt wæs god cyning*, the poet says of him, prescriptively.

Grundtvig's poem opens with an echo of these opening lines of *Beowulf*.[33] *Hwæt we Gardena in geardægum / Þeod-Scyldinga þrym gefrunon …* , "Lo, we have heard tell of the majesty of the Spear-Danes, of the people's Scyldings in days of yore". We note, however, that he has substituted "Scyldings" for the more general term "kings". It is soon clear why: he is intent upon asserting that, though in former times (*ærran mælum*, line 6) the dynasty may have suffered "wicked deadly evil" (*feorh-bealu frecne*, line 7), the dynasty has not been wiped out to the grief of the people (*folce to ceare*, line 7). The dynasty survives (to the joy of the people, implicitly). Frederik sits upon his father's throne, lord of men: *þæt is god cyning* – "he is a good king". The phrase in homage to Frederik VI, adapted directly from *Beowulf*, is placed, in effect, exactly where the *Beowulf*-poet placed his prescriptive exclamation upon the good king, Scyld, the founder of the dynasty. It would be myopic to conclude merely that Grundtvig is engaged in superficial pastiche here, opportunistically lifting a ready-made rhetorical unit from *Beowulf*. This is an act of strategy, matched by many others in this prefatory poem. Grundtvig is making, by allusion and nuance, a considerable and potentially very sensitive political statement – about the lineage and succession of the Danish royal house.[34]

Elsewhere, writing on *Beowulf* in *Danne-Virke*, II (1817), Grundtvig had already called Scyld "the blessed King Scyld" (den livsalige Kong Skjold, p. 216), and had summarised the *Beowulf*-poet's image of Scyld and the Danish people together as: "Scyld, gentle father of the land, and his loving and faithfully devoted Danish folk" (Skjold, den Landets milde Fader, og det ham kiærlig, tro hengivne danske Folk, p. 219). In his own poem, Grundtvig calls

33. *Beowulf* 1-2: *Hwæt we Gar-Dena in geardagum / Þeod-cyninga þrym gefrunon.* Grundtvig rather commonly transcribes Anglo-Saxon *dag-* incorrectly as *dæg-*.

34. The Danish royal house had faced crisis during the scandal involving Struensee and the English-born Queen Caroline Matilda in 1772 and during the revolution ("The Revolution, with all that gave folk to think on and talk about" (Revolutionen med Alt hvad den gav Folk at tænke paa, og tale om) was one possible reason for the delay in bringing Thorkelin's edition of *Beowulf* to publication: "Indledning" in *Bjowulfs Drape* (Copenhagen, 1820), p. xxx) resulting in the emancipation of the Danish peasantry from 1788 onwards as well as during the events of the Napoleonic Wars from which Denmark was not saved by neutrality and which led directly to national bankruptcy in 1813 and the loss of Norway from the Danish crown in 1814.

the Danish people, in line with this representation of king as father of the nation, "the children of the Scyldings" (*Scyldinga-bearna*, line 28).

In such a context, it can hardly have been an accident that by associating Frederik VI with the God-sent and God-favoured founder-king, Scyld, Grundtvig hints at a divine patronage of an absolute monarch who rules with his people's well-being at heart and with the love of his people.

All this, as I have said, is strategy. Read the prefatory poem in the light of the following translation; read the translation in the light of the preface. They speak together, and thus, in consequence, the ancient poet of *Beowulf* speaks timely truth and wisdom from out of antiquity into the present age. Similar exploitation could easily be demonstrated from the other Anglo-Saxon poems Grundtvig composed in association with his editions of *Beowulf* (1861) and *The Phoenix* (1840).[35] The proper context of much of this polemical use of Anglo-Saxondom must ultimately be within discussion of Grundtvig's attitudes to such issues as the emancipation of the peasantry, the renunciation of absolute monarchy in 1848, the drafting of the Constitution and extension of suffrage and the establishment of the Folketing in 1849.

Such, then, is the sophisticated use to which Grundtvig put the concept of historical continuity from a legendary antiquity, which attached to the documents of Anglo-Saxon, and the polemical use to which he put the poetic idiom and the poetic imagery – the picture language – in which he found them couched.

There is very much more that could be said on this subject. Grundvig's absorption of Anglo-Saxondom into the great complex of his other – and, of course, often far more eminent – preoccupations is surely one area of Grundtvig research in which advances wait to be made.

But I must move to some concluding thoughts. How far did Grundtvig succeed in building or persuading others to build the edifices he envisaged (those, at least, for the purposes of this paper, which were to rest in part upon Anglo-Saxon foundations or to be built to a blueprint at least in part Anglo-Saxon)? I mean, not simply his vision for Anglo-Saxon literature itself: that it should be a cultural element in the latter-day North especially in the enriching of language – "the blessed mother-tongue" as he called it[36] – and of

---

35. Very little attention has hitherto been paid to these compositions in Anglo-Saxon. I hope shortly to publish work in progress on the subject.

36. "Indledning" in *Bjowulfs Drape* (Copenhagen, 1820), p. lxxiv : His toil on the translation of *Beowulf* was, he said, "... et Arbeide, jeg dog i al Fald ei kan fortryde, da det har udvidet min Syns-Kreds, og gjort mig mere fortroelig med det velsignede Moders-Maal, hvis Bedste ogsaa jeg blev kaldet til at betænke" (... a labour which in any case I can never regret, since it has widened my horizons and made me more intimate with the blessed mother tongue, whose best interests I was called upon to consider as well).

literature and in the teaching of these to children;[37] and that it should be available in editions equipped with translation or paraphrase and polemical interpretative essay expounding its *relevance* for his larger didactic purposes.

I mean not simply all this, but also the greater visions of international awareness of a cultural – religious, ecclesiastical, economic and political – community within the North, arising at least in part from these foundations in Anglo-Saxondom. What of the objective so stirringly declared in his public lectures published as *Mands Minde*: " ... of all the great powers England is the one, both spiritually and temporally, to whom we wish all the good fortune that is consistent with the freedom of Greece and Scandinavia, and the one we must compete with to the best of our ability by removing all the bounds that impede our living industry"?[38] What of the same vision so movingly framed in his powerfully incipient *billed sprog*, his language of metaphor, in his verse preface to *Beowulfes Beorh* (1861), of the legendary and eponymous brothers Dan and Angul once more joining their brothers' hands across the North Sea?

That Grundtvig left a powerful following in Danish church-life, in scholarship and in the folk high schools; and that he indelibly imprinted his values upon the culture of modern Denmark there can be no disputing. But I hardly dare even begin to answer questions which move far afield from the study of literature[39] – though it is clear that any answer would have to include, alongside the evidence of more or less total failure in some respects, the history of modern relationships between Denmark and England within the context of the North Atlantic nations; consideration of both idealistic and practical aspects of Denmark's role in the Third World; not only the concept of the European Community but also the qualifications to that concept which are still evolving, with Denmark conspicuous among the shapers; and perhaps it should rightly include Denmark's self-exclusion from the Porvoo Declaration.

I end instead with an anecdote to remind us that Anglo-Saxon had meant much to Grundtvig, and indeed to his followers; an anecdote which also, at last, justifies my title, which you must then apply how you will:

A memoir of Grundtvig's last few days of life, by his old friend Frederik Hammerich, himself a scholar engaged in work upon "the oldest ecclesiasti-

---

37. This is an issue he takes up on various occasions, but notably, for the present context, within his preface to *Bjowulfs Drape* (Copenhagen, 1820), p. lii, where he commends the story for children's reading.
38. *Mands Minde* (1838), in Broadbridge and Jensen, *Anthology*, pp. 104-5.
39. I hope shortly to publish a collection of essays upon Grundtvig and Anglo-Saxondom which will give some attention to Grundtvig's immediate followers (one of whom was Frederik Hammerich, mentioned below) in the fields of Anglo-Saxon literature, history and spirituality, as well as to other issues discussed in this paper.

cal literature among the Gothic peoples"[40] (that is, Anglo-Saxon literature, in Grundtvig's classification and terminology),[41] may fitly serve here as a last word upon Grundtvig the Anglo-Saxonist.

Grundtvig, as is well known, had an old love for the Anglo-Saxons. Right from the start he was at home in their writings. He translated *Beowulf* and excerpts from Cæd-mon, both edited and translated *The Phoenix*, studied and transcribed their vellum co-dices on his English journeys, set forth plans in English for an edition of them and thereby drove and incited the English at last to get to grips with the rich remnants of antiquity. The last time he was at my place, the Wednesday (28.8.1872) five days be-fore he died, he had recently been sent a small English monograph on an Anglo-Saxon poem, "An ancient Saxon poem", by J. Earle.[42] [This is the poem now standardly titled *The Ruin*].

There was nobody in his immediate circle who could read it for him: his son, Pro-fessor S. Grundtvig, was away, and Professor Stephens[43] he had not found at home ... On the following Friday, three days before his death, I therefore went over to Tuborg to look at this small monograph and tell him what it contained ... I skimmed through the paper, gave him the main content and read some of it for him. There were no new things in it, except for the conjecture that the city in ruins which the old poet portrays so picturesquely could possibly be Bath. The poem, said Grundtvig, he knew well from Hickes' *Thesaurus*.[44] Amongst the rest I read for him its opening, which goes thus – I keep in translation as precisely as possible to the text: "Thou huge stone-wall, / top-pled by Fate! / shaken and riven / is the ring-wall's giant-work, / roofs gone, / towers

40. F. Hammerich, "Min sidste Samtale med Grundtvig" (My last conversation with Grundtvig) in *Danske Kirketidende* (1872), cols. 675-6; quoted in Johansen and Høirup, *Grundtvigs Erindringer*, pp. 262-63.
41. See "Indledning" in Bjowulfs Drape (Copenhagen, 1820): "Dansk, Norsk og Gothisk kalder jeg Siderne af Nordens historiske Trekant [p. liv] ... de Angel-Sachsiske Old-Sagn, som jeg kalder Gothiske ...[p. lv]" (Danish, Norse and Gothic I call the sides of the North's historical triangle ... the Anglo-Saxon ancient legends which I call Gothic ...).
42. J. Earle, "An Ancient Saxon Poem of a City in Ruins supposed to be Bath" in *Proceed-ings of the Bath Natural History and Antiquarian Field Club II* (1870-3), pp. 259-70; with text and literal translation.
43. George Stephens (1813-95), Professor of English and Anglo-Saxon in the University of Copenhagen. By this date, Stephens, a long-standing fellow Anglo-Saxonist for Grundtvig in Copenhagen, had published the first two volumes of his *Old Runic Mon-uments of Scandinavia and England* as well as (in 1860) the two leaves of an otherwise lost Anglo-Saxon manuscript of an epic poem *Waldere*, discovered in a book-binding in the Royal Library, Copenhagen.
44. George Hickes, *Linguarum veterum septentrionalium thesaurus grammatico-criticus et archaeologicus* (Oxford, 1703-5). Hickes' *Thesaurus* had been one of Grundtvig's earli-est sources of information on the survival of Anglo-Saxon manuscripts in English li-braries.

tottering, / the mighty gate-towers; / the masonry rime-encrusted, / shattered the bastions; / broken down, toppled all, / undermined / by the might of fire."[45]

"Yes," said Grundtvig, "here there's something of the grandiose, which the English have always had their strength in. Hearing this, you can't help coming to think of the whole of Anglo-Saxon literature for that is itself a truly proud ruin and so it can well be likened to the city in ruins that the old bard has sung of." We went on talking a bit about the Anglo-Saxons, and he gave me the poem to take home with me; so I left him, and had not the slightest suspicion that this was the last time I should see him in this life.

---

45. The Anglo-Saxon is: *Wrætlic is þ[æ]s wealstan wyrde gebræcon, / burgstede burston, brosnað enta geweorc, / hrofas sind gehrorene, hreorge torras hrungeat*. Oddly enough, though this was a poem enthused over by Thorpe (*Codex Exoniensis*, p. x) and plainly felt to be uniquely evocative by Grundtvig, it appears to be one of the very few omissions from Grundtvig's transcriptions of the Exeter Book in the Grundtvig Arkiv Fascicle 316, nrs. 1-8. When Hammerich here says that Grundtvig gave him the poem to take home with him, he must surely mean in context Earle's edition which they had just read together: but it is tempting to speculate that Grundtvig's original transcription is missing because it was given to someone such as Hammerich as a memento.

Grundtvig's "Education for Life" and the Cultural Challenge Facing the Baltic and Nordic Countries Today

By Gustav Björkstrand

In all probability we cannot fully understand how radical a change we have experienced in the Nordic countries and the Baltic Sea region during the last decade. Following the erection of the Iron Curtain after World War II, an event that broke the centuries-old natural links between peoples in the region, the 1990s have opened up an entirely new perspective. On the one hand, we have a clear orientation to the West and South in that Sweden and Finland have joined Denmark as members of the European Union. On the other hand, there is much talk of a Europe of regions and the Baltic constitutes one such natural region as it has since Viking and Hansa times. Who among us has pondered that Tallinn is not only Helsinki's but also Stockholm's nearest neighbouring capital? That the Danish flag waved above the battle of Volmer in Estonia in 1219 is well-known in Denmark but that is hardly the case when it comes to the fact that Riga was the second largest city during Sweden's period as a major power. Or how often is it recognized that Edith Södergran grew up in St. Petersburg with Russian, Swedish and German as daily languages before she moved to Raivola on the Finnish side of the border where she then became one of the Nordic countries' leading literary figures? Nor is it well-known that Icelandic literature today interests young people in Russia to an astounding degree.[1] The consequences of the political and cultural reorientation that we have embarked upon may clearly assume proportions at which we can only guess.

To relate Grundtvig to the Baltic region poses something of a problem. Denmark was for Grundtvig the focus of interest. It is not difficult to establish this if we take his important writings concerning the folk high school as our *point de départ*. Here we encounter *Det Danske Fiir-Kløver eller Danskheden partisk betragtet, Skolen før Livet og Academiet I Soer, Bøn og Begrep om en Dansk Højskole i Soer* and *Lykønskning til Danmark med det Danske Dummerhoved og den Danske Høiskole*.[2]

---

1. Cf. *Kulturens tredje pelare. Rekommendationer för det nordiska kultursamarbetet med Baltikum och nordvästra Ryssland*, Nordisk Ministerråd (Copenhagen, 1996), p. 1.

What will people say of the fact that *Danes* really try to create and spread among themselves a *Danish*, a national and patriotic education, which can both benefit and please
the entire people, from the highest to the lowest, and in every way bear desirable fruit
for good old *Denmark?*[3]

In truth, Grundtvig extends this perspective to cover the rest of the Nordic region, above all in his article *Om Nordens videnskabelige Forening*, in which he
makes a plea for discontinuing the four Latin universities and replacing them
with "a single Nordic university" that would put not only the universities in
Berlin, Göttingen and Wittenberg but also the giants in Paris, Oxford and
Cambridge in the shade. It is an absolutely fascinating picture that he paints
for his proposed university. At least 300 men would live for science and thus
– by means of their living interaction, a key concept for Grundtvig – would
become an honour, benefit and pleasure for the whole of humanity.[4]

Iceland also falls within Grundtvig's perspective. He speaks of the
mediaeval Nordic university in Iceland as being "without comparison in the
whole world".[5] But as far as I can see he passes over the Baltic countries and
Finland completely. Among the universities, he counts the older ones in Copenhagen and Uppsala and the newer ones in Lund and Kristiania but he
makes no mention of Åbo Akademi, which had newly burned down, or the
Alexander University founded shortly afterwards in Helsinki. Certainly he
could have referred to this, as I noted in my article *Grundtvig In Finland*, since
he was honoured with an appointment in 1834 as "foreign corresponding
member" of the Finnish Literature Society which had been founded in 1831.[6]
It is perhaps not so strange – as Roar Skovmand[7] has pointed out – that the
university library in Helsinki, which was otherwise well stocked, was slow to
acquire a single one of Grundtvig's folk high school writings and that for a
long time Grundtvig remained relatively unknown as a theologian in Finland. On the other hand, his importance for the Finnish folk high school
movement, which matured in the 1890s, was probably greater than in any
other country except Denmark.[8]

2. Grundtvig's works on the folk high school have been collected by K.E. Bugge,
    Grundtvigs skoleverden i tekster og udkast, I-II (Copenhagen, 1968).
3. Bugge, *Grundtvigs skoleverden*, II, p. 213.
4. Bugge, *Grundtvigs skoleverden*, II, pp. 134-41.
5. Bugge, *Grundtvigs skoleverden*.
6. G. Björkstrand, *Grundtvig i Finland – Grundtvigs oplysningstanker og vor tid*, Nordisk
    Folkehøjskoleråd (Jelling, 1983), p. 99; R. Skovmand, *Samspillet mellem Nordens
    Folkehöjskoler indtil Anden Verdenskrig*, Skrifter udgivet af Jysk Selskab for Historie, 41
    (Aarhus, 1983), p. 83.
7. Skovmand, *Samspillet*, p. 83.

Despite his strong Danish and general Nordic preoccupation Grundtvig, however, is the only person in the Nordic countries who has made any contribution of note to international educational development. This is rather surprising in view of the fact that Grundtvig did not actively teach for any length of time nor was he particularly familiar with international literature in the field of education. Consequently, he never developed a systematically thought-out educational programme. Nonetheless, throughout his life he took an enthusiastic interest in educational questions.[9] And the ideas that he put forward have proven to be of considerable importance even in quite different environments and times from those in which he himself lived. The explanation for this surely lies in the fact that in his work he addressed truly fundamental questions concerning the transmission of tradition, which means that his ideas have never gone out of fashion.

In various contexts K.E. Bugge has discussed Grundtvig's educational ideas and his view of an education for life, the theme of this paper.[10] Bugge sums up Grundtvig's views on upbringing in four points:

1) Emphasis on young people – as opposed to children.
2) Emphasis on oral teaching and not on book-learning.
3) Emphasis on the Danish-Norse cultural tradition instead of the classical Latin.
4) The linking of these ideas in some way with a Christian view of life.

When Bugge points out which of Grundtvig's ideas are relevant today, he selects three:

1) Grundtvig's ideas on freedom and responsibility.
2) Grundtvig's ideas on mutuality, that is, "living interaction".
3) Grundtvig's ideas of cultural identity.

After having been a supporter of a strong monarchy, Grundtvig became an advocate of freedom in all fields: in the church, in the school and in society.

---

8. G. Björkstrand, *Askov och finländska folkhögskolpionjärer – Kristen fostran i kyrka och skola*, Rapporter från Pedagogiska fakulteten, 6/1978 (Vasa, 1978), pp. 58-70. Cf. Skovmand, *Samspillet*, pp. 83-99.

9. K.E. Bugge, "Grundtvigs pædagogiske tanker" in *Grundtvig og grundtvigianismen i nyt lys* (Aarhus, 1983), p. 210; K.E. Bugge, "The School for life. The Basic Ideas of Grundtvig's Educational Thinking" in A.M. Allchin et al. (eds.), *Heritage and Prophecy. Grundtvig and the English-speaking World*, (Aarhus, 1993), p. 271. Concerning Grundtvig's educational ideas see also K.E. Bugge, *Skolen for livet. Studier over N.F.S. Grundtvigs pædagogiske tanker* (Copenhagen, 1965).

10. For the following see Bugge, "The School for life", pp. 271-80.

But freedom should be combined with responsibility for others, who must also be awarded freedom.

In Bugge's view living interaction cannot be seen as identical with dialogue or dialectics. Interaction contributes to illuminating human life. Dialogue has to have a dynamic perspective, dialectics a humane perspective.

Grundtvig's central concepts *folkelighed* and *historisk-poetisk* cannot really be translated. Education for life has to be *folkelig* in the sense that it must be true to life, true to a people's identity. This identity finds its expression in culture as a whole but above all in the people's history, myths and permanent values.[11]

By way of digression, I would like to underline the fact that *folkelighed* does not necessarily include an entire nation; it may also refer to part of a nation, for example the Swedish-speaking population in Finland. In a monograph *Den finlandssvenska folk-högskolan och allmogemobiliseringen* (The folk high school among the Swedish-speaking people in Finland and peasant mobilisation), I have tried to find the answer to the question of how it is that the densest frequency of folk high schools in the world is to be found just in the Swedish-speaking parts of Finland. There are 17 Swedish folk high schools in Finland, one for every 17,000 people. In a country with five million inhabitants this would mean approximately 300 schools. Folk high schools in Finland have emerged in three separate stages: 1. During the first period, 1891-1895, seven folk high schools were founded, evenly distributed throughout the Swedish-speaking parts of Finland. Their slogan was: against oppression. 2. The second period occurred in the years 1905-1908. It was at this time that Finland began electing a Diet with universal and equal franchise and it was a question of making people in Swedish-speaking regions aware of the importance of standing up for the Swedish language and Swedish culture. Once again seven schools were set up. 3. All the Swedish folk high schools that have been established since 1908 have been Christian schools and the ideological struggle has been against secularization.[12] The folk high school movement in Swedish Finland has, then, a strong stamp of *folkelighed* in a more restricted sense than is usually understood. It is encouraging to note that the same tendency exists in the Finnish-speaking population; in Finland the folk high schools did not become involved in language conflicts even in the most inflamed periods of lin-

11. Bugge, "The School for life," 1993, p. 279. Cf. H. Henningsen, "The Danish Folk High School" in A.M. Allchin et al. (eds.), *Heritage and Prophecy. Grundtvig and the English-speaking World*, (Aarhus, 1993), pp. 288-90.
12. G. Björkstrand, *Den finlandssvenska folkhögskolan och allmogemobiliseringen*, Kyrkohistoriska arkivet vid Åbo Akademi. Meddelanden 10 (Åbo, 1980, reprint 1981); G. Björkstrand, *Den svenska folkhögskolan – i kulturkampens tjänst – Frihed och anpassning. Hundra år av folkhögskolverksamhet i Finland*, Folkhögskolrörelsens jubileumsbok (Valkeakoski, 1989), pp. 79-85.

guistic differences. The explanation presumably lies in the fact that both forms of *folkelighed* could exist side by side.

But I shall now return to Bugge and his summary of Grundtvig's views on education. The question is how relevant these ideas of Grundtvig's are to the cultural challenges now facing the Nordic and Baltic countries as the Baltic Sea has once more, as in past centuries, become a uniting rather than a dividing element.

I should like to begin by establishing what general measures the Nordic countries have taken to meet this challenge. Since 1995 Nordic cooperation has been built on three pillars: the Nordic countries, the Nordic countries and Europe and the Nordic countries and their adjacent regions. Adjacent regions in this context meant not only the Baltic countries, even though this is the region we shall concentrate on, but also northwest Russia, including Kaliningrad, and Poland. If we look at the guidelines that the Nordic Council of Ministers has set up for its strategy concerning adjacent regions, we may note that the principal aims are:

1) to contribute to peace, security and stability in Europe.
2) to promote the development of democracy, a market economy, human rights and a sustainable use of resources.[13]

When it comes to the role of culture in achieving these aims, it is noted that well-functioning programmes of cultural exchange play a key role in furthering the development of democracy and political stability in the region. Culture can also act as a spearhead and battering ram in cooperation on a more general level.[14]

The information offices set up in the last decade play an important role in the achievement of the Nordic Council's aims. They are situated in Tallinn, Riga, Vilnius and now also in St. Petersburg, and they organise different cultural events, mediate cultural contacts in literature, film and art, arrange language courses and grant scholarships. In 1997 it was intended that 400 individual scholarships be awarded to civil servants, scholars, teachers, students and those active in non-profit-making organisations.[15] The Nordic Folk Academy in Gothenburg – a fruit, albeit somewhat belated, of Grundtvig's educational ideas – is constituted as a centre for the development of Nordic folk education and adult education and is an important resource in this respect.[16] In

---

13. *Arbetsprogram för Nordens närområden*, Nordisk Ministerråd (1997), pp. 3-5.
14. *Kulturens tredje pelare. Rekommendationer för det nordiska kultursamarbetet med Baltikum och nordvästra Ryssland*, Nordiska Ministerrådet (Copenhagen, 1996), p. 1.
15. *Arbetsprogram för Nordens närområden*, Nordisk Ministerråd (1997), pp. 13-14.
16. *Arbetsprogram för Nordens närområden*, Nordisk Ministerråd (1997), p. 27.

its general recommendations the Nordic Council of Ministers notes that cultural cooperation should be built on the principles of mutuality and equal participation. It should be guided by Nordic competence and Nordic know-how. It should be founded on the principle of networking and decentralization and be directed especially to weak, underdeveloped cultural areas. Furthermore, cooperation partners should be sought outside established structures of institutional cooperation.[17]

To what extent is it possible to discern the influence of Grundtvig's ideas on education for life in these aims and in the measures already taken?

First of all let me maintain that Grundtvig's ideas on education concerning *højskolen* have acquired a certain force in the Baltic countries during the 1990s. In answer to a questionnaire that I sent to the folk high school organisations in Denmark, Finland, Norway and Sweden prior to giving this paper it was interesting to discover that none of the organisations has taken steps to spread and put into practice the folk high school ideas. On the other hand, folk high schools themselves, especially in Denmark, Finland and Sweden, have had direct contacts and have thereby been wind in the sails of the folk high school movement in the Baltic countries.[18] It is hardly accidental that the current is from the bottom upwards and not vice versa, which is of course exactly the flow that Grundtvig aimed at in cultural life.[19]

A study undertaken in 1993 showed that about 20 percent of the Nordic folk high schools had had contacts with the Baltic countries. In the case of Denmark the figure was 23 percent, mainly with Estonia followed by Latvia and Lithuania. For Finland the percentage was as high as 38 (35 schools out of 92) but all contacts were with Estonia. The Norwegian folk high schools (20 percent) were interested in Estonia and Latvia, as was the case with Sweden (16 percent), which nonetheless also had contacts with Lithuania (two schools). The contacts were primarily in the form of study trips, participation in courses and conferences, and exchanges of teachers and students.[20] Folk high schools have been established principally in Estonia and Latvia, and they have specialised in particular fields. In Latvia, Kuldiga folk high school

17. *Kulturens tredje pelare. Rekommendationer för det nordiska kultursamarbetet med Baltikum och nordvästra Ryssland*, Nordisk Ministerråd (Copenhagen, 1996), pp. 4-16.
18. See, for example, *Baltic Dialogue*, no. 1, Nordic-Baltic Newsletter for Popular and Adult Education (1994).
19. E. Simon, *Grundtvigs syn på skola och kultur – Sorö och Göteborg – Grundtvig och folkupplysningen*, Nordiska Folkhögskolrådet (Odense, 1978), pp. 24-27. Cf. G. Björkstrand, *Folkhögskolan och antikulturen – Grundtvig och folkupplysningen, en samling artiklar som knyter an till N.F.S. Grundtvigs tankevärld*, Nordisk Folkehøjskoleråd (Odense, 1978), pp. 29-34.
20. *Baltic Dialogue*, no. 1, Nordic-Baltic Newsletter for Popular and Adult Education (1994).

has an ecological orientation, Ledurga has taken a special interest in art, while Rite and Aglona concentrate on life in a multicultural environment and on the Latvian language. In many cases the schools' activities are mainly in the form of courses of differing length since finance has proven a great problem.[21] Information about folk high school activity is provided on a continuous basis by the Nordic Folk Academy in Gothenburg through the magazine *Baltic Dialogue*, which has been published since 1994. While development has been rapid in the 1990s, it should also be remembered that in 1938-39 there were 15 active folk high schools in Latvia with 3,374 students, in effect more students than in the grammar/high schools at the time.[22] Seen in relation to this figure, only limited progress has been made if the aim is to re-introduce the folk high school as a real alternative in adult education.

If the new folk high school pioneers are asked why they wish to set up such schools in the Baltic countries, then the answer given by Marju Sarv, who works at the Alu Folk High School in Estonia is instructive. She believes that the folk high school can react more quickly to changes in society and to citizens' needs. Moreover, the folk high schools can do important social work of a preventive nature. At a time when there is little trust in political parties or movements, there is an obvious need for an institution which is not tied to political power and which can both teach people to fight for their rights and mould young people's characters so that a completely new generation of political leaders can emerge.[23]

To what extent can traces of the Grundtvig view of education for life in a broader perspective be detected in official Nordic documents? If, for example, we take the Nordic Council of Ministers' *Arbetsprogram för Norden näromrâden 1997* (Working programme for Nordic adjacent areas 1997) I did not find a single direct mention of folk high school cooperation. On the other hand, scholarships for education and research took up a large part of the budget. In the field of culture considerable sums are being invested in cultural festivals and media education. In this way it is hoped to contribute to democratic development based on stable Nordic values such as solidarity, the equality of the sexes, tolerance, openness, and the rule of law and order.[24]

In the document *Kulturens tredje pelare* (The third pillar of culture) guidelines are drawn up for future cultural cooperation. I have already reported

21. *Baltic Dialogue*, no. 1, Nordic-Baltic Newsletter for Popular and Adult Education (1997), pp. 8-10.
22. *Baltic Dialogue*, no. 1, Nordic-Baltic Newsletter for Popular and Adult Education (1997), p. 8.
23. *Baltic Dialogue*, no. 1, Nordic-Baltic Newsletter for Popular and Adult Education (1996). Cf. Antra Dukane's answer to the same question in the same magazine.
24. *Arbetsprogram för Nordens näromrâden*, Nordisk Ministerrâd (1997).

some of the principles in the document, which is founded on a conviction of the importance of cooperation between peoples for democratic development and on a strong interest in language as a bearer of culture. In identifying the target groups for these efforts, not only are mentioned journalists, authors, translators and other mediators of culture, but emphasis is also laid on the importance of initiatives on cultural work in schools and on youth exchanges.[25]

If we put this in relation to the principles emphasised by Bugge as characterising Grundtvig's thinking, we note that ideas of cultural identity, mutuality and living interaction, and of the importance of combining freedom and responsibility constitute a clear undercurrent in the documents when it comes to the Baltic. There is an obvious orientation towards young people in cooperative projects and also in the Nordic cultural tradition instead of an orientation towards Russia which has been so strong in past decades. To what extent these ideas can be traced back to Grundtvig and to what degree it is a question simply of a common Nordic cultural heritage is, of course, impossible to determine. For my own part I wish to stress that even if the importance of mutuality and equality between the Baltic countries and the Nordic countries is strongly underlined, it is clear that it is the Nordic countries that are implanting their basic view, instead of giving the Baltic peoples the resources with which to seek their own identity. Perhaps someone from the Baltic countries might claim that the Nordic countries are in fact laying a yoke on them!

This raises another question, namely the relationship between the Nordic countries and Europe. The cultural challenge of which we are in the midst affects not only Baltic-Nordic relations but also relations between the Nordic and Baltic countries and Europe and the European Union. Like Grundtvig we may well ask ourselves whether there is a risk that we shall once again come under the *"Romer-Aag"* in all its *"Skickelser*: som *Lænkerne I de Romerske Keiseres*, som *Krog-Kieppen I de Romerske Pavers*, og som *Riset I de latinske Skolmesteres Hand"* (the yoke of Rome in all its aspects: as the chains in the hands of the Roman emperors, as the croziers in the hands of the Roman popes and as the cane in the hands of the Latin schoolmasters).[26] I put the question even though I have myself been in favour of Finland joining the European Union. Is there a risk that the *folkelige* in northern Europe will fall victim to pressure from a pan-European and American culture, given the enormous flow of information that reaches us from that direction via television, films and telecommunication networks of different kinds? Here youth, oriented as they are towards the international and with their language skills, are in a special situa-

25. *Kulturens tredje pelare. Rekommendationer för det nordiska kultursamarbetet med Baltikum och nordvästra Ryssland*, Nordisk Ministerråd (Copenhagen, 1996), pp. 1-16.
26. Bugge, *Grundtvigs skoleverden*, I, p. 228.

tion. Is the national, the *folkelige*, necessary in an international environment? Do we lose something if we refrain from it or interpret it in an entirely new way in the European context and in relation to the rest of the world? And further: What role does our mother tongue play in cultural life? How can we create an identity of our own in our "new" Nordic countries with a pluralism of languages, cultures and nationalities? Has development in this respect overtaken the questions posed by Grundtvig?

In the Baltic countries Grundtvig's concept of culture and his view of education seem to play a role even if they are not always linked with him. People have found it important to create a strong national identity with the mother tongue as the principal factor. Stress is laid on safeguarding freedom, democracy and responsibility for future development. At the same time there is a strong trend towards enjoying the material fruits of the new order as quickly as possible, without stopping to think whether there might exist a connection between the Nordic welfare model and the ideology which has made it possible to develop such a system and put it into practice. At the same time there are efforts to join the European Union – for reasons of security rather than culture.

The situation in the Nordic countries is a complex one. I am not just thinking of the fact that Denmark, Finland and Sweden are members of the EU while the Faroes, Iceland and Norway remain outside. The whole of Nordic cooperation is hanging in the balance. It is true that at the sessions of the Nordic Council, leading Nordic politicians annually emphasise the importance of Nordic cooperation and, as has already been seen, careful plans for the future have been drawn up. In reality, however, eyes are on Brussels and the actual decisions made there. Carl Bildt has pointed out that the risk that the Nordic Council may become a reservation for increasingly irrelevant rhetoric has increased markedly. The feeling of fellowship that exists between the Nordic peoples and countries and their ability to work together flexibly should be transformed into political power. Paavo Lipponen was of the same opinion when he noted that Nordic cooperation has become non-binding almost to the point of self-destruction so that political commitment has been insufficient.[27] Both these leading politicians, who represent completely different political views, note, then, that Nordic cooperation is politically uninteresting at present. In the next breath it is noted that cooperation is positive and something needs to be done to make it more effective. The Nordic countries are dead. Long live the Nordic countries!

27. See K.-P. Mattsson, *Den europeiska integrationen; ett förnyet nordiskt samarbete och Baltikums ställning – nationalstaterna mellan öst och väst eller det nordiska samarbetet i EU-perspektiv*, Kansanopisto-Folkhögskolan nr. 6-7 (1995), p. 14.

The problem is made doubly difficult when decisions on the single currency have to be made as only Finland has joined the third stage of the European Monetary Union (EMU) from the beginning while the other Nordic countries remain aloof.

Nordic cooperation, Nordic culture and a largely common view of society do not depend on what leading political decision-makers do. Cooperation is so well developed and has such a comprehensive network in all sectors of society that it can very well continue even in the face of a completely new political situation. If the binding decisions are made in Brussels and not at Nordic meetings, it will create in the long run new cultural patterns and dependencies.

Can we imagine that in a distant, or even not so distant, future we will find ourselves in a situation where we are forced to turn back and seek our roots – our *Aand* (Spirit), our *folkelighed* (national identity) – when the wave of Europeanization and internationalization has washed over the Nordic and Baltic countries? This will not be the case if Grundtvig's ideas of education for life turn out to be time-bound.[28] But if there comes a time to cast aside what is experienced as the Roman yoke in the guise of false Europeanization and internationalization, then Grundtvig's prophetic views have really penetrated deeply into the very essence of human existence. Anyone who believes that this is so has of course reason to heed Grundtvig's voice and act accordingly.

28. On the question of the impact of Grundtvigianism in the third world see H.B. Hansen, "Grundtvig and the Third World. The Transfer of Grundtvig's Ideas to other Peoples and Cultures" in Allchin et al. (eds.), *Heritage and Prophecy*, pp. 299-322. Cf. E. Simon, *På sporet af national identitet: De nordiske lande som inspiration for Afrika – Grundtvig og folkupplysningen*, Nordisk Folkehøjskoleråd (Odense, 1978), pp. 104-22.

Adult Education in India: Relevance of Grundtvig

By Asoke Bhattacharya

India, a country with over 800 million people, bears the ignominious distinction of having half the world's illiterates, and, at the current growth rate, the population size will be of global concern in not too distant a future. When India achieved freedom 50 years back after nearly 200 years of foreign rule, thinkers and planners of the country were left with a host of problems to be addressed with unduly meagre resources. "Education for all" was voiced clear and loud but could not be accorded the priority it warranted and took a back seat in preference to economic developments through agricultural and industrial growth, infrastructure development, health and such. Input to education was limited to catering to the urbanised need for formal education – and even that was insufficient to cope with the growing demands. It was as late as 1988 that a countrywide comprehensive programme to eradicate illiteracy was seriously taken up and some of the regions could achieve success worth mentioning.

The present crisis should in no case be accepted as a pointer that India did not previously have an education system, folk and formal, or that there was previously no serious effort or experimentation in adult education. In fact Ashram-based education for the élite in society and orally-transmitted lore- and verse-based folk education have a distinguished history almost as old as the civilisation of mankind. But prolonged colonization not only prevented the growth of this culture but also led to its degeneration and destruction. Yet India produced a number of great personalities between the 18th and early 21st century who could weather the wrath of the colonial masters and who furthered the cause of education through the propagation of concepts and through efforts to expand educational facilities and experiments with novel ideas. However, all such efforts were individual or at best group activities and had only local bearing. An overview of such developments in Bengal, one of the leading States of India, is presented in the following pages to project a glimpse of the activities prior to the launching of the National Literacy Mission in 1988.

Raja Rammohun Roy and the *Brahmo Samaj*

Raja Rammohun Roy, born in 1774 and thus a contemporary of Grundtvig, earned the distinction of being the initiator of the Bengal Renaissance.[1] He was not only a great social reformer – he led a movement that culminated in the banning of suttee or widow-burning – but he was also the father of the modern Bengali language. Besides, due to his untiring effort, English language and education got introduced in India. Roy was also a great religious reformer who founded the *Brahmo Samaj* that sought to cleanse Hindu orthodox society of obnoxious practices. To understand and appreciate the real contribution of Roy it is necessary to remember that the British East India Company started its rule in India in 1757. When Rammohun Roy was a young man the euphoria of making money by any means resulted in the disappearance of all ethics and morality from urban society. In a bid to find favour among the English and other European settlers the *nouveaux riches* used to amass wealth through all sorts of unethical practices and spend it on grand feasts, betting, musical extravaganzas, brothel-visits and such. The so-called Bengali "Babu" culture had its origin there. The British, fearing that the natives might go against colonial rule if they intervened in their religious, educational or social "customs", turned a deaf ear to any call for progress or reform.

The state of education was alarming. According to a survey[2] conducted in 1801 by Hamilton, a Briton, there were large districts in which not a single primary school existed. As the rulers continued the administration of justice in Persian, there were a few *madrasas* which trained pupils in that language and Arabic. There were also a few *tols* where Hindus could learn Sanskrit. However, in actual practice these traditional schools were degenerated orthodox institutions and were opposed to all sorts of enlightenment in the society. There was hardly any institutionalised form of education in the country. In its absence the primary schools, *pathshalas*, which were founded mostly by half-educated people, became the only place of learning available in the community. Each household sending its wards to these schools had to pay fees in cash and kind. Wards from poor families were severely treated. They used to be caned, beaten and punished – the various forms of punishment could be the subject of a dissertation – upon the least pretext. Boys used to shudder at the very proposition of going to these schools. Raja Rammohun Roy was the foremost exponent of opening up the doors of education. With his direct involvement and support, on January 20, 1817, Hindu College, the

1.   Susobhan Sarkar, *Bengal Renaissance* (Calcutta, Dipayan, 1991), p. 12 (in Bengali).
2.   Shibram Shastri, *Ramtonoo Lahiri and contemporary Bengali Society* (Calcutta, Bishwabani Prakashan, 1983), p. 54 (in Bengali).

most important national institution, was established in Calcutta and grew to be the hotbed of the Bengal Renaissance that churned out the most progressive and revolutionary individuals over the centuries.

The same year European and Indian intellectuals founded the School Book Society.[3] Its members took earnestly the task of publishing textbooks in Bengali and English. Previously, missionaries like William Carey and Marshman had started a great intellectual activity in the Danish colony of Serampore.[4] There they translated the Bible into Bengali and other Indian languages. They also wrote books on Bengali grammar. These activities were of immense significance in the history of the development of the Bengali language.

By 1801 the British government had established a college at Fort William in Calcutta for training English civil servants in the language and custom of the local people. Need arose to translate and write books in Bengali. Ishwar Chandra Vidyasagar, the greatest social reformer after Rammohun – he successfully conducted a great social movement for widow remarriage – joined this institution and started writing Bengali texts for English students. His great literary activity gave the Bengali language its modern flavour. It may be interesting to note that in 1855 Vidyasagar wrote the most popular primer which is still used to teach children.[5]

With time the British began to appreciate the importance of modern education for the Indians. As shrewd colonial masters, their aim was not to universalise education but to create a small section of upstarts who would act as buffer between the British masters and the people of India. In 1857 the University of Calcutta was established.

However, as early as the 1870s Keshub Chandra Sen, one of the leaders of the *Brahmo Samaj* and himself a great social and religious reformer, started a host of activities. He inspired his disciples to take up publishing low-priced books to popularise Bengali literature and initiated movements against drinking, for the establishment of schools for the toiling masses, for the education of women and for the promotion of charitable work.[6] Thus Keshub Chandra Sen can be considered the pioneer of adult education in India.

3. Susobhan Sarkar, *Bengal Renaissance*, p. 23.
4. Sri Pantha, *When the printing press arrived* (Calcutta, Bangiya Sanskriti Sammelan, 1977), p. 13 (in Bengali).
5. Biman Basu, *On Vidyasagar* (Calcutta, Bangiya Saksharata Prasar Samity, 1991), p. 415 (in Bengali).
6. Shastri, *Ramtonoo Lahiri*, p. 203.

Rabindranath Tagore

Rabindranath Tagore was born in 1861 to an illustrious family of Bengal. His father Debendranath revived the *Brahmo Samaj* movement after the death of Raja Rammohun Roy, whose principal associate Dwarakanath was Rabindranath's grandfather.

Rabindranath hailed from a large joint landlord family and was brought up by many servants and maid-servants. It was from them that Tagore learnt the stories of the Indian epics – the Ramayana and Mahabharata. Tagore had a lasting impression from the wisdom of these illiterate people, just as Grundtvig learned from his nurse, Malene, how great the contribution was of common people to the culture of a nation.[7]

Tagore was admitted to a normal school in his early childhood. Here his experience showed a marked parallel with that of Grundtvig. The uncouth teachers used vulgar language in the classrooms. They were rude and rough with the children. Tagore expressed his displeasure about teachers in later years by portraying some of his well-known characters in the short stories drawing on his childhood memory. He was equally disgusted with the host of private tutors who had the uncanny ability to turn unique literary pieces into most uninteresting subject-matter. Tagore changed schools a number of times over the years until finally he ceased going to school at all. Thus the greatest Indian of the 20th century, on whom at a later date many institutions from all over the world conferred honorary doctorates, did not possess even a school leaving-certificate.

However, by great insight Tagore understood the malaise of the prevalent Indian education system. He came to espouse the view that the mother tongue should be the only vehicle of imparting real knowledge. In a colonial set-up, education through English would produce an English-speaking élite isolated from society. It is well-known that Grundtvig held the same view regarding the medium of instruction.[8]

Tagore wrote a number of articles on education in his late 20s. These writings were widely accepted by the Indian intelligentsia for their thought-provoking arguments against many aspects of the colonial education system. In an article on education written in November 1892,[9] he expressed his opposition to learning by rote in order to cross the hurdle of examination. He also

7.   A.M. Allchin, *N.F.S. Grundtvig, An Introduction to his Life and Work* (Aarhus, Aarhus University Press, 1997), p. 27.
8.   Niels Lyhne Jensen et al. (eds.), *A Grundtvig Anthology. Selections from the Writings of N.F.S. Grundtvig (1783-1872)* (Cambridge, Clarke and Viby, Centrum, 1984), p. 74.
9.   Satyendranath Roy, *Thoughts of Tagore (Education)* (Calcutta, Granthalaya, 1985), p. 65 (in Bengali).

pointed out the utter futility of learning through a foreign language, marked by the absolute absence of imagination in the child.

In his early 40s Tagore thought of developing a system of education in line with the ancient Indian tradition of Brahmacharya where a student would be educated in harmony with nature in the residence of the guru, away from the affluence and distraction of city life. One could find the echo of Kold[10] in the Tagorean scheme. Tagore founded the *Brahmacharyashram* – the school – at Shantiniketan in 1901.

In a concurrent article Tagore emphasised the need to organise country fairs which would bring together entrepreneurs and consumers to bridge the gap between people's needs and innovative solutions and thus to give rise to a national awakening and self-reliance.

Tagore always believed in sustainable development. He felt that development could be brought about not from above but by the effort of each individual dedicated to a national cause. He despised big talk and little action. In 1905 a great political movement took shape against the partition of Bengal. In this period of political turmoil the British government issued a number of black circulars to restrain the students of schools and colleges from joining this movement.[11] To protest against these repressive measures, some educationists contemplated developing what was termed national education, through establishment of national schools; and the idea was mooted of establishing a National University. Many national schools were organised at various locations in Bengal. Tagore was fully supportive of these ideas although he doubted how many of these mushrooming institutions would stand the test of time.

During the movement for restoration of unity to Bengal, Tagore started his own movement for self-reliance. He took a number of measures in his estate in this direction. He firmly believed that in a country like India, with an overwhelmingly large rural population, self-reliance of the rural people was the most important weapon for achieving self-sufficiency. In 1905 he founded a cooperative rural bank with the participation of local peasants. It may be pointed out that cooperative concepts had not yet gained ground in India. He also started a night school for adults in a village of "untouchables".

The movement for repealing the partition of Bengal also witnessed widespread boycotting of British goods. Tagore felt that without a viable alternative the movement would fizzle out. He therefore started a school for the revival of the Bengal handloom. All these programmes were to be incorporated

10. Thomas Rørdam, *The Danish Folk High-Schools* (Copenhagen, Det Danske Selskab, 1980), p. 42.
11. Prabhat Kumar Mukhopadhyay, *Tagore's Life and Works*, Volume II (Calcutta, Vishva Bharati Granthanbibhag, 1989), p. 174 (in Bengali).

in the Visvabharati University which came into being later. In 1907 under a village improvement programme he took the initiative in the construction of roads, the digging of ponds, the clearing of bushes and such. He believed that *Swaraj* (self-rule) called for all these and also for a raising-up of the so-called lower strata of society. His activities in regard to development of village infrastructure, formation of cooperatives, introduction of labour-saving machinery in agriculture, development of diverse cottage industries, diversification of agriculture and such earned the wrath of the British colonial administration against his *Brahmacharyashram* at Shantiniketan. A circular was issued to restrain government servants from sending their wards to his school.

In 1913 Tagore received the Nobel Prize for literature. He kept the prize money (£8,000) in the cooperative rural bank he had created, in order to boost the local economy and help the development work which was being carried out in the rural community.

In 1916 Tagore initiated a village development programme in his estate in North Bengal.[12] His scheme consisted of:

1) Improvement of health and hygiene of the rural people with measures to treat the ailing in the village itself.
2) Organisation of the village library.
3) Construction of roads, digging of ponds and wells and clearing of bushes.
4) Protection of peasants from money-lenders.
5) Resolution of local disputes through negotiations.

These programmes had a direct relationship to his own scheme of things at Shantiniketan. His concept of Visvabharati evolved out of his concept of development. In all other countries, he wrote, education had a link with the life of the people. Only in colonial India, he lamented, was education linked up with qualifying for a waged livelihood. Where the peasants were producing, where the oilseeds were being crushed, where the potter's wheel moved, our education did not reach there. The reason was that our universities did not have any root in our soil. If we really had a national university, this would utilise its knowledge in such areas as economics, agriculture and health, for the development of the village and the people residing there. This university would employ superior methods in agriculture, animal husbandry and cottage industries, and would develop economic self-sufficiency through cooperation. All these would bind together the students, teachers and the local community. He declared that Visvabharati, established in 1918, would be such. And he realised these ideals when on February 6, 1922, he established the Rural Reconstruction Wing at Visvabharati.

12. Mukhopadhyay, *Tagore's Life*, p. 568.

Tagore's concept of a national university developed through his visits to different countries of the world and not least through his visits to Sweden and Denmark. He first visited Denmark on May 21, 1921. On his arrival at Copenhagen Railway Station he was given a warm reception; and two days later, after he had addressed the students at the University, they followed him to his hotel in a candlelight procession. He met the Danish philosopher Harald Høffding (1843-1931) on this visit. He also went to see the ailing literary critic Georg Brandes (1842-1927) at his residence. There is no doubt that these visits made Tagore aware of the strides the Danes had achieved in the field of education and development. There is another significant Danish connection which might have made Tagore conversant with Denmark. Amiya Chakraborty, Tagore's secretary for many years, had married a Danish lady named Sigurd who later adopted the Indian name Haimanti.[13] She came to India from Europe with Tagore's family in 1926 and married Amiya in December 1927. Tagore again visited Denmark in 1930 to attend the conference of the New Education Fellowship at Elsinore.

It may be pointed out here that even before he visited Denmark he was aware of the Danish contribution in the field of cooperation. In an article on cooperation in 1918 he referred to the cooperative method adopted in the Danish dairy industry which, he said, went a long way towards alleviation of poverty of the rural people in that country.[14] However, the later visits and direct connection with Danish intellectuals definitely enlightened him more about Denmark.

Post-independence era

At the dawn of independence some great Indian thinkers were engaged in preparing a document under the aegis of the University Education Commission to serve as a guideline for a national education policy.

The University Education Commission had its tenure of existence from December 1948 to August 1949. Members of this Commission included Dr. S. Radhakrishnan, Dr. Meghnad Saha and Dr. Zakir Hussain. All of them were leading lights of the pre-independence period and adorned high positions in the post-independence period. Radhakrishnan was the first Vice-President of the Indian Republic. He later became President. Dr. Zakir Hussain also became President of India. Dr. Meghnad Saha was a renowned physicist and a member of the Parliament. All three were intimately connected with the Indian Freedom movement.

---

13. Mukhopadhyay, *Tagore's Life,* Vol. III, p. 406 (in Bengali).
14. Satyendranath Roy, *Thoughts of Tagore (Native Land)* (Calcutta, Granthalaya, 1989), p. 189.

In their report the members observed at the very outset that with the adoption of the new Indian constitution the achievement of democracy had only barely begun. Fundamental changes of attitude "will be necessary before what is written on paper can become the prevailing way of life. One of the points at which democracy will fail or succeed is in the kind of education which will be made available to the common people". Thus there is no doubt that the founding fathers of independent India considered education to be of utmost importance and to be ultimately linked with the success or failure of democracy. Here we hear the echo of Grundtvig's thought on the eve of the transition of Denmark from absolute monarchy to democracy. The report continues: "Even after a vast extension of basic education, a large proportion of Indian rural boys and girls may not attend formal school beyond the seven or eight years of basic education. How after that, they will enter into the life of the nation, is not only important to them but may determine whether or not democracy becomes a reality in India. The university and especially the rural university, has a vital relation to this problem. To indicate what that relationship may be, and how the university may contribute to the further education of this great majority of the Indian people, is essential to an understanding of the right place and work of the rural university." Do we not hear the echo of thoughts of Tagore? There is no doubt that Tagore's Sriniketan (the Rural Reconstruction Wing of Visvabharati) is at the back of these observations. "For helpful guidance in this matter", the authors continue, "we may turn to the programme of the People's Colleges of Scandinavian countries, especially to those of Denmark. Sir Richard Livingstone, England's foremost figure in adult education, called the Scandinavian People's College the only great successful experiment in educating the masses of a nation." Thus the introduction comes to the gateway of the Danish folk high school.

"When the People's College movement was initiated in Denmark, a century ago," the report continues, "the Danes were a defeated, poverty-stricken, largely unschooled, privilege-ridden and dispirited people. In considerable degree, as a result of the People's College movement the Danish people have risen from ignorance and poverty to about the highest general level of education and well-being. Their social legislation has been sane and liberal. Danish agricultural practice has changed from a primitive state to among the most scientific and best organised in the world. All this change has been brought about with an increase rather than a loss, of the human element."[15]

These observations are of paramount importance for India. Comparisons are often made with our neighbour China though we tend to forget that

15. Asoke Bhattacharya, *Empowering the Neoliterates: Relevance of Danish Folk High-School and Cooperative Movements for Adult Education in India* (Calcutta, Raktakarabee, 1994), pp. 108-27.

China and India have two different systems of government. In a recent study made by Dreize and Sen the authors favourably compare the achievements of Kerala, a state in India, in such fields as literacy, population growth and health care, with those of China. They lay stress on the persuasive element inherent in the Indian system. In the same vein it can be argued that comparison with many Western countries – England or France for example – often offers very little for emulation in the Indian context.

It is to their credit that the authors of the report under consideration took note of Denmark and her methods. "The part which the People's Colleges have played in this transition", the report continues, "is suggested by the fact that a third of the rural people attend them, while another third come under their direct influence. More than 30 percent of the members of the national legislature, and 80 percent of the cooperative leaders in a country where cooperatives play a dominant economic role were educated at the People's Colleges rather than at the universities."

"A paraphrase of a recent description of the philosophy and method of the Danish People's college", say the compilers of the document, "will indicate how it might suit Indian conditions and how the rural university could further its development." As for the role of democracy, the authors assert, "while democracy requires well qualified men and women in positions of importance and authority yet Government by and for the people requires also that fine resources of culture, leadership and wisdom shall be maintained with good distribution throughout the population. The ranks and file of men have often been deprived of their best elements and potential leadership as a result of a typical attitude toward democracy, which is not that it eliminated privilege but that it gives everyone an equal chance to get ahead of others in the competition to escape from the mass of men and join the more privileged classes". This appreciation of democracy may help us understand the following observation of the authors: "Important as it is to keep open avenues of development for the specially gifted, society has an even more fundamental need. In leavening bread we do not aim to have the gas escape from the mass and rise to the top, but rather we desire to trap the gas in small bubbles all through the dough, so that the entire mass will rise with uniform light texture. Our ideal for the gifted person among the common people, that he shall escape in an environment of culture and economic privilege, results in his leaving behind a yet more sodden mass of uninspired and unenlightened people. With this prevailing ideal, the very equality of opportunity of a political democracy accelerates the tendency towards a population composed of subject masses and ruling classes. For a continuing democracy it is essential that our programme of liberal education shall not promote the escape from the common people of the culture which that education generates, but shall inspire able students to remain common people, in and of the people, acting as their servants and leaders and raising the whole social lump."

Deliberating on who should be recipients of liberal and vocational education the authors contend: "The chief issue is not where young people come from to get an education, but where they go with an education." The authors did not touch the problem of brain-drain as it was not so acute at that time. However, they were aware of the exodus from the rural to the urban, from a place with less developed infrastructure to a place with more developed infrastructure. They wrote: "Democracy requires leadership steadfastly loyal to the whole people. Throughout history the people's cause has often been lost by leadership becoming estranged from and even turning traitor to the people, though often it has only recently emerged from the common people. The philosophy of rule by an intellectual élite, which characterised Plato, was the object of criticism by Bishop Grundtvig, originator of the Danish People's College. He wrote: People in our day shout themselves hoarse about freedom and culture, and that is certainly what we need, but the proposals of attaining them usually have the same fundamental faults as Plato's *Republic* where the guardians of freedom and culture themselves swallow them both up, so that people for all their labour get only proud tyrants to obey, to support, and if that can comfort them, to admire and deify."

"Leadership which cannot express itself in the shoes of the common man is rather rulership than leadership. Was not that Gandhiji's message?" the document reads. "How to achieve intellectual discipline and culture which give quality to leadership, and yet to maintain identity with the common people, is a problem which seldom has been solved. Because the Danish People's College has contributed greatly to the solution … the rural university may make a significant contribution to its solution here."

The intention, realisation, conception and direction of educating the mass thus did not lack intellectual fervour. But governmental support remained limited to consolidation and expansion of the educational infrastructure inherited from the British. Educating the masses for gainful economic and social development was low in priority. However, sporadic efforts continued. National bodies like the Adult Education Directorate were formed. Many policies and directives were enunciated in the following years. But strangely enough nowhere was the Danish experience referred to, and in 1983 the bicentenary of Grundtvig was totally ignored at the national level though a few universities observed the occasion with the solemnity and grace it deserved.

In 1988 a countrywide movement, the National Literacy Mission,[16] was launched with the aim of educating a targeted age group within a specified time-frame through involvement of people from a cross-section of society and of social and socio-political organs existing in the country. States like

---

16. Asoke Bhattacharya and Tandra Mitra (eds.), *Role of Universities in Post-Literacy Continuing Education* (Calcutta, Jadavpur University, 1995), pp. 1-10.

Kerala and West Bengal achieved phenomenal success – so much so that Kerala was declared a totally literate State and many districts of West Bengal were conferred full literate status. But this movement has already started to show signs of withering because of some inherent shortcomings in its conceptualisation. The role of post-literacy continuing education in integrating the neoliterate mass into the mainstream of improvement of the quality of life has been well demonstrated.[17] The present movement in India could not break the shackles of the colonial concept of linking education with income-generation only. The post-literacy movement thus requires a major shake-up, and the need for an ideological turn-about is urgently felt. It is at this juncture that analysis of the activities of Danish folk high schools and co-operative system assumes immense importance, as the only successful movement to achieve popular enlightenment carried out anywhere in the world in the democratic way is the Danish experiment. India, the largest democracy in the world, therefore, can find the Danish experience and the ideas and contribution of N.F.S. Grundtvig in relation to people's enlightenment highly relevant. However, one cannot deny the wide differences between 19th-century Denmark and 20th/21st-century India. The multi-ethnic, multicultural, multilingual background of India may not apparently provide fertile soil for adopting any imported ideology. But who can deny the unity in diversity prevalent in India? Moreover, it would be foolish to argue that great thinkers would be confined in their thoughts and practices within the four walls of a geographical location. Had it been so, Lincoln and Jefferson, Gandhi and Tagore, Jesus and Buddha would have remained confined within narrow boundaries. The history of ideas does not corroborate this view. Buddha's non-violence became a political weapon in Gandhi's hand. Christianity spread from the Middle East to Europe and America. Similarly, given a chance, Grundtvig's thinking might prove extremely useful for India.

A comparative study of the educational philosophies of Tagore and Grundtvig would reveal that both these thinkers hated prevailing educational systems – so much so that Tagore could not pursue his studies in the conventional mode and became a drop-out. Both these thinkers thought profoundly as to how education could be made relevant to life. Tagore even tried to implement his philosophy at Visvabharati. Though Grundtvig never succeeded in establishing the Academy at Sorø, his contemporaries took useful suggestions from him in order to implement his ideas in the folk high schools. This comparison will throw light on why Grundtvig's ideas had takers throughout Scandinavia and beyond. Tagore achieved considerable success in his own University but could not spread the message further. As both thinkers had their cups filled with success and failure, we can think of a syn-

17. Bhattacharya and Mitra (eds.), *Role of Universities*, pp. 1-10.

thesis in which the best of Grundtvig and of Tagore could be taken up and implemented.

Some International Varieties of Grundtvig Inspiration

By K.E. Bugge

In 1992, the management of the Grundtvig Museum (Grundtvigs Minde-stuer) in Udby decided to produce a world map illustrating the world-wide spread of Grundtvig's ideas. Hung up upon a wall and furnished with small coloured dots and a few photos this map would enlighten the visitors about where traces of Grundtvig influence were to be found internationally. The idea of producing such a map was inspired by a similar map composed by Svend Erik Bjerre and exhibited at the Museum of National History at Frederiksborg Castle in 1983, the year of Grundtvig's bicentenary.[1] Shortly afterwards, Nornesalen, the new research center in Ollerup under the man-agement of Dr. Lilian Zøllner, decided to launch a series of studies of Grundtvig's influence in countries outside Scandinavia. Consequently the two institutions, the Grundtvig Museum and Nornesalen, very sensibly de-cided to cooperate in the implementation of the two closely related projects.

During 1992-93 two young assistants working at Nornesalen, Birgitte Ingsø Laursen and Brian Lorentzen, established an extensive and updated collection of materials. The collection comprises letters and interviews, re-ports from the International Committee of the Association of Danish Folk High Schools, newspaper clippings, articles from certain periodicals, espe-cially *Højskolebladet*, extracts from books and finally maps showing the exact location of institutions mentioned in the material. My own research during this period was limited to the investigation of other literary sources, mainly books on the folk high school movement. The idea was that from 1995 on-wards the two projects should become ever more closely coordinated.[2]

The project initiated by the two institutions has proved to be much more complicated than originally envisaged. The aim of this brief introduction to the project is to put on record some of our problems in order that we may re-ceive some advice and some feedback on our tentative conclusions. Space does not allow me to enter into much detail. Let me then outline some of the problems[3] we have encountered:

---

1. Povl Eller, *Grundtvig og Danmark. Exhibition Catalogue* (Hillerød, The Museum of Na-tional History Frederiksborg, 1983), pp. 88-90.
2. The lecture upon which this paper is based was given in 1994.

I. What kind of "traces" should we be looking for?

"Traces" of Grundtvig's influence could be:
1) Grundtvigian congregations and churches
2) Folk high schools
3) Other educational institutions
4) Cooperative movements
5) Books and articles by individual authors, who do not represent a specific institution or movement, but who are writing more generally on Grundtvig and his ideas
6) Elements in certain nationalist movements.

The possibilities are indeed manifold. For practical reasons, in order to reduce the scope of our investigation to manageable proportions, we decided to limit our investigation to folk high schools and to educational institutions closely related to these. However, in situations where for example a Grundtvigian church or congregation has constituted the basic context for the founding of a folk high school, then of course such information should be briefly presented. This applies for instance to the early folk high schools in North America and in Argentina.

II. Should previous but no longer existing institutions be recorded?

It is well-known that in Poland, the United States and Canada quite a number of folk high schools existed for a short period of time and have since been closed. It is our good fortune that new information continues to be uncovered concerning earlier initiatives of institutions that once had notable influence but are no longer existent. An example of such recently presented information is the article by A.M. Allchin on a folk high school movement in Wales during the first half of the 20th century.[4]

However interesting such new information may be, we have found it necessary in this respect as well to reduce our project to manageable proportions. The resources for extensive new historical research are simply not available. Therefore we have decided to focus mainly on the situation of the present day. Previous initiatives will be recorded only insofar as such information is necessary to understand the present situation.

3.   Some of the problems and conclusions have been briefly discussed in the introduction to the book by Lilian Zøllner, *Grundtvig's Educational Ideas in Japan, The Philippines and Israel* (1995).
4.   A.M. Allchin, "Grundtvig and Nationalism in Wales" in *Grundtvig Studier* (1992).

III. Which geographical areas should be investigated?

As already briefly mentioned, we decided to concentrate on countries outside Scandinavia. There are two reasons for this decision:

a) The history and present situation of the folk high schools in Scandinavia has been thoroughly and recently described, for example by Erica Simon, Roar Skovmand and others.[5]

b) It is of crucial importance that the development of folk high schools in the Third World is recorded now, while the written sources are still available. Due to the well-known difficulties pertaining to the maintenance of libraries and archives (for example insufficiency of funds, humidity, termites) in these parts of the world, such sources may disappear within a very short span of time.

IV. Are we actually talking about a Grundtvig inspiration?

During the recording process we have now and then had some difficulty in recognising the educational institutions we have encountered as expressions of Grundtvig's ideas. According to our knowledge of Grundtvig's original vision and our familiarity with the Danish folk high schools, the distinctive characteristics of the Grundtvig tradition can be summarized as follows:

a) The folk high schools are *residential colleges*, where students and teachers learn to live and to work together.

b) The folk high schools cater to the *adult* population.

c) The main purpose of the folk high schools is to offer an opportunity for life-enlightenment (*Livsoplysning*), that is, to offer an opportunity to study and discuss the fundamental question of what it means to be a human being. Consequently the folk high schools offer no courses for the attainment of specific qualifications which can be documented through examinations. In Denmark a certain relaxation of this stance has been observed in recent years. The main principle is, however, still adhered to.

---

5. Erica Simon, *Réveil national et culture populaire en Scandinavie* (Paris, 1960); Roar Skovmand, *Samspillet mellem Nordens Folkehøjskoler indtil Anden Verdenskrig* (Århus, 1983); Thomas Rørdam, *The Danish Folk High Schools*, 2nd ed.(Copenhagen, 1980).

d) Usually the *time-span* of these courses is approximately half a year. When shorter courses are now and then offered, they are usually considered to be a supplement to the normal, longer courses.

Studying the material now available we have discovered that:

– some of the institutions, for example in Israel, are not residential colleges.
– some of the institutions, for example in India, cater only or primarily to teenagers and are in this respect more closely related to our Danish *Efterskoler* than to the folk high schools.
– some of the institutions studied, for example educational establishments in Nigeria and Japan, are primarily geared to vocational training courses or high-level academic studies and are more or less integrated into an official examination system.
– some of the initiatives, for example in Canada, offer a series of short courses covering a few days, a week or at the most a fortnight.

After careful deliberation we have decided to register these initiatives as new types of Grundtvig inspiration, ones in which his ideas have been modified on certain points in compliance with the necessities of a socio-economic situation or with an indigenous cultural tradition.

The conclusive arguments in favour of this decision were:

1) It would be an expression *of cultural imperialism* to expect all people throughout the world to interpret Grundtvig's ideas in exactly the same way as we have done.

2) "Facts are stubborn things." This expression, which Grundtvig had heard in England, was often quoted by him. It is not only a fact that several of the educational initiatives recorded deviate from Grundtvig's ideas on important points. It is also a fact that the people involved claim both to be inspired by Grundtvig and to be working in accordance with his ideas.

3) It is a fundamental point in Grundtvig's educational thinking that the School for Life envisaged by him should be *folkelig*. In other words, it should always reflect the cultural identity of a particular people. Furthermore, it should respond to the challenges of a particular historical and political situation. Striking illustrations of such responses are the Highlander Research and Education Center of Myles Horton in the USA and the folk high schools currently developing in the Philippines.

These have been some of the most important points in our mutual discussions on the basic principles of the investigation in hand. Let me mention some supplementary issues which have caught my personal interest in connection with our research project.

V. Patterns of dissemination

Through which channels have Grundtvig's ideas become known in countries outside Scandinavia? Five main patterns have emerged:

1) In their endeavour to preserve their Danish cultural heritage Danish emigrants to North and South America have among a number of institutions also established folk high schools.

2) Non-Danish educators in foreign countries have read or heard about Grundtvig and have subsequently visited Denmark in order to gain a personal insight into the folk high school movement. Then on their return they have implemented these ideas in their own countries. Examples of this type of Grundtvig tradition are numerous. Let me from the post-war era just mention the works of Erica Simon from France and Paul Röhrig from Germany.

3) Over the years some persons working within the Danish folk high school movement have felt a special responsibility to act as ambassadors for Grundtvig in foreign countries. An outstanding example of this type of dissemination is the lifelong activity of Peter Manniche, the former principal of The International People's College in Elsinore.

4) Some present-day educators in non-Scandinavian countries pick up and revitalise an older tradition, which for political reasons has been broken for a very long time. At the present time this pattern is recognizable in the Baltic states, which were isolated from the rest of the world through more than 40 years of Soviet occupation.[6] To some extent this also applies to the German folk high schools after the period 1933-45.

6. See, concerning Estonia, Jiiri Uljas, *On the Historical Background of Estonian Voluntary Associations* (Tallinn, Folk Culture Center of Estonia, undated but 1992-93); and, concerning Latvia, Ingrid Sokolova, "Grundtvig and Latvia" in *Grundtvig Studier* (1993), pp. 39-46.

5) Finally the possibility of an indirect influence from Grundtvig's ideas has been encountered. In this respect some German "Heimvolkshochschulen" provide an example. In the former Federal Republic of Germany more than 40 such institutions are functioning today. According to Dr. Norbert Vogel, who has meticulously studied the history of the German Grundtvig reception, some of the last links in this chain of tradition may, however, be inspired by the model of older German institutions rather than by Grundtvig and the Danish folk high schools.[7] Another example of indirect inspiration is the institution for adult education founded in Ethiopia by representatives of the folk high school movement in Sweden. Concerning these two examples from Germany and Ethiopia it might be appropriate to borrow a phrase from nuclear physics and speak of a spiritual "chain-reaction".

VI. The phenomenon of immunity to Grundtvig's ideas

Some countries seem to have been almost immune to Grundtvig's ideas. Why? Must it continue to be so?

Although exceptions are to be found, it seems to be a general rule that Southern Europe, the former Soviet Union and the Muslim World are major geographical areas that in the past have been remarkably resistant to influence from Grundtvig's ideas. In these cases, we are dealing with countries dominated by strong ideologies such as Roman Catholicism, Russian Communism and Islam. However, at the present time we are witnesses to some interesting breaks in this general pattern. In the Philippines, where the Roman Catholic Church enjoys a strong position, the folk high school movement is now gaining momentum. In St. Petersburg in Russia, a folk high school was established in 1993.[8] And in the Muslim country Bangladesh five folk high schools have been established during the 1980s and the early 1990s.[9]

In all these cases the driving force behind the initiatives has been the need for an alternative education of a free, voluntary and democratic nature. The main difficulty these new institutions are facing is the obvious fact that Roman Catholicism, Russian Communism and Islam are deeply ingrained in the *folkelighed* – that is, in the cultural identity – of these countries. This fact poses a serious challenge to these interesting new initiatives. However, an opening may be provided by reform movements within these traditions.

7.   Personal communication from Norbert Vogel, dated November 16, 1992.
8.   As reported in the daily newspaper *Politiken*, March 27, 1993.
9.   Bjørn Hamre, "Højskoledrømme mellem Grundtvig og den bangalske virkelighed" in Anna Bojsen-Møller et al. (eds.), *Vartovbogen* (Copenhagen, 1994), pp. 33-44.

VII. The language of discourse

My final reflection concerns the vocabulary employed in our discussions of the spread of Grundtvig's ideas. Quite a few different terms have been used to describe this process. The vocabulary can be categorised in three main groups:

1) Early in the post-war era the term *export* was frequently in use.[10] The idea was that just as factories, washing machines and Coca-Cola were deemed beneficial to the modernization of the non-Western world, similarly the export of the folk high school idea was judged to be Denmark's special responsibility. Basic to this line of thinking was the conviction that such export articles could be transferred to other parts of the world and function there in the same way as in Denmark. This kind of language was clearly derived from the economic and technological context of development aid programmes.

2) In the late 1960s another type of language became predominant. The background was the experience gained: that the transfer of ideas is a much more delicate and complicated affair than the export of machinery. This realization was succinctly expressed by Dr. Kachi Ozumba from Nigeria: "Carbon copies of the Grundtvigian ideas and the Folk Highschool idea never work."[11] In view of this development, the term "adaptation"[12] was found to be more appropriate. But also a kind of gardener language emerged. The seed of the folk high school idea should be planted in foreign soil. Or the vigorous branch of the Danish idea should be grafted into the stem of a foreign culture. Inherent in this type of language was a dawning realization that the final outcome of such a process might in some ways be something different from what we had known before.

3) During the 1980s and early 1990s a third stage was reached, one at which the language of discourse was derived from the world of the spirit. Dis-

10. Holger Bernt Hansen, "Grundtvig and the Third World" in A.M. Allchin et al. (eds.), *Heritage and Prophecy. Grundtvig and the English-Speaking World* (Aarhus, 1993), pp. 208-310.
11. Quoted by Holger Bernt Hansen in *Grundtvig Studier* (1993), pp. 122, 131. According to Peter Manniche, the folk high school idea can not be exported, only imported, cf. Max Lawson, "Extending the Grundtvigian Vision: Peter Manniche (1889-1981) and the International People's College, Helsingør, Denmark" in Lillian Zøllner (ed.), *Enlightenment in an International Perspective* (Copenhagen, 1995), pp. 65-86.
12. Steen Folke & Jens Herluf Jensen, "Indien, Mysore, Shivaragudda" in *Internationalt samarbejde*, ed. by *Mellemfolkeligt Samvirke*, 17 (Copenhagen, 1968), p. 36.

course on export, transfer, adaptation and gardening was replaced by inspiration. What does such a change of language imply? It is well-known
that the spirit like the wind "blows where it wills" (John 3.8). In other
words, the final result of inspiration is unpredictable. This means that we
must face up to the fact that the outcome of an encounter between Grundtvig's educational ideas and an indigenous, non-Scandinavian culture will
most likely be radically different from what has become our local version
of that idea. It will be different not only in some minor aspects but also regarding fundamental issues.

Such an understanding of what inspiration from Grundvig means is actually
not new. It was expressed in the concluding passage of P.G. Lindhardt's
Grundtvig biography from 1963. Here the author sharply criticises all mindless repetition of Grundtvig's words and ideas. But Lindhardt winds up this
criticism by saying that "if you follow [Grundtvig's] inspiration, then your
journey is without any limitation whatsoever."[13]

---

13. P.G. Lindhardt, *Grundtvig* (Copenhagen, 1964), p. 130.

Education for Life or for Livelihood?
Grundtvig and the Third World Revisited

Holger Bernt Hansen

Around 1960 when Denmark first became aware of the developing world and the first aid programmes were started, the name N.F.S. Grundtvig was frequently mentioned and almost ascribed with "ancestral power". With reference to his writings, to his influence on educational thinking and to his impact on the development of Danish society it became very common to link Grundtvig with the developing world – or to use a term often heard in those early days: the underdeveloped countries.[1]

The inclusion of Grundtvig into this new Danish enterprise was primarily based on three premises. According to the first premise, Grundtvig's analysis of 19th-century Denmark as subdued and culturally colonized by the major cultures of Europe was seen as applicable to the newly decolonized nations in the Third World. Grundtvig had fought against "the Roman yoke" and worked for the revival of forgotten Danish values lying dormant in the Danes' history, poetry, mother tongue, myths and the whole realm of religion. His major aim was for man to be aware of his own position in history and thereby overcome the alienation – a key concept in Grundtvig's thinking. People should be aware and conscious of their own potential and ready to assume responsibility for their own destinies.

This whole analysis of the Danish situation in the 19th century was considered very suitable as a description of the new nations and for emphasising the challenge of fighting the "yoke of colonialism" on culture and values; one should value one's own heritage as it unfolds in history, nation and mother tongue – aptly summarized in the title of the African book *Decolonizing the Mind*.[2]

The second premise takes as its point of departure the influence of Grundtvig's ideas on the direction of change in Danish society. Although in

---

1. This topic has been dealt with in two earlier works. Holger Bernt Hansen, "Grundtvig and the Third World: The Transfer of Grundtvig's Ideas to Other Peoples and Cultures", in A.M. Allchin et al. (eds.), *Heritage and Prophecy. Grundtvig and the English-Speaking World* (Århus, 1993), pp. 299ff. Holger Bernt Hansen, "Grundtvig, Europe and the Third World", in *Grundtvig Studier* (1993).
2. By the Kenyan writer Ngugi wa Thiong'o, published in London (1990).

the era of Grundtvig fighting colonialism was not an issue his ideas had a political dimension in the sense that they were linked with the process of democratization which was on the agenda for most of the 19th century in Denmark. Grundtvig's emphasis on awareness-raising and on adult education was to a large extent geared towards enabling and empowering ordinary people, first and foremost the ignorant and subdued peasantry so that they could have influence and be included in the decision-making in the local community as well as at the national level.

Corresponding to the political dimension, a social message was also read into Grundtvig's thinking. There was clearly a strong criticism of the established ruling elite and a call for more equality aptly expressed in the often quoted sentence from one of Grundtvig's patriotic songs: " ... then we have gone far when only a few have too much and even fewer too little".

In relation to the newly decolonized nations and the many challenges they were facing, both the political dimension and the social message in Grundtvig's thinking were seen as highly relevant. For some of the people most influenced by Grundtvig's thinking this set of ideas came close to constituting a development theory as it laid down the guiding principles for the whole development process.

Consequently the third premise for transferring Grundtvigian ideas to developing nations takes its point of departure in the operationalization of these ideas in Danish society. The two major instruments were adult education as practised by the folk high schools and the organization of the peasants in cooperatives formed to manufacture and market their products. These two instruments have later been seen as the major forces of transformation of Danish society in the latter part of the 19th century. This transformation has been seen as a success story since it brought Denmark close to realising Grundtvig's ideas and thereby setting it on the path towards realising, later, the idea of the welfare state.

It follows that such a success story and the underlying experiences gained during the process of transformation were considered worth transferring to the newly independent nations that faced challenges similar to the ones that the Danish nation had faced a century earlier. In 1960 one of the founders of the Danish aid programme could confidently proclaim: "The Folk High Schools and the cooperatives are our biggest export products." As a small nation with a forgotten record as a colonial power many people took pride in the discovery that in the Grundtvigian heritage we have a unique model for development which is bound to work just as well in other societies that exhibit symptoms of malaise similar to those of Denmark in the 19th century.

There is no doubt that this whole approach has been one of the important factors in swaying public opinion into a remarkable support for the Danish aid programme right from the beginning. And what is possibly even more remarkable, these ideas became widely shared by officials in the Foreign Ministry who were responsible for the implementation of the Danish aid programme.

On the other hand it is worth noticing that the warning lights inherent in Grundtvig's own way of thinking were not taken into account. Judged from Grundtvig's own scepticism towards Christian missionary activity and his constant argument that the time was not yet ripe it could be questioned whether the transfer of the Grundtvigian-inspired "Danish model" to developing countries was the right thing to do.[3] If the people were not ready in the sense that they had not "decolonized their minds", would there not be a risk of creating a feeling of alienation? Grundtvig would certainly have warned against such a risk. It is also questionable whether Grundtvig would have approved of dispensing with the rule of time and place in history by carrying over experiences from one century to another and from one continent to another. In Grundtvig's universe the driving forces of history were likely to have warned against such a procedure.

This was exactly the reaction which came from Indian delegates when in 1980 they took part in a workshop examining the many attempts to transfer the folk high school idea to developing countries.[4] Their response was that what was good in one part of the world in one century was not necessarily the right thing at a different time and place. This attitude is usually echoed in comments by students from Third World countries when at the University of Copenhagen they attend seminars on Grundtvig's ideas and the relevance of the Danish – Grundtvigian-inspired – "model" for the developing world. They find the well-known emphasis on history, myths, the religious heritage and the mother tongue to belong to an unfamiliar and outdated context.

Even the concept of nation is foreign to them and is seen as dangerous in view of the risk of its lapsing into nationalism, which has had so disastrous consequences, not least in Europe. For them there is often a distinction between state and nation. While they try to come to terms with the former with all its weaknesses in the post-colonial era they find it more relevant to seek their identity within primordial groupings constituted by ethnicity or religion than in the nation. When Grundtvig is presented to them as "the revered ancestor of the Danish nation" they fail to acknowledge his importance outside the Danish borders. And they are astonished to sense the atmosphere of self-glorification which often accompanies the presentation of "the Danish model" and which carries reminiscences of colonial paternalism.

---

3. Grundtvig's attitude to missionary activity has been discussed in Holger Bernt Hansen's "Grundtvig and the Third World", in *Heritage and Prophecy*, pp. 302ff.
4. See Holger Bernt Hansen, "Grundtvig and the Third World", p. 314.

This leads to the obvious suggestion that one initial condition for discussing the theme of Grundtvig and the developing world will be to undress Grundtvig from his special Danish garment and look for universal values in his thinking. At a minimum it will be necessary to separate Grundtvig's educational ideas from the Danish folk high school institution. Grundtvig's ideas on education should be judged on the basis of their inherent worth and not be seen as succeeding or failing on the basis of the way in which they have been put to practice in the Danish context.

But the need for a new paradigm goes further. It has been the customary point of departure to take for granted that Grundtvig's relevance and importance for developing countries is beyond dispute. It would almost amount to sacrilege if that assumption were questioned. It is ingrained in the Danish self-understanding that the Grundtvig-inspired idea of adult education as practised by the folk high school institution has proved its value again and again, and it cannot be questioned that it will make a major contribution to the development of the societies in the Third World. Even if it has to be modified in accordance with the local situations the basic idea is sound and has proved its value.

Nevertheless, the latter assumption has to be questioned. In 1990 as part of an earlier work on Grundtvig and the Third World I carried out a survey of Danish-funded projects in Africa and Asia within the area of adult education based on the folk high school model.[5] The tendency was fairly clear. The more faithful a project was in upholding the original principles, the more foreign it was felt to be and correspondingly the less successful it was in influencing the situation of the target group. And the more a project dispensed with the usual practices and adapted to the lives of the people, the more relevant and integrated those involved felt it to be.

One major explanation of this outcome could be ascribed to a lack of understanding of the special needs of these people and of the kind of development needed to reduce poverty and improve living conditions. Education for life and awareness-raising were not seen as the right instruments; higher in demand were literacy classes and skilled education. And the educational institutions should be compatible with the rhythm of people's daily lives and the requirements of the surrounding community.

This leads to the suggestion that the customary Danish approach, which stipulates education first and then development, should be reversed. It would be more relevant to speak of development and education, development being the key concept. An assessment of development comes first, including people's own priorities, and education in a broad sense is then seen as an important tool for development.

5.   See Holger Bernt Hansen, "Grundtvig and the Third World", pp. 311ff.

This latter point emphasizes the need for a new paradigm. If we combine the arguments presented so far they lead to the radical suggestion – possibly by some condemned as heretical – that Grundtvig and the Grundtvigian heritage may not at all be relevant for the situation which the developing countries are facing. We will have to start without assuming both that Grundtvig *per se* is relevant for the Third World and that a substantial contribution to change and progress in people's lives follows the transfer of Grundtvigian ideas and practices based on earlier Danish experiences. It means that an analysis should not take its point of departure with Grundtvig, nor with the Danish experiences, but it should start in the developing world. Development should be the heading, and the needs and priorities of the people themselves should be the point of departure. Only then will it be meaningful to bring Grundtvig back and ask whether his way of thinking, not least within the area of education, has any relevance for the process of change and development.

To demonstrate what is meant by suggesting a new paradigm and to discuss the underlying hypothesis, a Danish supported educational project in Bangladesh will be introduced. It serves our purpose as during the project cycle attempts have been made both to draw inspiration from Grundtvig's ideas and to introduce elements from the folk high school model. This is directly spelled out when it is stated that one of the objectives of the programme is «to act as a centre of inspiration for social development based on the concept of the Danish Folk High School Movement» (p. 63).[6]

The Gonobidyalaya project: a case study from Bangladesh

The Gonobidyalaya project was started in 1981 with financial support from the Danish International Development Agency (Danida). Its purpose was an innovative non-formal education programme for the underprivileged youth, not least women, in rural areas of Bangladesh centred around four, later five, so-called Gonobidyalayas, that is, community schools at village level. The local partner was the Non-Governmental Organization (NGO) Bangladesh Association for Community Education (BACE). After the first phase the Danish Folk High School Association (FFD) was asked in 1991 to join the project in order to strengthen it by contributing with some of the experiences from the long Danish tradition of adult education. The project is now in phase three (1996-2001) with a grant of DKK 11,2 million.

---

6. *Bangladesh Country Study*, Danida (Copenhagen, September 1999). Page numbers given in the text refer to this report.

The Gonobidyalayas were briefly included in the above-mentioned survey from 1990 of Danish supported adult-education projects with roots in the Danish folk high school tradition. Since 1991 this element has been strengthened by the direct involvement of the FFD. During the 1990s a number of appraisals and evaluations have been undertaken. Most relevant for this paper is a major impact study carried out in 1999 as part of an overall *Danish NGO Impact Study*. The assessment of the Gonobidyalayas is included in the *Bangladesh Country Study*, and the report constitutes the main source for the following case study.[7]

When the project first started in 1981 it was not designed in accordance with the folk high school model. The request for Danish support came from BACE, and Danida agreed to grant support for mainly two reasons. Firstly, the project combined education with vocational training in a non-formal way in order to integrate general subjects and practical work, which at the time was seen as unusual and innovative in the Bangali context. Secondly, the target group was solely the rural poor and in particular women, and the aim was twofold: to address the unequal access to educational and vocational training which prevailed in rural areas; and to improve the living conditions in the rural communities through the skills and attitudes gained by the young people.

While the latter motive was in full accordance with the overall Danish aid policy, the former one reflects the Danish adult-education tradition from the folk high schools. This was borne out by the way in which the project was put into practice. From the beginning it was centred around four Gonobidyalayas, which were not only seen as educational institutions carrying out the non-formal education programme but also as centres of inspiration for promoting social development in the surrounding local community. This latter aim was helped by the fact that the Gonobidyalayas were not residential institutions but day schools without any tuition fee, and in addition the schools had the great asset of providing a free midday-meal and a stipend to compensate for any income loss.

Apart from the fact that the Gonobidyalayas differed from the folk high schools by not being residential they were supposed to have an impact on the surrounding rural communities like a traditional Danish folk high school. Like the first Danish folk high schools, they were also supposed to gradually raise more funds by income generation in order to reduce the dependency on Danida grants. Finally and still following the Danish model the curriculum included not only general education and training in basic skills including literacy and numeracy, but great emphasis was also put on awareness-raising, on making people aware of their own potential to achieve a better quality of life.

7.   *Danish NGO Impact Study*, Danida (Copenhagen, September 1999).

As we can tell the Danish approach to the educational project was clearly rooted in the folk high school tradition, and important elements from that tradition were included in the project design. Further emphasis was put on that particular point when – in an evaluation from 1987 and later in an appraisal from 1990 – it was pointed out that there was a need to strengthen the understanding of the pedagogic concepts behind the Gonobidyalayas. The suggestion was that this could best be done by handing over the responsibility for the project to the FDD. This was done from 1991 onwards, which has meant that the Gonobidyalayas have put more emphasis on «the participatory and 'empowering' approach to education» (p. 67), in other words have strengthened the awareness curriculum.

The outcome has so far and not surprisingly been that the project management in its response to the team doing the impact study has underlined that "the Danish Folk High School model has been replicated through the Gonobidyalayas after adaptation for the Bangladesh context" (p. 67). By adopting this approach the project has so far proved itself to be relevant and successful especially when measured by the employment rate of the ex-students and the general improvement in their living conditions. The importance attached to the adapted Danish model is also indicated by the arguments in favour of continuing the long courses over eight months as the core activity of the schools. When the team questioned the high costs of running these long comprehensive courses compared to far shorter, more specific courses which would improve the cost-effectiveness, it was maintained that the eight-month courses are a distinctive feature of the Gonobidyalayas.

An indication of the support for the employment of the adapted folk high school model can also be seen from the donor's patience and leniency in relation to the otherwise crucial issue of sustainability. Already before the present phase three of the project was approved in 1996 it was recommended that more attention should be given to the question of sustainability as "none of the five Gonobidyalayas are likely to be able to continue their operation for long without external support" (p. 71). The team conducting the impact study has observed that the project has not made much progress in raising its own funds by income-generation activities. The leaders of the project admit that they will only be able to earn five percent of their total costs within the present phase and cannot hope to do better during the promised phase four from 2001. The project is heavily dependent on external support, but they are optimistic that in the case of Danida withdrawing its funding the Bangladesh government will step in and secure the future of the Gonobidyalayas.

The Danish donor has so far been willing to dispense with the principle of longer-term sustainability. Priority has been given to the continuation of the non-formal adult education based upon the folk high school tradition and aiming at the poorest segments of the population. The values of the project and the results achieved so far justify this kind of priority. The expectation is that over time this Danish approach to adult education will prove itself so valuable that the Bangladesh government will make it a part of its educational policy and budget for the Gonobidyalayas and even replicate the model on a larger scale.

It remains to be seen whether this optimistic scenario is at all realistic given the many constraints on a poor country's resources. It depends on the willingness of the government to give priority to this particular approach to education at the expense of the more customary way of organizing the educational system, which is based on a different set of values far from those of the folk high school tradition. If that fails the donor is left with a paradox: Does it make sense to continue the funding with no prospect for longer-term financial and institutional sustainability or has the value of this particular educational model proved so strong that the donor is justified in dispensing with the principles normally guiding activities under the development programme.

This leads to the question of effect and impact of the project and how the basic idea of the project is understood by the people involved. First and foremost, the report from the impact study confirms that the project has to a large extent reached its primary target groups, which are from landless families or from families of small farmers and of which women constitute a substantial segment. The non-formal education and skills training have helped the poor to reduce their poverty by increased employment and some increase in income. There has been a sustained improvement in literacy and good use is made of the skills training. This has meant some improvement in living standards and a significant change in gender attitudes, although traditional values still tend to dominate.

From reading the report it is difficult to measure the progress in quantitative terms, but it is beyond doubt that living conditions have improved for the students and their families. However, it is less clear whether these students are able to have a wider impact on their communities. This corresponds with the observation that the Gonobidyalayas remain somewhat isolated from other local structures although ten community-based adult literacy centres have been established under each of the five Gonobidyalayas.

So far we have seen that the combination of general education, literacy courses and vocational training have been geared towards developing the students' capacities and skills and thereby helping the rural poor to gain access to economic and social resources in order to give them a better livelihood. The main goal is clearly a better livelihood within society. In this respect the Gonobidyalayas differ substantially from the essence of the folk high school idea which emphasizes human development as the precondition for any kind of change and which does not grant such direct prominence to the societal dimension.

Still the Gonobidyalaya concept does include the "classical" element of the folk high school tradition: consciousness-raising, also called the awareness curriculum. Only recently a new six-month course "on literacy, numeracy and awareness development" has been introduced (p. 65). This is further elaborated in the objectives of the Gonobidyalayas:

Literacy and numeracy skills are also taught along with awareness training among the poor. An immediate objective of the Gonobidyalayas is to improve the trainee's understanding of life and society and to upgrade their skills and literacy proficiency in order that they themselves might be able to better their lives (p. 63).

Compared with the well-known Grundtvigian concept of "education for life" it is characteristic that the idea here is expanded to be "education for life and society", and that it emphasizes the chances for bettering life by acquiring new skills and greater capacity. Awareness development is directed towards the individual's ability to improve his or her family's living conditions. Hence it comes as no surprise that when former students were asked to rank the significant changes in their lives as a result of their training at the Gonobidyalayas the overwhelming trend was to rally around the option which stated: "It boosted my self-confidence" (p. 70).

What is understood by awareness development is aptly described in a summary made on the basis of interviews with 20 ex-students:

Level of awareness achieved by former students: the gender attitude of most ex-students (male and female) has changed positively. They believe that the women should be given the opportunity to attend school and that men and women should work together for eradicating their poverty. Also they are now aware about their civil rights and can contribute to changing their physical and social environment. Their health consciousness and attitude towards family planning have also changed positively (p. 69).

The change in gender attitude is a remarkable achievement in such a male-dominated society as we used to find in Bangladesh. But what is at stake is rather the question of equality between men and women in connection with granting women equal rights to receiving an education and earning an income in order to reduce poverty. In general the awareness curriculum is geared towards developmental issues such as eradicating poverty and improving the living conditions of the poor segments of the population. We do not meet the usual Grundtvigian categories like the necessary relationship between language, culture and nation, and neither do we meet the concern about alienation. Adult education with its strong emphasis on awareness-raising, that is, education for life, is not conceived as a necessary precondition for enabling people to improve their lives as human beings.

The earlier suggested hypothesis that the order has to be reversed is confirmed by the experiences from the Gonobidyalaya project: development first, education next. Education has to be geared towards development needs and the aim of the awareness curriculum is to enable people to make use of their opportunities and to influence the direction of change. It will probably be more accurate to replace the term awareness with the word empowerment which is much used in today's development terminology. It is of crucial importance to empower people to have influence on their own destinies and not to be victims of the elite; to give them sufficient confidence to go against inherited traditions and accustomed power structures; to have confidence to challenge leaders to show accountability and not engage in corruption; to enable them to influence the agenda setting and last but not least to increase their share of the decision-making power so that they can influence the handling of topics which have a bearing on their living conditions, be it gender issues or land questions.

Education for life or for livelihood?

Two observations follow from the case study of the Gonobidyalayas. First, the folk high school tradition has been decisive for the Danish engagement in the project, and the project leaders are conscious of the fact that the project is based on an adaptation of the folk high school model which has inspired the pioneering and innovative activities within adult education, which the schools are carrying out. But the schools are not replicas of Danish folk high schools with regard to their curriculums. In their recruitment and teaching they are geared towards the development needs of society, especially towards alleviating poverty and improving the living conditions of the poor. This direct link with the development agenda makes the Gonobidyalayas very different from the folk high schools and raises the question of how much is really left of that idea.

This first observation leads to a second question: how much is left of Grundtvig's ideas of education as they have been practised within the Danish folk high school tradition? The essential element in Grundtvig's educational thinking is the awareness-raising attached to people's place in history, culture, religion and nation. In the Gonobidyalaya programme this crucial part of Grundtvig's thinking has clearly been scaled down, if not left out, and priority has instead been given to literacy, numeracy and skills training combined with "an understanding of life and society" in order for the poor segments of the population to face the challenges stemming from a lack of development and to achieve better living conditions. Education is linked with the concept of development, and it is clearly the social dimension which prevails and penetrates the present adult-education programme.

This leads to the conclusion that it is not relevant to introduce typical Grundtvigian categories when analyzing the Gonobidyalaya adult-education programme. *Education for life* does not constitute the major principle of the curriculum. This again leads to the alternative suggested in the title of this paper: *education for livelihood*.

The inspiration to make a distinction between education for life and for livelihood comes from the Indian poet and Nobel Prize winner Rabindranath Tagore. During a visit in January 1999 to the Visva-Bharati University founded by Tagore and the adjoining Tagore Museum, there was an exhibit of photographs illustrating and commenting on the surprisingly few contacts there had been between the two great Indian contemporaries, Mahatma Ghandi and Tagore. On the accompanying guide-sheet the following sentence was quoted: "Greater attention had been paid to livelihood than life". From the context it was not clear to whom of the two the sentence should be ascribed, and that question deserves a paper of its own. But the distinction between the two concepts is most appropriate for a discussion of Grundtvig's educational ideas in a Third World context.[8]

Tagore was certainly aware of both concepts and of the need not only to concentrate on life but also on the necessity to move on to livelihood. This is made clear in an often quoted statement in which he outlined his ideas for improving "life and livelihood" for the vast majority of the people living in rural areas:

Today for various reasons, villages are fatally neglected. They are fast degenerating into serfdom compelled to offer to the ungrateful towns cheerless and unintelligent labour for work carried on in an unhealthy and impoverished environment. The object of Sriniketan is to bring back life in its completeness into the villages making them self-reliant and self-respectful, acquainted with the cultural tradition of their own country and competent to make an efficient use of the modern resources for the improvement of their physical, intellectual and economic condition.[9]

Tagore put his ideas into practice by setting up the *Sriniketan* unit in 1922 under Visva-Bharati University. It has later been named "Centre for Applied Rural Education, Extension and Research", but all the time the objective has been to promote social change and development in rural areas through confidence and competence building.

8. The visit to Visva-Bharati University and Tagore's home area was part of the programme for the conference "Grundtvig International Conference on Education and Development", organized by Professor Asoke Bhattacharya and held at Jadavpur University, Calcutta, 15-16 January, 1999. I am grateful to Dr. Asoke for inviting me to participate in the conference and to present a paper.
9. The quotation appears in several of the Sriniketan pamphlets.

For Tagore, life and livelihood were complementary but judged from the activities he started the order is "livelihood first, life next". This is not least borne out by his openness to use research and "modern resources", that is, new knowledge and technology whenever appropriate, in order to speed up the improvement of the living conditions of the rural poor. This is closely connected with his conviction that leading intellectuals and educationists at university level have an obligation to engage themselves in the problems of the rural poor and to contribute by working together with them and not practice the usual top-down approach. Tagore was an early advocate of the later well-known Participatory Rural Appraisal approach closely identified with the name Robert Chambers.

For Tagore it was essential not to leave "life" out but to include as he said "the cultural tradition". He talks about joy across the village coming from music, dance and recitations. In particular literacy serves as the link between livelihood and life. It is not enough to make people, especially women, literate, it is just as important to maintain literacy by providing opportunities for access to a variety of books covering broad cultural areas like history, religion, novels and so on. That explains why a number of small rural libraries still function in villages in Tagore's home area in West Bengal.

Tagore drew up an impressive rural development strategy, in which he included both dimensions: livelihood and life. In that respect his ideas about education are closer to reality in societies under development and change than Grundtvig can be. Tagore responded to an historical situation quite different from Grundtvig's. In such a situation education for livelihood must have the priority as we have seen in the Gonobidyalaya programme. Yet Tagore would almost certainly have wanted more emphasis on education for life in the activities under the programme. It should be added here that with regard to the overall issue of education for life or for livelihood there is a great need for a comparative study of Grundtvig and Tagore similar to the one that A.M. Allchin has already pioneered.[10]

The obvious question is now why BACE, the NGO responsible for the Gonobidyalayas, turned to the Danish folk high school idea instead of seeking inspiration closer to home. Tagore had after all lived and worked in the neighbouring West Bengal. Apart from the attraction of Danish funding, there may in the case of the Gonobidyalayas have been national, political and religious reasons involved going back to the division of the Indian subcontinent between India, Pakistan and later Bangladesh.

Yet, it is still interesting to speculate why BACE and other educationists from the Indian subcontinent concerned with adult education are interested in the Danish folk high school tradition and in Grundtvig's educational ideas

10. In his paper at the conference at Jadavpur University in January 1999.

instead of taking a greater interest in their own educational traditions origi-
nating from such great figures as Tagore and Ghandi. And there are similar
examples from other parts of the Third World. Why does Grundtvig have
such a special appeal?

As argued earlier the transfer of the Danish folk high school institution
and of the special Grundtvigian thoughts and ideas has in most cases been
problematic and not the most fruitful way of arriving at an answer. As suggested above Grundtvig should be removed from his Danish context, and his
educational ideas should not exclusively be identified with the folk high
school concept. Furthermore, the Danish presumption that Grundtvig per se
is relevant and important for developing countries should not be taken as the
starting point.

Instead Grundtvig should so to speak be "internationalized" as we
should look for the general value of his thinking and its universality, not least
in regard to education. Then we should ask in what way Grundtvig is perceived to be addressing essential problems in developing societies and how
he is interpreted and seen as relevant by the major actors. In other words,
how are Grundtvig's thinking and ideas linked with the process of transformation which is going on in the Third World?

One first and typical answer can be found in the case from Bangladesh. At
an early stage it was pointed out that there was a need to strengthen the understanding of the pedagogic concepts behind the educational activities, and
in that situation Grundtvig's educational ideas ingrained in the folk high
school tradition were seen as highly relevant. Why was and is that so? Five
interrelated observations can be put forward.

Firstly, in his pedagogic thoughts Grundtvig advocates a break with pa-
triarchal and patronizing teaching methods. Likewise he rejects the idea that
the educational system should reflect the wider society's hierarchical structure and corresponding pattern of authority. This attitude falls on fertile soil
among people who are struggling for reforms of inherited structures and
breaks with elitist attitudes and who argue for a change in the relationship
between those who rule and those who are ruled.

Secondly, this first point corresponds with Grundtvig's ideas of equality
and justice. He is concerned about the less privileged, be it for political or social reasons, and he is seen as a strong advocate of their "empowerment", a
concept which is equally as important as his emphasis on awareness-raising.
This again is relevant for people who are concerned that the educational system should be geared to meet the need for empowerment coming from
marginalized and unprivileged people. From here there is a natural link with
Grundtvig's advocacy for freedom and people's rights to influence their own
destinies, in modern language called human rights and democratization.

Thirdly, in this latter context Grundtvig's fight against "the Roman yoke" is interpreted as a struggle to overcome the alienation from which people suffer in societies under rapid transformation. Not least the need to "decolonize the mind" is relevant in former colonial societies.

Fourthly, and following upon the three earlier points, what appeals to people in Third World countries is the gist of Grundtvig's message: his emphasis on adult education as the best way of making people conscious of their positions in life and society and of their potential to remedy their situations and by their own efforts to improve their conditions of life.

Fifthly and lastly, Grundtvig's pedagogic ideas are reflected in his advice and suggestions as to which methods to use in adult education. In that area he is seen as an original and pioneering educationist with a "modern" message about teaching methods based on equality and participation.

Hence there are many and solid reasons for Grundtvig's appeal to educationists and reformers in Third World countries. His educational ideas are stimulating for the process of change in which they are engaged. But Grundtvig must be understood and used in the right context which is the core argument of this paper. There is a long distance from Danish surroundings to societies where development is on the top of the agenda. The challenges are different and that necessitates an affirmative answer to the main question presented in this paper under inspiration from Tagore: greater attention has to be paid to livelihood than to life.

List of Authors

Canon, Professor, Dr. Arthur Macdonald Allchin
1 Tren Yr Wyddfa
Bangor, Gwyneda
LL Bangor 57 2ER, North Wales
UK

Professor Dr. Jakob Balling
Voldbækvej 3
8220 Brabrand
Denmark

Director, Professor Dr. Asoke Bhattacharya
Jadavpur University
Centre for Adult and Continuing Education
Culcutta-700 032
India

Vice-Chancellor, Professor Dr. Gustav Björkstrand
Academy of Aabo
Domkyrkotorget 3
20500 Aabo
Finland

Reader S.A.J. Bradley
University of York
Department of English Literature
Heslington, YO 1 5DD
England

Professor Dr. Knud Eyvin Bugge
Dronningeengen 22
2850 Vedbæk
Denmark

Dean, Professor Dr. William Franklin
Berkeley Divinity School at Yale
363 St. Ronan Street
New Haven, Connecticut 06511
USA

Professor Dr. Holger Bernt Hansen
Center for Africa-Studies
University of Copenhagen
Købmagergade 44-46
1150 Copenhagen K
Denmark

Professor Dr. Phil Hefner
Lutheran School of Theology at Chicago
1100 East 55th Street
Chicago, Illinois 60615
USA

Rev. Norman A. Hjelm
624 Sussex Road
Wynnewood, Philadelphia 19096
USA

Professor Dr. Axel Kildegaard
6946 Lake Drive
Circle Pines, Minnesota 55015
USA

Professor Dr. Michael Root
Trinity Lutheran Seminary
2199 E. Main Street
Columbus, Ohio 43209-2334
USA

Professor Dr. Jens Holger Schjørring
Faculty of Theology, University of Aarhus
Taasingegade 3
8000 Aarhus C
Denmark

Professor Dr. Christian Thodberg
Thunøgade 16
8000 Aarhus C
Denmark

Professor Dr. Vítor Westhelle
Lutheran School of Theology at Chicago
1100 East 55th Street
Chicago, Illinois 60615
USA